TRAINING ESSENTIALS FOR
ULTRARUNNING

TRAINING ESSENTIALS FOR
ULTRARUNNING

HOW TO TRAIN SMARTER,
RACE FASTER, AND MAXIMIZE
YOUR ULTRAMARATHON
PERFORMANCE

JASON KOOP

WITH JIM RUTBERG

BOULDER, COLORADO

Acute Training Load, Chronic Training Load, Training Stress Balance, Normalized Pace, and Training Stress Score are trademarks of Peaksware, LLC.
Ironman® is a registered trademark of World Triathlon Corporation.

▼velopress

3002 Sterling Circle, Suite 100
Boulder, Colorado 80301-2338 USA
(303) 440-0601 · Fax (303) 444-6788 · E-mail velopress@competitorgroup.com

Distributed in the United States and Canada by Ingram Publisher Services

Library of Congress Cataloging-in-Publication Data
Names: Koop, Jason, author. | Rutberg, Jim.
Title: Training essentials for ultrarunning : how to train smarter, race
   faster, and maximize your ultramarathon performance / Jason Koop with Jim
   Rutberg.
Description: Boulder, Colorado : VeloPress, [2016] | "Distributed in the
   United States and Canada by Ingram Publisher Services"—T.p. verso. |
   Includes bibliographical references and index.
Identifiers: LCCN 2015048379 (print) | LCCN 2016007183 (ebook) | ISBN
   9781937715458 (Paperback : alk. paper) | ISBN 9781937716806 (ebook)
Subjects: LCSH: Marathon running—Training. | Ultra running.
Classification: LCC GV1065.17.T73 K66 2016 (print) | LCC GV1065.17.T73
   (ebook) | DDC 796.42/52—dc23
LC record available at http://lccn.loc.gov/2015048379

For information on purchasing VeloPress books, please call (800) 811-4210, ext. 2138, or visit www.velopress.com.

This paper meets the requirements of ANSI/NISO Z39.48-1992 (Permanence of Paper).

Cover design by theBookDesigners; cover photograph by PatitucciPhoto
Interior design by Erin Farrell/Factor E Creative

16   17   18 / 10   9   8   7   6   5   4   3   2   1

For Liz, the best crew chief I could ever ask for

CONTENTS

FOREWORD

When I first met Jason Koop, I was skeptical. He had been assigned to train and prepare me to run 50 marathons in 50 states in 50 days. What could this ultra rookie, from an organization that specialized in training cyclists, possibly teach me? I'd completed many ultramarathons, including the Western States 100-Mile Endurance Run and the grueling 135-mile Badwater ultramarathon, without a coach. How could "Koop" help me?

The answer surprised me. Koop began by assessing my current training program and diet. Without being pushy or overbearing, he suggested ways that I might adjust my routine and practices to improve my endurance and overall level of fitness. I was reluctant at first, but what he was saying made sense. I was largely self-coached at the time, as there wasn't a lot of information about training and preparation for ultrarunning in 2006. Much of what I'd learned was through conversations with other runners at various events or by attempting to scale existing marathon training programs for ultrarunning.

Much has changed since that time. Ultrarunning has experienced a boom in popularity, and the number of participants and events has multiplied exponentially. A whole new generation of ultrarunners has emerged, and the level of energy and excitement is like never before. However, there still remains a dearth of reputable and vetted training resources that have demonstrated proven results. Until now.

Training Essentials for Ultrarunning is a breakthrough work that brings together sound scientific principles and years of coaching experience to create the definitive training manual of our time. An elite runner, and now an accomplished ultramarathoner himself, Koop is uniquely qualified to author such a work. He taps into his extensive background, experience, and formal professional training to create a resource that is comprehensive and complete, covering everything from proper fueling and hydration to technology and data tracking. The book is logically organized into chapters that provide rich context and perspective, flowing naturally from one section to the next in a hierarchy that builds the reader's knowledge and insight, with key lessons and practical advice peppered throughout.

Yet you don't have to be an elite ultramarathoner to benefit from this book—it speaks to people of all ages and abilities. *Training Essentials for Ultrarunning* draws upon the expertise of some of the sport's top athletes—with contributions from the likes of Dylan Bowman, Kaci Lickteig, and Dakota Jones—bestowing upon the reader the lessons and practices of these remarkable athletes. Koop does a masterful job of translating how you can use the advice of these champions to better your performance, whether you're a front-of-the-packer or just starting out.

A timely work, *Training Essentials for Ultrarunning* offers a comprehensive look at the state of the sport as it stands today, examining everything from popular North American ultras to the everyday demands of the sport. Koop offers practical advice for ultrarunners managing the demands of everyday life along with a sport that commands its own brand of toughness and perseverance. He provides an inclusive road map for training, nutrition, hydration, and environmental factors—such as heat or cold—along with a proprietary ADAPT strategy for problem-solving and decision-making. As I have experienced firsthand, such knowledge can help build confidence and self-assurance, two qualities that are invaluable in finding the courage to start an ultra and summoning the strength to finish one.

Having worked with Coach Koop, and having known him for many years, I can attest to his passion and devotion as a coach and trainer. He takes his responsibility seriously and is a student of science-based logic, constantly seeking and researching the latest studies and trends in the field of endurance sports. Koop lives for this stuff and is tireless in his quest for more information and greater insight, which he applies to his profession and to his own racing career.

Where once there was only anecdotal inferences and self-prescription, now there is a complete resource for ultrarunners, one that is vetted and proven. And having such information doesn't take the fun out of it; on the contrary, it makes running and racing all the better. Whether you're an aspiring ultrarunner looking to tackle your first race or a veteran looking to take your training and fitness to the next level, *Training Essentials for Ultrarunning* positively belongs on your bookshelf and is sure to remain there for the long run.

—*Dean Karnazes*

CHAPTER 1

THE ULTRARUNNING REVOLUTION

There is nothing like the experience of finishing an ultramarathon. As the final miles click by, there's a lot of time to think about how far you've come, not just over the past day or two but also through the months of training and lifetime of experiences that led to that moment. As a runner, I have been fortunate to experience the final rush of emotion that seems to sweep us over the finish line, and as a coach, I have had the privilege of experiencing it again and again with the athletes I work with.

The beauty of ultrarunning is its accessibility; ours is a sport that is open to everyone. But the sheer magnitude of 50- and 100-mile races is intimidating to many, and for a long time information about preparing for ultramarathons has been hard to find and largely based on "it worked for me" anecdotes. This is the problem I set out to address when I started coaching ultrarunners more than a decade ago.

What I've learned, and what I hope to teach in the following pages, is: Training for ultrarunning isn't as complicated as it may seem, and there's a logical progression that yields measurable and meaningful improvements regardless of your starting point. I'm not here to make ultrarunning easy; it's not. Instead, I've devoted my career to applying sound sports science and effective coaching methods to the unique demands presented by ultradistance running so you can push yourself farther and have more fun every step of the way.

THE BIG IDEAS

Before I explain more about my history and what led me to develop a unique coaching philosophy and training system for ultrarunning, I want to give you a preview of some of the main ideas you'll find in this book.

- **Fitness makes everything better.** This seems like an obvious statement, but when you look at how most ultrarunners train, by simply running as many miles as possible, you see that improving cardiovascular fitness isn't their priority. Being more fit isn't just about going faster or being more competitive, either. Fitness enables you to run more comfortably, with more control, and with better technique. It not only gives you the ability to get yourself out of trouble if things go wrong but also keeps you out of a lot of trouble in the first place.

- **Structured training is the best way to build fitness.** "Just go run" works for a little while, but you quickly reach a plateau where progress stops. More mileage alone isn't the answer, but unfortunately it's the default solution for most athletes. In order to make progress, your training has to have structure, with workouts that target specific energy systems, purposeful recovery periods, and a progression that applies the correct amount of training stress.

- **It takes more than fitness to reach the finish line.** What separates ultrarunning from other endurance sports is the impact of everything else beyond fitness in determining whether or not you will reach the finish line. If you have successfully finished a marathon, you have the physical capacity to finish a 50K, 50-mile, or even a 100-mile race. But ultramarathons are not simply longer marathons. Your limiting factor isn't your physical capacity but rather your habits, nutrition and hydration strategies, gear selection, knowledge of the course, decision-making capabilities, and forged toughness.

- **Your mind is your greatest weapon.** Ultrarunning is hard. The training is difficult, and the events are even more so. The conditions, the course, and your body will conspire against you. Ultrarunning is an intellectual sport; you have to think your way through the challenges. In events that last up to (and sometimes beyond) 30 hours, there's a lot of time for plans to go awry as well as a lot of time to right the ship. You have to find solutions to the puzzle, often when you're tired, hungry, wet, and cold. To be successful, you need to train your mind just as much as you train your body.

STARTING FROM SCRATCH

I have been a coach for nearly as long as I've been an athlete. At the age of 16, I got my first gig coaching a summer track team, the Texas Stars Track Club. Twice a day, every day, in the searing Texas summer heat, I herded dozens of kids through simple drills and conditioning regimens. Although it would be a stretch to say I was a legitimate "coach" at that point, one thing was certain: I fell in love with seeing people improve. Helping an athlete "get" the Fosbury Flop (a high-jumping technique), spring out of the blocks properly, or run a personal record (PR) captivated me. As you can imagine, tangible improvement came easily for these young teens. Many of them had never run before. No matter what they did, they were almost sure to do it better, faster, or higher the next day. But what also captivated me was seeing how a logical approach to training helped them understand the "why" behind what we were teaching. You can't simply tell 12-year-old high jumpers to "get your butt over the bar" and magically expect them to flop over the bar like a pro. You have to logically introduce each aspect of the high jump before they get how to flop. You need to establish their run-up, their penultimate step, and how their shoulders should line up while they are in the air. I discovered that summer that if you do this methodically and in the right order, they get it. Tell them to simply "get your butt over the bar," and it's a disaster. Coaching had a wonderful logic: You instructed an athlete on a series of tasks, they accomplished those tasks, and they became better athletes.

Fast-forward to 2001. I accepted a coaching internship at Carmichael Training Systems (CTS) in Colorado Springs, Colorado, and began to work with cyclists, triathletes, and marathon runners of all levels. I was surprised to find that the coaching process I had fallen in love with as a teenager still applied: Have an athlete perform a series of workouts in a logical order, and he or she improves. But instead of standing in 100-plus-degree Texas heat watching kids run around in circles, now I was coaching mostly from behind a computer and by telephone. Maneuvering an athlete into starting blocks gave way to analyzing training files. The series of tasks morphed into structured workouts that built up into weeks and phases of endurance training.

When I started coaching cyclists, triathletes, and marathon runners, I had been a runner, and only a runner, for my entire life. I knew very little about the sports of cycling and triathlon and had no practical experience in either sport. Early in my coaching career, I did not fully understand the nuances of power profiling, drafting, or how to run off the bike. But as strange as it sounds, that initial lack of knowledge proved crucial to how I ultimately developed an effective coaching philosophy for ultramarathon runners.

Because I knew nothing, I was forced to learn everything. Rather than relying on my own experiences, I was forced to look at things from an unbiased, unobstructed, and unfiltered point of view. I had to break the demands of the sport down to their component parts, so I examined and analyzed the aerobic system, muscular function, race tactics, heat stress response, and myriad other components. This process—breaking down a sport, figuring out the key components, and optimizing those components to make a better athlete—molded my coaching. As the years went on, I worked with every kind of athlete in nearly every endurance sport save one: ultramarathon. Initially, I found this strange. The most complicated sports benefit the most from the guiding hands of a professional coach. To me, ultramarathons seemed arduous and complicated enough to make ultramarathon runners good candidates for coaching. The events are long, and there are myriad physiological, tactical, and nutritional considerations to take into account. Some ultras have success rates of only 50 percent. Yet virtually no ultrarunners had coaches or even a semblance of a structured training plan. If I went to the local criterium or road race, nearly all the cyclists had a coach, logged their training in some program, could chart out their peak heart rate values, and knew every nuance of their power profile. Triathletes took it to an even higher level. They trained, used proper periodization methods, absorbed every aerodynamic advantage they could find, ate right, and planned their race tactics at a level normally reserved for a military operation.

But when I went to an ultra event, it was as if I had been transported back in time. Training logs, if they existed at all, were paper. Nutrition was water and a quartered PB&J sandwich. I would ask ultrarunners what they did for training, and the resounding answer was "Run." I likened this response to my previous experience as a teenaged track coach: "Get your butt over the bar." While nearly all other endurance sports accepted coaching and the application of sound sports science principles, in ultrarunning these ideas were met with a lukewarm reception at best. In fact, many elites in the sport were proud and vocal that they trained by feel and that their training had no structure. In social settings, I often found myself defending coaching within the sport, something that doesn't happen in any other endurance sport. Though I coached a handful of ultrarunners at the time, I concluded that ultrarunning was not ready for coaching.

Nearly 10 years later, I read a profile of Dakota Jones in which he mentioned wanting to find a coach. I asked if I could help with his training, and he agreed.

I began the coaching process as I had hundreds of times before. Dakota's next race was Transvulcania, a notorious early-season kickoff for many elite ultrarunners. I put him through a fairly standard round of lactate threshold work (the kind I'll talk about in detail throughout this book), anticipating that Transvulcania would demand that system be tuned to its max. The race went very well, and this happy-go-lucky kid from Durango won, beating some of the best runners in the world, including the incomparable Kilian Jornet. To give credit where credit is due, Dakota was a fine athlete before I started working with him. He has a great engine and is tough as nails. The two months that I spent coaching him probably had a marginal impact. Nonetheless, he won, and ultrarunners started to take notice.

Since that time, I have never had to convince an ultraunner that coaching is a good idea. The awkward moments in which I defended coaching have been replaced by question-and-answer sessions on training, nutrition, and physiology. Runners come to me from many different athletic backgrounds and experiences: fledgling athletes on the cusp of something great, others at the top of the sport, and still others looking for a fresh approach. Some want to be fast as hell and win races; others just want to do what they can to ensure they cross the finish line.

///// DAKOTA JONES MY FIRST ULTRA

While I was still in high school, I volunteered at the Hardrock 100, which gave me my first and best look at the type of outdoor adventure that has captivated me for nearly a decade. Hardrock is an event that has changed the lives of many people, and I was lucky to start there. I was 17, and I watched 140 people complete an extraordinary feat in an extraordinary place. They made me think that I could do something similar—indeed, that I could do anything I wanted. And instantly, all I wanted to do was Hardrock. So I signed up for a 50K that fall and, having no idea how to train for it, just proceeded to run. A lot.

And it went well. Despite my inexperience, I had big hopes for the race. No matter that it was a poorly attended first-year race in the desert—when I finished in third place, that performance spurred me to think that maybe I could be good at this sport, which in turn made me want to try all the harder. I immediately went back into training mode, working furiously to reach a standard that I hadn't quite divined yet. I wanted to be a successful athlete, whatever that meant, and to reach that goal I ran long and hard all through the winter, training alone and on a plan I patched together from reading blogs and websites and thinking things like "Well, if I want to run really far, I should probably just do that a lot in training." It apparently worked well enough because at my next race—a more competitive 50K—I took fourth place. This fueled my passion even more, and I began to consider going bigger.

Fast-forward nearly three years, to December 2011. In that year I had won a 50K in Moab, taken fourth at an extremely competitive 100K in California, won a 50-mile race in Idaho, and finished second in the Hardrock 100. That fall I trained intensely for the year's most competitive 50-mile race, the North Face Endurance Challenge Championships, which attracts all the fastest runners, largely because of its prize purse of $10,000. I had run the race twice before, taking 14th in 2009 and then 4th in 2010, and I wanted to do even better this time. I was attending college in Fort Collins, Colorado. I spent my mornings running, my days in school, and my evenings sleeping. And for the first time in my ultrarunning career, I made a point to incorporate speed training into my regimen. I had enough race experience amassed by now to know I could run the distance, but I also knew that the North Face race would be fast and that the key to doing well would be maintaining a fast pace for the whole distance.

With this mind-set, I was part of a small vanguard of people who were no longer running ultras just to finish. Of course, these events had always been "races," and races by definition delineate who wins from who doesn't. But my segue into the sport came from Hardrock, which is so difficult that the first runner is often almost 20 hours faster than the last. Hardrock has a strict policy of calling the event a "run" rather than a race, and this mind-set gives the event a unique character, a camaraderie that has begotten a self-styled "Hardrock family." I wasn't changing the world or anyone's concept of sport by trying to compete in ultramarathons, but the fact is that ultramarathoning was not a professional sport for most of its history. This began to change for some of the more competitive races, and by the fall of 2011 I found myself very much a part of this transition to competitive-minded ultramarathoning.

While I had experienced some success to that point, I still had no clear concept of how to train. The problem was that as the sport got faster and I wanted to keep up with it, the stakes became much higher. In a desperate attempt to stay relevant, I did random sets of tempo runs. Twice a week or so I'd go out for fast sprints on hilly roads and see how long I could keep up the pace. I worked off of logic, trying to balance speed work and distance runs with enough rest to make each workout count. But my plan was vague, and I had little confidence in it because my training did not have a scientific foundation. When the race arrived, I ran well enough, but I wasn't satisfied. I knew I could do better. I could feel deep inside that my knowledge of training, rather than my experience or fitness, was now my limiting factor. I needed to continue to improve but had no idea how. How do you get better when you've already done everything you know how to do?

Well, apparently you wait until the perfect thing falls into your lap. Early the next year I had made no progress toward finding a coach when one   >

day, out of the blue, I received a call from a guy named Jason Koop. I had only vaguely heard of him, but after some conversations and Googling, I decided that it was worth a shot. So I agreed to work with him for a few months.

He immediately sent me out on a dirt road doing 3-minute intervals. For those of you who haven't run 3-minute intervals, just think about how fast you can run an 800-meter race, then keep going again and again. They're short enough that you can run really fast but long enough that you can hardly believe time hasn't slowed down when you look at your watch after forever, only to find that you have several more minutes to go. Jason made me do about five of these workouts over the first two weeks, and they confirmed my impression that I had a lot of improvement ahead of me. They really hurt.

Soon we started working up to longer intervals. The idea sounded simple. You pick a goal race (for me, it was Hardrock 2012) and then start by running workouts the least like that race (for me, 3-minute intervals). As the race approaches, you transition into training that is more similar to the goal race, until the month or so before the race you're running almost exactly like you will be during the race. There is a lot of science behind this, and all that science will be detailed in other parts of this book. But as an athlete, this was all I needed to know. Jason made sense, I believed him, and I followed his plan.

I have now been working with Jason for nearly four years. I have run a lot of races in that time, and I have been proud of most of them. Not every race has been a spectacular success. The reasons for success are as varied as the courses we run on. I don't know why some days are good and some days aren't. I simply know that when I line up for a race, I'm going to run as well as I possibly can, and that I have worked really hard to be prepared for the event.

At Hardrock in 2012 I lived the experience that had coursed through my dreams since volunteering at the race years earlier. My body was strong and my mind stronger, and I moved through the huge mountains that constitute the course with an efficiency that will always make me proud. In the end I finished in third place, in one of the race's then top-five times.

/////

In the years I have been involved in ultrarunning, it has been great to see sports science and coaching gain acceptance at all levels of the sport and yield improved performances for athletes of all abilities. I am truly humbled by the athletes I've been able to work with and the opportunities I have been given, including the opportunity to publish this book and help you achieve your goals.

CRACKING THE CODE ON ULTRARUNNING TRAINING

As I began working with ultrarunners (even before working with Dakota), my process started as it always had in other sports. I looked at the demands of the sport, dissected the critical components, and sought out the research to guide me in how to improve athletes. This time, however, there was a big problem: Minimal literature and practice existed to quantify the unique demands of an ultramarathon. There were no power files, few heart rate files, and relatively little academic research to draw upon. The content that did exist was rooted in blogs, personal anecdotes, hundreds of N's of 1 (see page 11), and strategies based on an ultramarathon simply being a longer marathon. Everyone had an opinion on how best to train for an ultra, but no one actually knew. No one *knew* the relative intensity one could run at for a 50-mile mountainous race because no one was really looking at it. No one *knew* what your aerobic power should be because no one was looking at it. Few people truly *knew* how to make you a better climber or train you to tolerate thousands of feet of descending because no one was looking at it. Trying to find answers, I searched, scoured, and rifled through the content that did exist. Initially, I was not satisfied. I failed to find unbiased, unobstructed, and unfiltered information on what it took to be a successful ultramarathoner. So I sought to create what I could not find. As I had done before in other sports, I broke down ultramarathon racing into its component parts. I looked at these parts and found ways to make better ultra athletes.

At first, it was an educated guessing game. While the first few athletes I worked with saw success out on the racecourse (always the most important indicator), I did not have proof that I was, in fact, helping them improve. Yes, they raced well and were satisfied with their performances, but I wanted concrete evidence that their success was the result of applying the correct training principles. With a cyclist or triathlete, improvements are easy to mark. You look at the athlete's power (on the bike) or speed (on the run) profiles week to week and month to month, and the evidence is right there in front of you. The training formula is relatively simple. Apply a training stimulus, track week-to-week training, determine how the training is impacting the athlete in terms of fitness and fatigue, adjust the training appropriately, and the athlete improves. When I spoke with cyclists and triathletes, they intuitively felt they were improving, and I could back up that intuition with training data. After a race, we could look back at their training and say, "Yes, that performance makes sense." With ultrarunners, however, it was different. The early ultrarunners I worked with would tell me that they felt faster, better, and stronger. But often I could not definitively show that they were.

Over the years, I have pored over thousands of heart rate and GPS files to find correlations I could use for ultrarunners. I wanted something I could look at and say, "Yup, you are better because of X, Y, and Z." Unfortunately, there is no discrete data source that ultramarathon runners (specifically trail ultramarathon runners) can rely on to track training, like cyclists (who use power) and triathletes (who use power and speed) can. For ultrarunners, speed is a useless tool unless running on roads (something ultrarunners rarely do with any consistency). Even the same section of trail can change with the seasons and over time. Heart rate varies too much with temperature, time of day, and fatigue. Running power is still an emerging, fledgling technology. The fact is, there are few good ways to mark improvements with an ultrarunner. So how do you know if what you are doing in training is, in fact, working?

The question of how to measure improvement is still difficult to answer, so I developed some tools that bring light to the subject. I've tested ultrarunners to see how their VO_2max and lactate threshold (LT) improve over time. I've analyzed GPS files, normalized graded pace, and graded adjusted pace over multiyear time frames to better understand how ultrarunners respond to training. I have analyzed race performances as the ultimate test of whether the training process is successful. By breaking down the sport into its component parts and then tracking how athletes improve, I developed an ultramarathon coaching method that consistently delivers improved performance for athletes of all ability levels.

THE TOP FOUR TRAINING MISTAKES IN ULTRARUNNING

The world of ultrarunning is changing. People are starting to pay far more attention to their training and are realizing that if they do the right things leading up to the event, they will give themselves the best chance at success. Still, there are many misconceptions and errors in current training methodologies for ultrarunners. Time and time again, I see ultrarunners making the same mistakes. They unnecessarily prioritize mileage over focused training. They train too slow. They do not train for the specific demands of a particular event. Correct training methodology not only fixes these problems but will also optimally prepare the athlete for success.

Later in the book I will dive deep into the whys and hows of best training practices. For now, let's take a 10,000-foot view of the top mistakes I see in training.

MISTAKE 1: THE N OF 1

I have my share of personal ultramarathon experience. I have finished a lot of ultras and competed in some of the toughest races in the world. I've had both great days and very bad ones. I've DNFed when I shouldn't have, and I've finished races when I should have dropped out. I've trained for speed, vertical, endurance, and every other aspect I preach to my athletes. And I've improved tremendously as an ultrarunner. Despite all this, I use very little of my personal experience when coaching an athlete. In research papers, the number of subjects in an experiment is referred to as the *N*, and the best studies benefit from a large *N*. I acutely realize that I am my own N of 1. If I ever use an "I" statement in my coaching, I consider it a flaw. A coach should certainly take his or her own experience into account. However, *relying* on that experience, the N of 1, is the ultimate coaching flaw. Yet it's one I see over and over again. I have seen dozens of athletes fail to improve because they are relying on an N of 1 to guide them. Ultrarunning coaches routinely regurgitate their personal training for their athletes. And runners who coach themselves tend to insert too much of their own bias into the process. Others ask their peers what they have done, relying on small likelihood that the N of 1 will also work for them.

MISTAKE 2: TOO MUCH FOCUS ON VOLUME

Ultramarathons are long, sometimes taking a day or even two to complete. Athletes often look at the prospect of locomoting for hours on end and feel overwhelmed, thinking, "If I'm going to be out there forever, I better run and hike in training as much as possible." They make the classic sacrifice of substituting more volume in place of intensity. They train low and slow, and they do it all the time. While this type of training does produce limited benefits for the ultramarathon athlete, it carries significant risk, and the point of diminishing returns is reached quickly. Quite simply, you run more miles but don't get enough out of them.

MISTAKE 3: NOT ENOUGH INTENSITY

Athletes often think, "I'll be running slowly during my race, so I don't need to run fast during training." This thinking is not entirely flawed. It's not that you need to run spectacularly fast but rather that you need to focus on a range of different intensities. Developing specific parts of your physiology, through focused intensity during different parts of the year, produces a more fit and ready athlete, regardless of your background and goals. For those of you reading this book who do in fact incorporate some sort of intensity, I applaud you and encourage you to give yourself a pat on the back. However, even when athletes incorporate intensity, I have often found it to be sporadic and unsystematic. They do different intensities during the week (say, a speed session on Tuesday and a tempo run on Thursday) or not enough of the same intensity all at once. Yes, some intensity is better than none, but focused and concentrated intensity, applied systematically over a period of weeks, is the best way to become a complete athlete.

MISTAKE 4: LACK OF SPECIFICITY

It's easy to generalize that all ultramarathons are long and done at a low intensity. Although this is oftentimes the case, you can train and prepare for specific elements within individual races. How steep are the climbs? How hot is the race? How far apart are the aid stations? What is the terrain like? These are elements of specificity you can train for. For example, consider trail versus road. Athletes understand that if the goal event is on trail, they need to train predominantly on trail. Simple, right? Yet many athletes, even the best, make the mistake of changing their terrain specificity in the weeks leading up to a critical race. There is fantastic track in Chamonix, France, just next to the starting line of the Ultra-Trail du Mont-Blanc (UTMB). It's a picturesque setting, with the stunning Alps framing the background. For some odd reason, when thousands of athletes descend upon Chamonix every August for the 100-mile UTMB and its companion races, many of them feel the need to do mile repeats and 5K time trials around the pristine, smooth track surface. The last time I checked, there's not one speck of track surface on any of the trails around Chamonix.

The concept of specificity extends beyond the surface under your feet. You can, and should, extend that concept to every aspect of the race. The degree to which you can apply specificity to training makes you better prepared for all the elements on race day, including the intensity, duration, environmental conditions, and whatever other troubles and tribulations you might encounter.

BOILING IT DOWN: WHAT YOU NEED TO GET IT RIGHT

I'm often asked, "What is your training philosophy?" Athletes ask about it. The media ask about it. Our CTS coaches learn it. As you are reading, you are probably wondering about it, too. So just what is it? Though it is difficult to express in a sound bite or elevator pitch, my training philosophy encompasses physiology, psychology, emotional support, communication, personal values, risk-taking, and a host of other aspects. It has taken me over a decade to flesh out a comprehensive coaching philosophy, and I continue to do so as I evolve as a coach. Several books would be needed to explain it down to the minutiae, which I will spare you. But for the purposes of this book, it can be broadly divided into two components: a philosophy around relationships and a philosophy around how to comprehensively prepare an athlete for success.

CARE MORE ABOUT THE PERSON THAN THE PERFORMANCE

One of the best coaches I know is Adam Pulford. If you are an ultrarunner, chances are you have never heard of him. But if you have been anywhere near a mountain bike race in the United States in the past several years, you surely have. Adam came to CTS not as an endurance athlete but as a collegiate wrestler (with the cauliflower ears to prove it). He was chunky, almost doughy, and had a lot to learn—far more than even I did. In fact, some of our senior coaches wanted to let him go because his knowledge gap seemed just too big. He had to learn *all* the nuances of the different endurance sports. During his internship, he meticulously analyzed the critical components of cycling, triathlon, and running. About the same time, he snagged an entry into the Leadville 100 mountain bike race. It was one of his first personal endurance events, and it was a complete cluster. Before the race, he broke his bike. During the race, he had four flats, almost broke his bike in half, and was a complete train wreck less than halfway through. I worked one of the latter aid stations and noted when Adam came crawling in, dehydrated, bonking, and in a very bad mood. I silently gave him little chance of finishing. Worse than having a rough day on course, he clearly wasn't following any of the advice he would regularly dish out to his athletes. He was a new coach who was not able to talk the talk or walk the walk. He did miraculously finish the race under the 12-hour cutoff, but not without a tremendous amount of suffering and unnecessary duress.

Despite watching Adam implode at the Leadville 100, I had no reservations about hiring him as a coach. The mistakes he made as a novice endurance athlete were correctable. He was clearly smart and resourceful, and we could fix the knowledge gap. Most importantly, though, he already possessed a quality I have found to be unteachable—a quality that is far more important than suffering through any race or being able to run a lactate threshold test: He cares. He cares for his athletes and about his work with more passion and fervor than anyone I know. Since I hired Adam, he's expanded his knowledge base and is one of the smartest coaches we have. But what still sets him apart, what makes him a truly great coach, is that he cares about the athletes he works with as people first and athletes second. He embodies the often-quoted idea: "Your athletes will not care how much you know until they know how much you care."

I care about performance deeply, but I care about people first. Conversations start with questions about my athletes' lives, not about their training. I do not coach "clients"; I coach athletes, and they are not machines or a collection of data points. The people I have the privilege of working with are athletes, fathers, mothers, breadwinners, the soccer coach, and my personal friends. They are the people I will travel to far-flung races for and stay up with at all hours of a cold, shivering night simply to hand them a gel and give them a hug when they need it most. It is why I don't deliver static "training plans," and you will not find one in this book. Coaching goes far beyond a training plan that is packaged, delivered, and then blindly followed. Training plans cannot care. By starting from a perspective of caring for the person first, I can deploy strategies necessary to make that person a better athlete. All athletes should remember that point. Before you are an athlete, you are a person. You play many different roles in life, including your role as an athlete. Training needs to take those roles into account. Training should encompass you as a father, mother, breadwinner, and soccer coach as well as an athlete. Remember that as you work through your own training process, regardless of whether you work with a coach, follow a training program, or coach yourself.

FITNESS MATTERS THE MOST

If you focus on just one thing in your training, it should be it your fitness. For purposes of this book, I define fitness as cardiovascular fitness, or the total amount of oxygen your body can utilize and the economy with which it does so. I always strive to put the most fit athlete on the starting line of an ultramarathon. This means organizing training in a strategic way to maximize the gains that an athlete can make during the season. I think all athletes would agree that being more fit is better than being less fit on the starting line, yet I can definitively say that most training plans do not meet the objective of producing maximum fitness. Rather, many athletes choose to focus on other aspects in lieu of developing their cardiovascular fitness. They hit the weight room to improve their strength. They pound the downhills to season their quads. They restrict carbohydrate to burn more fat. As I'll discuss in more depth in Chapter 2, these training techniques, though well intended, are actually likely to hinder you from achieving your best cardiovascular fitness—and ultimately your best race-day performance.

You may be dubious. After all, one of the greatest things about ultrarunning is its accessibility, and you don't have to be incredibly fit or talented to participate. Most races have generous cutoffs, aimed at encouraging more participation. Take the Javelina Jundred 100 in Fountain Hills, Arizona, where the cutoff is 30 hours (a common cutoff time for many 100-mile events), or 18 min/mi. The preferred walking speed for humans is 19:21 min/mi (Levine and Norenzayan 1999; Mohler et al. 2007; Browning et al. 2006). Let that sink in for a moment. This means that if you observe people walking by, chances are they are walking at approximately 19 minutes and 21 seconds per mile. If you stop reading this book, put it down, and walk to the fridge (or the coffeepot to stay awake), you are probably walking at around 19 min/mi, merely 5.6 percent slower than the necessary speed to beat the cutoff for the Javelina Jundred. I use this as an illustration of how accessible ultramarathoning is and how most people have the fitness to locomote at the required speed for an ultramarathon finish. They need not improve their fitness to simply run at that speed. Compare that scenario with running a 30-minute 5K, which is an admirable goal for many runners (median finishing times for the 5K are 28:46 for men and 34:53 for women according to a Running USA state-of-the-sport report for 2014). Not all people are able to run a 9:40 mile, the necessary pace to run a 30-minute 5K. To do so, one would need to become more fit so the body could handle that pace, even for 1 mile. Not so for most ultramarathons. Just about everyone toeing the line for an ultramarathon has the fitness to run 1 mile, or even many miles, at or significantly faster than the cutoff pace. Why, then, focus on becoming more fit if you already have the fitness to complete an ultramarathon? The reason is that there is a difference between merely participating in an ultramarathon and working to assure your success in a race.

Being as fit as possible gives you the best chance for success. Fitness gives you options and allows you to fix problems you encounter on the trail. Fitness enables you to comprehensively address many of the stresses you are likely to encounter during an ultramarathon. When you are more fit, you spend less time on your feet, finish faster, and reduce the risk of injury. You spend less time between aid stations, are exposed to the elements for a shorter duration, and have the capacity to run faster at certain points to avoid inclement weather. If you are fit, you can afford to spend extra time at an aid station, and you have a buffer against getting lost and losing time; heck, maybe you can even have a little more fun out there. Your cardiovascular fitness is the key to unlocking your best ultramarathon running, and thus it is a central focus of this book.

In order to keep focus on your fitness, it is important that training be oriented toward the fundamentals. Athletes and coaches are quick to add extraneous stuff to training programs. They want to try the latest equipment, experiment with the newest diet, or start sleeping in an altitude tent before actually focusing on nailing down the basics of training. But it's a fool's errand to chase marginal gains on the fringes while neglecting the fundamental and known principles for improving endurance performance. Don't misunderstand me: I am a proponent of innovation in training, gear, and nutrition. I use advanced protocols for altitude training and heat acclimatization. But innovations should enhance sound training, not attempt to circumvent it.

To arrive at the starting line completely prepared for an event, you must maintain a tight focus on eight fundamental areas. When I coach an athlete, all decisions about training, nutrition, racing, and equipment are filtered through this list of eight. Simply put, if an activity doesn't address and enhance your performance in at least one of these fundamental areas, it isn't going to make you a faster, stronger, or better runner.

1. **Develop the cardiovascular engine.** The more oxygen you can take in, deliver, and process in working muscles, the better. The workouts necessary for this are not complicated or particularly sexy. Some could even be called boring, yet I don't apologize for that. Gimmicks sell but fade out; sound training principles will never let you down.

2. **Improve lactate threshold climbing speed.** You spend a lot more time going uphill than downhill, and that's where you can most dramatically improve your pace and your race-day performance. Lactate threshold is also one of the most trainable aspects of performance, which means that LT work yields the greatest improvements for the amount of effort you put toward it in training.

3. **Concentrate your workload.** Training stimulus has to be sufficient to cause an adaptation, and as athletes get more fit, a bigger and more concentrated stimulus is needed. In practical terms, this means creating training blocks and maintaining focus on one area of training long enough to squeeze as much adaptation from it as possible.

4. **Train the gut.** The best cardiovascular engine in the world won't help you if you overheat, fall short on calories, run out of fluids, or suffer from gastric distress. How, what, when, and how much you eat and drink can all be trained so you can supply your body with the fuel and fluid it needs.

5. **Do the most specific things last.** Each event has its unique nuances, and preparing for them is important. The most effective way to do that is to start with the broadest aspects of training (aerobic endurance, time on your feet, etc.) and gradually work your way to the most specific aspects, such as event-specific intensity, environmental adaptations, and terrain and grade specificity, closer to your event.

6. **Race with a purpose.** Ultramarathons are too hard, long, and difficult to race on a whim. When the going gets tough—and it will—it is purpose that will help drive you forward. Why are you doing this? It does not have to be a

world-changing purpose. In my experience, athletes with deeply personal reasons for racing are able to better leverage their purpose than those with grander but perhaps less personal reasons.

7. **Rest with purpose and intensity.** It is all too easy to run yourself into the ground. Have confidence that past a certain point, the amount of running you can do does not correlate with an increased chance of finishing an ultramarathon or improving your finishing time. Training is a balance of stress and recovery. Recovery is a part of training, not the absence of it.

8. **Comprehensively prepare for all the stresses you will face on race day.** To paraphrase Scottish poet Robert Burns, "The best-laid plans of mice and men often go awry, and leave us with nothing but grief and pain." Some race-day stresses are easily visualized and anticipated, like the chill of the night or the distance between aid stations. Others will present themselves at inopportune times and in the worst places imaginable. Such is the nature of the sport. Everyone faces tough moments in ultramarathons, and you have to be prepared to deal with those you can predict and be ready to think your way through the ones you didn't see coming.

The methods I have developed are for anyone wishing to complete or improve at the ultramarathon distance. There is a lot of information to cover in the coming pages about training, the science of ultrarunning, and proper periodization. My ultimate goal, however, is to inspire athletes. By giving you the tools to correctly apply sound methodology to your ultramarathon preparation, I hope to inspire you to take on bigger, badder, more audacious goals.

WHY THE 0.5 PERCENT MATTERS TO THE 99.5 PERCENT

The "schedule review" is a frequently used coaching education exercise at CTS. The approach is simple: Throw your athlete's training plan up on a computer monitor, provide a brief background on the athlete, and listen to what the other coaches in the room tell you is right and wrong about the plan. We banter, philosophize, criticize, delve into physiology, and generally (but not always) engage in a civil discussion. I have participated in hundreds of these schedule reviews over the years, but I vividly remember one in particular. One of our younger coaches had just started working with a national-caliber athlete. He loaded up that athlete's training plan on the big screen and gave an overview of the training phase. The training plan had the normal small flaws you'd expect from a young coach. Usually, we simply discuss these flaws and how to correct them. However, I could tell early on that this was likely to be a more heated discussion, one in which people's feelings could get hurt and a few four-letter words might come out (there's a big difference between "I don't understand what you are doing" and "I don't understand what the hell you are doing"). The crux of the actual problem was small, revolving around the proper length of interval to use for a particular adaptation. To put it in perspective, the amount of workload we were at odds over amounted to 12 minutes in one particular workout in one particular phase of training. The athlete was training nearly 40 hours, or 2,400 minutes, during that phase, yet here we were arguing over 12 of those 2,400 minutes, or just 0.5 percent of the total training for the month. We spent a heated two hours arguing about whether those 12 minutes were right or wrong. The young coach dug in his heels. Our more seasoned coaches ripped him apart. Finally, the young coach asked in desperation, "It's 12 minutes; why does it matter?" Arguing over a mere 0.5 percent of the total training load seemed ludicrous. After a painful pause from the group, the simple retort was, "When you are working with elite athletes, you better get it right."

For elite athletes, 0.5 percent matters. The United States Olympic Committee's physiologists have calculated the difference between a gold medal and *no medal* to be about 0.5 percent (Pyne, Trewin, and Hopkins 2004; Hopkins 2005; Saporito 2012). This means that, in any Olympic-level competition, the athlete at the top of the podium listening to her national anthem is only 0.5 percent better than the athlete who finished in fourth place and is sitting in the stands. This fact is not lost on seasoned coaches who work with Olympic-caliber athletes, which is why they're willing to spend two hours making that point to a more junior coach.

So what does this 0.5 percent matter to the average runner? Do elites have something to teach us, or are they part of a unique club to which only the gifted need apply? The truth is, you can do a lot wrong while coaching novice or amateur athletes, and they'll still improve. Usually there's so much space between their current level and their ultimate potential that even a poorly designed plan will nudge them in the right direction. Some coaches rely on that ambiguity. They don't know how what they're prescribing will actually improve performance, or to what extent, but then again neither do the athletes.

The reason coaching elite athletes matters is that it teaches us what actually works and what doesn't. Elite athletes are closest to the limits of human performance. They have already optimized and wrung all the improvements out of many aspects of training, nutrition, recovery, and race-day strategy. While they are reaching for that last 0.5 percent, they do so from a foundation made strong by proven training methods that worked not once but consistently over a period of years. That's the piece that is most relevant to amateurs, and it is the reason my work with elite athletes improves the training methods I utilize with athletes of all ability levels.

A CAST OF CHARACTERS

Much of this book is based on my practical coaching experience with ultramarathon runners. It is a smorgasbord of science, philosophy, practical application, and coaching intuition. It is a representation of what I do day-to-day as a coach and what my athletes do to succeed. The athletes I work with live and breathe the coaching practices detailed in this book. It seems fitting, then, that they offer their own perspectives on the process. In that spirit, throughout this book they have provided their own anecdotes of their training experiences. These accounts were carefully chosen so they can be applied to a variety of runners, from the front of the pack to the back and everyone in between. You may recognize some of these athletes; others you may not. Either way, I hope you find the input from this cast of characters inspirational and informative.

DAKOTA JONES (aka "Young Money.") I hope I have the opportunity to work with Dakota until he's "old, used, and out of circulation" money. That's how much I enjoy seeing him succeed. Fortunately, he's got a long, long time to reach that point. A runner in high school, Dakota found ultrarunning through his love of the mountains and the tight-knit ultrarunning community in Durango, Colorado.

Dakota began working with me when he was an aspiring elite ultrarunner, having won several races and looking to further improve his abilities. Since then, Dakota has taken his happy-go-lucky approach all over the globe, racing and running in some of the most high-profile ultra events. Make no mistake: When the gun goes off, he is a fierce competitor. He cares about the preparation and training he does in advance of an event. If you ever get the chance to meet him, ask him for some of his world-famous baked goods. The walnut chocolate chip cookies are my favorite.

RUNNING HIGHLIGHTS

2015
Transvulcania 83K—4th place, 7:28

2014
North Face Endurance Challenge, San Francisco 50-mile championships—2nd place, 6:12 | Moab Trail Marathon—1st place, 3:02

2013
San Juan Solstice 50 Mile—1st place and course record holder, 7:35 | Ultra Race of Champions 100K—2nd place, 9:32

2012
Lake Sonoma 50—1st place, 6:17 | Transvulcania 83K—1st place, 6:59 | Hardrock 100 Endurance Run—3rd place, 25:45

2011
Grand Canyon Rim-to-Rim-to-Rim—6:53 | North Face Endurance Challenge, San Francisco 50-mile championships—2nd place, 6:21 | Hardrock 100 Endurance Run—2nd place, 27:10 | Pocatello 50—1st place, 8:17 | Moab Red Hot 55K—1st place, 4:02

2010
North Face Endurance Challenge, San Francisco 50-mile championships—4th place, 7:01:55 | White River 50 Mile Endurance Run—2nd place, 6:49:20 | San Juan Solstice 50 Mile—8:13:00 | Desert R.A.T.S. 50 mile—1st place, 7:15:17

DYLAN BOWMAN (aka "DBo.") The master of stoke and a true bro's bro. Life is good for Dylan as long as he has a buttery singletrack trail to run and a burrito to devour afterward. Originally from Boulder, Colorado, Dylan had an unconventional path to ultrarunning from a college lacrosse career at Colorado State University. Although lacrosse is not a traditional endurance sport, his role as team "hustler" paid dividends for him as an elite ultrarunner. He works hard, communicates well, is disciplined and tough, and is a first-class person through and through. His nickname, "DBo," comes from his passion for the Denver Broncos and their former quarterback Tim Tebow.

RUNNING HIGHLIGHTS

2015
Tarawera Ultramarathon 100K—1st place, 7:44:58 | North Face 100K, Australia—1st place, 8:50:13 | North Face Endurance Challenge, San Francisco 50-mile championships—2nd place, 6:20:28

2014
Sean O'Brien 50 Mile—1st place, 6:23:17 | North Face Endurance Challenge, New York 50 Mile—1st place, 6:51:52 | Western States 100—3rd place, 15:36:41 | North Face Endurance Challenge, San Francisco 50-mile championships—5th place, 6:23:48

2013
Ray Miller 50 Mile—1st place, 6:47:36 | Miwok 100K—1st place, 4:49:56 | Western States 100— 5th place, 16:32:18 | North Face Endurance Challenge, San Francisco 50-mile championships— 5th place, 6:37:48

2012
Bandera 100K—4th place, 8:40:07 | Leona Divide 50 Mile—1st place, 6:00:38 | Western States 100—7th place, 16:03:24 | Speedgoat 50K—8th place, 5:47:39 | Run Rabbit Run 100 Mile—2nd place, 19:56:45 | North Face Endurance Challenge, San Francisco 50-mile championships—7th place, 6:02:48

2011
Moab Red Hot 55K—4th place, 4:15 | Antelope Island Buffalo Run 50 Mile—1st place, 6:15 | Collegiate Peaks 50 Mile—2nd place, 6:57:54 | San Diego 100—1st place, 18:00:15 | Leadville Trail 100—2nd place, 17:18:59

2010
Desert R.A.T.S. 50 mile—7th place, 8:20:54 | Quicksilver 50K—4th place, 4:04:01 | Ultimate Direction Dirty Thirty 50K—2nd place, 4:55:20 | Silver Rush 50—2nd place, 6:52:45 | Leadville Trail 100—3rd place, 18:36:16 | Run Rabbit Run 50 Mile—4th place, 7:50:00

2009
Run Rabbit Run 50 Mile—6th place, 8:51:00 | Silver Rush 50—7th place, 7:45:56

KACI LICKTEIG (aka "the Pixie Ninja.") If niceness, humbleness, and tenacity could be bottled, I'd label it "Pixie Ninja Potion." Kaci found ultrarunning after running for the University of Nebraska at Kearney. This collegiate running background has given her the physical fundamentals to excel at ultradistance events. Kaci is also what I affectionately refer to as "vertically deprived." Her training ground in Omaha, Nebraska, is about as flat as it gets, yet she has tackled many of the toughest mountain ultras, including the Western States 100-Mile Endurance Run. The terrain she has available and how she successfully works around that limiter is a lesson for many ultrarunners. Aside from being an elite ultrarunner, Kaci is an even better human being. She is also a physical therapist, which helps her better understand the training demands that I put her through.

RUNNING HIGHLIGHTS

2015
Lake Sonoma 50—5th place, 8:04:14 | Silver State 50—2nd place, 8:01:48 | Western States 100—2nd place, 19:20:31 | Ultra Race of Champions 100K—3rd place, 10:56:22

2014
Rocky Raccoon 100 Mile—2nd place, 15:45:32 | Lake Sonoma 50—3rd place, 7:37:42 | Ice Age Trail 50—1st place, 6:41:39 | Western States 100—6th place, 20:07:10 | Psycho Psummer Run Toto Run 50K—1st place and course record, 4:14:51 | The Bear Chase 100K—1st place, 8:40:45 | Market to Market 50K—1st place and course record, 3:27:33 | Javelina Jundred 100 Mile—1st place, 15:40

2013
Kettle Moraine 100K—1st place, 9:47:12 | Black Hills 100—1st place and course record, 19:12:01 | Psycho Psummer Run Toto Run 50K—1st overall, 4:19:35 | Lean Horse 50K—1st place and course record, 3:43:50 | Hawk Hundred 50 mile—1st overall and course record, 7:25:38 | The Bear Chase 50 mile—1st overall, 6:54:15 | Market to Market 50K—1st overall, 3:38:02 | G.O.A.T.z 50K—1st place and course record, 3:54:17

MISSY GOSNEY. A badass momma, Missy is a tough-as-nails mountain woman living in Durango, Colorado. Throughout my coaching relationship with Missy, I know I can count on one thing—she will set outrageous, audacious goals. Whether it is the Hardrock 100, the 200-mile Tor des Géants, or the Nolan's 14 line, I'm never lacking for a new problem to help her solve. Before working with me, Missy had two decades of Outward Bound wilderness experience, which translates perfectly to rugged mountain courses and is an illustration of her spirit of adventure. She's a helluva mom, a helluva competitor, and a helluva inspiring person to work with.

RUNNING HIGHLIGHTS

2015
Zane Grey 50 Mile—2nd place, 11:18:36 | Hardrock 100 Endurance Run—4th place, 33:22:21 | Part of a duo who were the first women to complete the Nolan's 14 line in under 60 hours

2014
Cedro Peak 45 miles—3rd place, 9:04:43 | Bighorn Trail 100—1st place, 24:30:40 | North Face Endurance Challenge, San Francisco 50-mile championships—26th place, 9:41:09

2013
San Juan Solstice 50 Mile—4th place, 11:01:09 | Jemez Mountain 50 mile—5th place, 10:57:22 | Tor des Géants 330K—122nd place, 5 days, 3 hours, 16 minutes, and fun the whole way

2012
Zane Grey 50 Mile—6th place, 11:37:36 | Jemez Mountain 50K—2nd place, 6:14:54 | Bighorn 100—2nd place, 24:46:51 | Speedgoat 50K—10th place, 7:51:17 | Cascade Crest 100—1st place, 23:48:30 | Durango Double 50K—3rd place, 6:21:00

2011
Moab Red Hot 55K—12th place, 6:06:59 | Zane Grey 50 Mile—6th place, 13:13:48 | Jemez Mountain 50 mile—12:18:49 | San Juan Solstice 50 Mile—2nd place, 11:32:49 | Speedgoat 50K—3rd place, 7:20:03

2010
Jemez Mountain 50K—4th place, 7:06:37 | San Juan Solstice 50 Mile—10th place, 12:44:15

ERIK GLOVER. I first began working with Erik when he was a triathlete. At a certain point, the Ironman® distance was just too easy, so he decided to take a crack at an ultra. Eventually he got the bug for 100-milers and completed his first in no-drama fashion at the 2015 Lean Horse 100. Erik is usually the smartest person in the room, with a degree from the Massachusetts Institute of Technology. Despite his intelligence, he's still an ultrarunner. Erik is as entertaining as they come, always the life of the party. Yet at his core, he is a down-to-earth father and always puts his family first. Originally from Anchorage, Alaska, Erik now lives and trains in New York City, so I can always count on a good story from him about dodging roller-bladers in Central Park.

RUNNING HIGHLIGHTS

2015
American River 50 Mile—25th place, 7:55 | Vermont 100K—6th place, 11:16 | Lean Horse 100 Mile—5th place, 21:17

2014
American River 50 Mile—174th place, 9:40 | North Face Endurance Challenge, New York 50 Mile—77th place, 10:56

2013
American River 50 Mile—145th place, 9:09 | North Face Endurance Challenge, Washington, D.C. 50 Mile—18th place, 5:16

2012
American River 50 Mile—116th place, 8:45

COME JOIN THE REVOLUTION

Ultrarunning is ready for a revolution. The old methods of training have reached their natural limitations; athletes can no longer simply run more and treat ultramarathons as longer marathons in order to perform better. A performance revolution happens in every sport, and the time has come for it to happen in ultrarunning.

As Leadville Trail 100 founder Ken Chlouber is famous for saying, each one of us has an "inexhaustible well of grit, guts and determination." If you do an ultramarathon, it is guaranteed that you will have to dig into that well at some point. When that point comes, it is important to be tough. But well-trained ultrarunners are more than tough. They are also fit, confident, and prepared for success. I want you to be all of these things, and I have the plan to get you there. So let's get going!

CHAPTER 2

THE HIGH-PERFORMANCE ULTRARUNNER

I have been fortunate to work with and run alongside many elite ultrarunners, and each one of them has a unique story of how they became one of the best. Some have formal sports backgrounds, having spent their formative years running around in circles on tracks. These athletes typically continued that process in a collegiate program, often running sequential seasons of cross-country, indoor track, and outdoor track. Some elites discovered running later in life, and they work to make the most out of their remaining competitive life span in a newfound sport. Still others developed into elite ultrarunners from a team sports background, bringing with them attributes and physical skills developed on the field rather than the track or trail. None of this is unusual, as there are no established development pipelines for ultrarunners. You can come into this sport at any age and from any background and still experience success, at a personal level certainly, and perhaps even at a competitive level.

In league sports such as football, basketball, baseball, and hockey, there are established pipelines for athlete development. Peewee leagues, middle school, high school, and collegiate programs systematically guide athletes from the fundamentals to high performance. Track running has a similar flow, with summer track programs, high school athletics, and the collegiate system. These established pipelines

///// DYLAN BOWMAN   HOW I GOT INTO ULTRARUNNING

Ever since I can remember, I've been an enthusiastic follower of sports. I have a photographic memory for useless sporting facts and possess the often annoying ability to regurgitate obscure statistics about a variety of athletes, teams, and events. I've always admired athletic greatness and been fascinated by the icons. When I was growing up in Colorado, my first sporting hero was the legendary Bronco quarterback John Elway. My mom still has a video of me wearing a head-to-toe Elway costume, complete with helmet and shoulder pads, to a family member's wedding when I was 3 years old. Apparently I refused to attend wearing anything else at the threat of an extreme tantrum.

My love for sport developed into an adolescence filled with soccer, basketball, and football. While I appreciated the great characters of individual sports, when it came to my own athletic ambitions, I always gravitated toward a team environment. As is the case for many young boys, I dreamed of one day being a star professional athlete for a first-tier NFL franchise (ideally, quarterback for the Denver Broncos). I had a decent amount of success and a tremendous amount of fun with these sports, but I found my true calling when I started playing lacrosse in eighth grade. I ended up having a solid high school and college career, with many successes and friendships.

My lacrosse career ended with my college eligibility, and suddenly I was without an organized sport for the first time in my life. It's not an exaggeration to say I felt lost and even a bit depressed. Athletics had been an enormous part of my life, and suddenly I didn't have the daily ritual of practice. I no longer had a craft to hone or a goal to achieve. It was a foreign and uncomfortable place. As luck would have it, in the summer after I graduated, I came across an article in the *Aspen Times* about an individual who would eventually become my very good friend and ultrarunning mentor, Zeke Tiernan.

Zeke had finished second at the Leadville 100 that year (2008), and the article focused on his preparation for and execution of that race. This was the first time I'd heard of ultrarunning, and I was captivated. It was one of those rare and precious moments in life when you are conscious that things will never be the same. I was awestruck by the scale of the undertaking and questioned whether it was even possible. I too craved the challenge of the Leadville 100. Suddenly, I had a goal again.

At the time of this writing, I've now done more than 30 ultras, 7 of which were 100-milers. My love for the sport has grown every year and with every race. What was once just a recreational hobby has become my passion and my lifestyle. Ultrarunning has provided me with the most powerful experiences of my life and a community of friends around the world. As a lifelong athlete, I think I finally found my calling.

/ / / / /

also feature talent identification systems, so the young baseball player who shows promise can be identified, nurtured, and developed to his potential. There are no analogous systems in ultrarunning. The elites in the sport today are a hodgepodge of postcollegiate runners, mountain athlete converts, and athletes who found running by happenstance as adults. Dylan Bowman, for example, played college lacrosse. Kaci Lickteig ran competitively in college and stereotypically graduated into longer distances. Dakota Jones was pulled into ultrarunning through his love of the mountains and the running community. These athletes came to ultrarunning from varied backgrounds and have followed different paths to success. This is possible because ultrarunning rewards diversity. Instead of rewarding an athlete's ability to perform a technical skill (shooting baskets, hitting baseballs, swimming with perfect technique, etc.) over and over again, ultrarunning has room for athletes with varied talents and skills to excel. The traditional trail running aspect of the sport favors athletes brought up through track and cross-country programs. The steep climbing, hiking, technical terrain, and high-altitude traverses are places where mountain sport athletes shine. Athletes with league sports backgrounds are experts at leveraging teamwork, tenacity, and toughness to elevate their individual performances. All this makes for a wonderful mix that keeps the sport fresh and accessible to new talent. The diversity of athletic backgrounds serves as a catalyst for new ideas on training, free from the bias of traditional run coaching and the opinion that ultrarunning is merely a longer marathon.

CHARACTERISTICS OF ELITE ULTRARUNNERS

Despite their diverse backgrounds, elite ultrarunners share three common characteristics. You have them too, to some degree. And all three can be developed by any runner to improve performance!

- **Talent.** All elite ultrarunners (and elite endurance athletes in general) have a high genetic potential for aerobic power. If you want to run fast for long periods of time, you have to be able to suck in a lot of air and use it to metabolize food into energy. The takeaway for any runner is that no matter your starting point, working to optimize your aerobic power will make you a better ultrarunner.
- **Toughness.** All elite ultrarunners are tough as hell—almost to a fault. The good news for all runners is that anyone can harness their inner toughness with focused training.
- **Emotional engagement.** Ultramarathons are hard. The best runners have an emotional attachment to the races they compete in. They care about the race and the community surrounding the event, not just their own performance. I encourage my athletes to pick races they have a genuine, visceral attraction to, the type of attraction that makes you excited, giddy, and just a bit scared all at the same time. I would encourage you to do the same.

The best ultrarunners possess the highest levels of talent, toughness, and emotional engagement. It is the harmonious intertwining of these qualities that ultimately allows them to perform at their peak. While we all wish to run as fast as an elite athlete, reality dictates that most of us will be much slower (sorry to break the news). The key is to optimize what you have by tapping into, leveraging, and developing your own innate talent, toughness, and emotional engagement.

TALENT

My formal educational background is in biochemistry and genetics. I spent the better part of five years toiling away in labs behind pipettes, graduated cylinders, and beakers, studying gene expression and its role in the development of living organisms. So it is with a bit of bias that I consider talent to mean your genetic predisposition for athletic activity. All elite ultrarunners are born with a high degree of innate talent. This gift bestowed on them by their parents is completely out of their control. Genetics sets some of the parameters and physiological limits of athletic potential. It plays a large role in determining the height of our highest-possible jump and the speed of our fastest-possible run, even if we could optimize everything else, like training, nutrition, and recovery. For an endurance athlete, physical talent is largely (but not exclusively) measured through the amount of oxygen one can consume, more commonly referred to as VO_2max.

This measure, the maximum volume of oxygen an athlete can consume, transport, and process, is usually expressed as milliliters per kilogram of body weight per minute (ml/kg/min). Typical VO_2max values for elite athletes in a variety of sports are shown in Figure 2.1. For endurance athletes, the rate of oxygen consumption is your most significant limiting factor, or your greatest advantage. The oxygen you consume is used to burn fuel in your body. The more oxygen you can consume, the more rapidly you can burn fuel and, therefore, the faster you can run. To be an elite athlete, you have to be able to consume the oxygen required to keep you at the front of the pack. When an athlete has the necessary VO_2max values, we typically say he or she is "in the club." In long-distance running, for example, a typical elite male will have a VO_2max around 77.4 ml/kg/min (Nevill et al. 2003). This does not mean that all elite runners have this level of maximum aerobic output. Nor does it mean that one can't be an elite runner with less than a 77.4 VO_2max. Instead, it means that in order to be an elite runner, you have to at least be close to that number. Someone who comes into our physiology lab and tests at only 40 ml/kg/min has no realistic chance of "getting into the club" in elite marathoning.

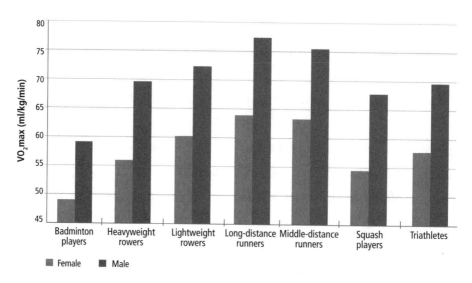

FIGURE **2.1** *Typical VO₂max values for elite athletes in various sports*
Source: Nevill et al. 2003.

Elite ultrarunners don't have VO₂max values as high as tose of other elite runners, but they still have to be able to consume oxygen at or above a certain rate in order to compete at the top of the sport. In my testing of elite ultrarunners, males can be successful with a VO₂max of approximately 60 ml/kg/min and female athletes with a VO₂max of approximately 55 ml/kg/min. This means simply that if you want to win a big, competitive race, like the Western States 100, Leadville Trail 100, or Lake Sonoma 50, your VO₂max values need to be in those neighborhoods.

In spite of how much emphasis I put on the aerobic system, I am the first to admit that an athlete's aerobic power is not the only physiological variable to consider. If races could be won simply by having a higher VO₂max, athletes could skip the running part and just show up with VO₂max test results to claim their prizes. But to be a contender to win a major ultrarunning competition, an athlete needs many different physiological talents, even more so than for other running events. (I expand on this concept in Chapter 4, "Failure Points and How to Fix Them.") Elite ultrarunners are naturally skilled over varied terrain, with good balance, reflexes, and an innate sense of where to put their feet. They have a talent for coping with environmental stressors; they are able to consume food and fluid in great quantities in the middle of heated competition without getting sick. The fact of the matter is, elite ultrarunners are elites because they are talented across many physiological variables, not solely aerobic power.

It is important to note that these aspects of talent are trainable. Even an athlete with an elite VO_2max can improve with proper training. I know this because it has been demonstrated in elite athletes in other endurance sports. Additionally, several of the top runners I coach, many of whom won ultrarunning competitions before starting to work with me, are still able to achieve measurable increases in their VO_2max values. For beginning runners, VO_2max can improve by well over 20 percent. In elite athletes, improvement can also be attained, if to a lesser degree (usually 5 percent). Other aspects of innate talent can be similarly improved. You can train to consume more food, run over technical terrain, and handle heat and cold. In these respects, all athletes are maximizing their innate talents; elite athletes just have a higher ceiling.

Why Talent Matters

Very few athletes have the constellation of physical gifts required to be an elite ultrarunner, but talent is nevertheless important for all of us. Every athlete has some level of talent, and it is important to identify the areas where genetics and predispositions are well suited to ultrarunning. Maybe you don't have a world-class VO_2max, but you have a better-than-average ability to maintain your lactate threshold pace for long periods. That's useful for long climbs in events. Maybe you adapt remarkably well to high altitude, so your performance and pace don't drop as much at high elevations. Or perhaps you are able to sustain a heavy training workload week after week because you recover and adapt to training stress quickly. These are all naturally derived traits you can optimize and leverage in training and competition.

When elite ultrarunners line up at the start of a major race, they are very similar to one another in terms of talent. On paper, this would appear to be a race among equals, yet the runners' real-world performances vary greatly on any given race day. Where these athletes differ is in how much they have closed the gap between their actual performance level and their maximum potential. Because the athletes have very similar levels of talent, those who can operate closest to their physiological ceiling have the advantage. No matter where your own physiological ceiling is, the goal of training is to close the gap between your current performance level and your maximum potential. The great thing is that there is always room for improvement because none of us, not even Olympic-caliber athletes, operate at our maximum. We can get very, very close to that theoretical maximum, but we always come up a little short. That gap, which always exists, is the reason we can all improve given proper training.

TOUGHNESS

Four to one is my typical rule of thumb. For every four workouts I give an elite athlete, I'm holding him or her back in some way on one of them. This is because elite athletes are naturally very tough. All too often, they are too tough for their own good. They have a tendency to push through injury and illness, sometimes to the point where these problems become unnecessarily serious. This can be a bad thing in day-to-day training, but toughness is a golden quality on race day. Elite ultramarathoners train a lot. That's one of the bigger advantages they have over the rest of the pack. They organize their lives so they can train for many hours. However, even elite athletes can only prepare so much for race day. The goal is always to be 100 percent prepared, but reality dictates that they will show up at the starting line with at least a few chinks in the armor. Maybe they left mileage on the table. Sometimes they can't get in the vertical (Kaci Lickteig, for example, who lives in Nebraska). In these instances, toughness can take over where training leaves off. The elites bridge this gap better than the rest of the pack.

Why Toughness Matters

No matter how well you prepare for an ultra, it is nearly impossible to be fully ready for everything the race will throw at you. The elites have to be tough to maintain a performance level that will keep them in contention for victory; sometimes, when victory is no longer within reach, they have to rely on toughness just to keep moving forward. For a nonelite ultrarunner, toughness may be even more important because you are out on the course longer. There's more time to be affected by adversity, more opportunity for unfavorable weather to creep in, and several extra hours for your stomach to turn against you. You have to battle through fatigue at hour 23 or 27, whereas the elites were at the finish line hours earlier. Fortunately, toughness is a quality that can be developed and honed. It is forged through day-to-day training and through learning to endure specific challenges as you prepare for your ultramarathon event. Rising to those challenges by pushing through difficult workouts, working through bad patches during long runs, and venturing out for runs when it's rainy, snowy, windy, or dark increases your toughness. Being willing to be uncomfortable is essential for building toughness; it's a characteristic that will pay dividends when honed to its fullest potential.

EMOTIONAL ENGAGEMENT

Elite athletes have a high level of emotional engagement in the events they compete in, and it shows. They have a tendency to care about the community surrounding the event, not solely their own performance on race day. During interviews, the elites have a sense of history, past winners, and every rock, nook, and cranny of the racecourse. Many times, they know the aid station captains by name. After they are done competing, they often volunteer for the races they have won and come to love. In 2015, Western States 100 winner Rob Krar ran the final mile with the last finisher, in flip-flops. Think about that for a second. After running 100 miles and resting for about 14 hours, this guy had the energy and emotional investment to escort the final finisher all the way to, and around, the Placer High School track. He could have easily sat in the bleachers with the rest of the crowd and perhaps mustered the energy to join the standing ovation. But he did so much more. He took his emotional engagement several hundred steps farther. He cared about the overall race, and he cared about that last finisher. He has an emotional engagement with the Western States 100 that surpasses his own planning, preparation, and rigors of race day.

A large part of success in any elite competition is the athlete's emotional engagement with the event. We have all seen extremely talented, well-trained athletes underperform on the field of battle because they were "checked out."

It happens in every sport, at every level of competition, even in elite ultrarunning. The elites I work with are able to go to almost any race on the planet. When I sit down with them at the beginning of every season, the number of opportunities on the table is unmanageable. During this process of picking and choosing events, it is easy to identify the characteristics of the races that would best suit the athlete's physical abilities. It is easy to look at a race to match up how much climbing and descending it includes, consider how hot or cold it will be, and look at whatever other variables exist and say, "Well, you are good at X, Y, and Z, so go do the races with X, Y, and Z." However, I always begin with finding events the athlete is most emotionally engaged in. I put my athletes in a position for success by first encouraging them to train for events they genuinely care about, then building their physical tools around that event, not the other way around.

Why Emotional Engagement Matters

For the last four years I have been working with an athlete who has been attempting to complete the Leadville Trail 100 within the required 30-hour cutoff. Unfortunately, she has been unsuccessful in this endeavor thus far. Based on her innate talent, the 30-hour cutoff for that race is within the limits of her physical capabilities, but only by a razor-thin margin. For her to be successful, everything has to go right. In training she has to make the most of every day, completing each workout to the fullest and resting with purpose. During the race she needs perfect weather and flawless race execution, and she has to dig further into her training-honed well of toughness than ever before. If, and only if, all these things go right, she has a chance to be successful.

On her very best day in her very best year, this athlete is capable of a 29:45 finish. Unfortunately, for the last four years, she has been on the other side of that coin, yet she continues to go back, and I wholeheartedly encourage her to do so. I could easily coax her into an easier race with a more generous cutoff—perhaps a 100-miler at sea level. There are numerous events that would greatly increase her chances of finishing her first 100-miler, on paper at least. Yet, despite what I know from the rudimentary mathematical exercises of cutoffs, paces per mile, and probability ratios, I refuse to talk her out of racing Leadville. The sole reason for this is that she is 100 percent head over heels, obsessed, infatuated, and in love with the Leadville Trail 100. She is more emotionally engaged with that event than with any other race. So, even though on paper another event might be "easier" for her, I would argue that her best chance of success in a 100-mile foot race is in the race she's most passionate about.

Many people race in events they simply have no attachment to. I honestly don't know why. Even when you love the sport and the event you're preparing for, at some point you will want to quit. When you're exhausted, wet, cold, and nauseous, a part of your brain will tell you it's just not worth it, and you will quit. Training for and running an ultra are extremely hard. You'd better like what you are doing.

Missy Gosney's story of her Nolan's 14 odyssey (see sidebar, page 38) is a great example of how emotional engagement can drive the perseverance necessary in ultramarathoning. What she decided to take on was big. The route had never been completed by a woman. Previous finishers of the route were far more accomplished ultra athletes. As she puts it, success was "on the edges of my capabilities." As she initially undertook this endeavor, I emphasized the role that emotional engagement would play in maximizing her commitment to training and overcoming the hardest moments of the event itself. Three years of planning and waiting is a very long time, and many athletes would have given in to doubt, become frustrated, and ultimately given up. Missy didn't do that. Her high degree of emotional engagement with the goal ultimately enabled her to finish what she set out to accomplish.

TRAINING TIES TALENT, TOUGHNESS, AND EMOTIONAL ENGAGEMENT TOGETHER

Because this book centers on training for an ultramarathon, I'd be remiss if I neglected to tie together how training affects talent, toughness, and emotional engagement. Quite simply, training is the catalyst that maximizes these qualities. You can improve by training more. You can improve by training harder. However, the most successful athletes also train smarter than the rest. They utilize training to harmoniously maximize their innate talent, hone their inner toughness, and reinforce the emotional engagement for the event they are training for.

///// MISSY GOSNEY MY NOLAN'S 14 ODYSSEY

Mount Massive, Mount Elbert, La Plata Peak, Huron Peak, Missouri Mountain, Mount Belford, Mount Oxford, Mount Harvard, Mount Colombia, Mount Yale, Mount Princeton, Mount Antero, Tabeguache Peak, Mount Shavano. The Nolan's 14 route is nothing more than an unspecified connection of the 14 aforementioned 14,000-foot peaks in the Sawatch Range of central Colorado, dreamed up by a few mountain runners. The route is hemmed in by a loose set of rules—in fact, you make many of your own rules. For reference, the Nolan's 14 route is about 100 miles, climbs more than 44,000 vertical feet, and is a mixture of standard trails and find-your-own-adventure bushwhacks. The specified time limit is 60 hours. As of 2015, there had been only about 14 finishers, and none had been women.

I was captivated by the Nolan's 14 route when two friends of mine became some of the rare people to finish it in 2012. Both were far better runners than I, but I was fascinated by the route, and something about it made me think that it would just barely be possible for me to complete. It surely would be a big endeavor, something just on the edges of my capabilities. The fact that no women had finished the route was petrifying and intriguing at the same time. Additionally, I had spent 20 years teaching at the Outward Bound School in nearby Leadville, Colorado, so I had an attachment to the area.

To prepare, I learned the topography through maps and reconnaissance. I studied other people's attempts and successes and practiced different fueling and hydration techniques on long runs and in races. I failed at my first two attempts. In the first, I couldn't even get to the starting point. The logistics and enormity of the line made an attempt a nonstarter. The following year, a team consisting of me, my husband, and my coach made 12 of the 14 peaks over 55 grueling hours. Though the failure of two consecutive years was devastating, I was still drawn to the area and to the route. The challenge and the area were special to me.

For the third year, I teamed up with Anna Frost. Our goal was to finish the route, no matter what. As in previous years, I trained and studied the course. We assembled an excellent crew, who set up high alpine shelters, tracked the weather, and stayed up all hours of the night to assist us. The route was as difficult as always; after all, mountains don't get any smaller. Anna and I were successful that third year, summiting all 14 peaks in the required 60 hours. Though I still love the Sawatch, I think I'll call it good.

/ / / / /

Training maximizes talent by pushing your raw physical capabilities ever closer to their predetermined genetic limits. Even rudimentary training moves you in the right direction, and training that is well designed further enhances your progress. The better, more intelligent, and more precise the training design, the closer you will get to your physical talent ceiling.

As for toughness, its importance cannot be exaggerated. As much as I am an advocate for intelligent, precise training, I still want my athletes to work hard and push themselves when required. After all, physical adaptation to training is Darwinian in nature. Training should be difficult because you need to impose enough stress in order to adapt. In this way, training hones toughness. The weekly act of pushing yourself in training reinforces and builds toughness you will draw upon come race day.

Training is elective—with rare exceptions, we are not running to earn our next paycheck—which is all the more reason that emotional engagement is a key part of training. You choose to lace up your shoes, head out the door, and put in the miles. This ritual is a daily reminder of what you are ultimately training for, serving as reinforcement of the emotional engagement you have with your goals. How many of you reading this book post the elevation profile of the race you are training for on the wall or refrigerator? That is a form of emotional engagement. The hills you run, the intensity of your efforts, and nearly all aspects of training should remind you of the event you have chosen to undertake.

PRIORITIZING WHAT MATTERS

Training maximizes talent, hones toughness, and reinforces emotional engagement. But to do any of these things well, training also requires logic and precision. You need to do the right things, at the right time, and in the right amount in order to succeed. Many people have tried to describe the process of training, and for some reason, many endurance coaches seem to favor culinary analogies: *Training is like baking; you need the right proportion of ingredients. Training is like cooking; it's better to use a slow cooker than a microwave. Training is like a pizza.* I have always wondered whether the world's best chefs describe cooking using sports training analogies!

Despite good intentions, using the metaphor of ingredients, oven temperatures, and baking times to describe elements such as duration, intensity, and recovery misses the mark. It implies that the process of training is neatly compartmentalized and culminates in the creation of a finished, complete product. While I will describe these nice, neat components of training later in the book, it is important to understand that as an athlete, you are capable of more than a sum of ingredients and processes. Furthermore, training itself is continuous. Each race is simultaneously a performance goal and a training stimulus, and fitness builds incrementally as races and seasons accumulate.

The fact is that first and foremost, the training process should improve the athlete. The improvements are derived from the right mix of component parts such as duration, intensity, and recovery. Coaches and athletes who stick with the culinary mind-set insist on first finding the right type of intensity (oven temperature) and amount of volume (baking time) and then mix these two "ingredients" to produce an adaptation. This approach is backward. I focus first on the set of prioritized adaptations I want an athlete to achieve, as described in Figure 2.2. From this set of prioritized adaptations, in the order presented in the next section, I can then apply the right mix of training components to achieve performance gains that continue to build on themselves over the course of months and years.

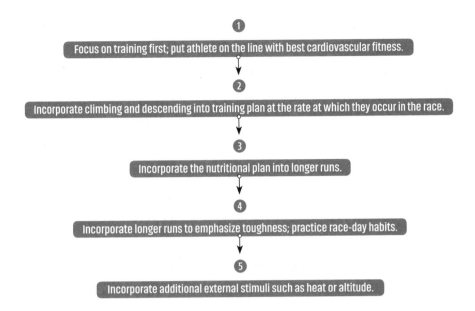

1 Focus on training first; put athlete on the line with best cardiovascular fitness.

2 Incorporate climbing and descending into training plan at the rate at which they occur in the race.

3 Incorporate the nutritional plan into longer runs.

4 Incorporate longer runs to emphasize toughness; practice race-day habits.

5 Incorporate additional external stimuli such as heat or altitude.

FIGURE **2.2** *Prioritized adaptations for ultrarunning*

FITNESS ALWAYS COMES FIRST

"What is your desert island workout?" This is an exercise we use in every CTS Coaching College (our in-house education program) for new coaches looking to join the company. The gist of the question is: If you could prescribe only one workout, what would it be? Recovery runs? Long endurance? Speed work? There is no right or wrong answer, but the exercise is great for revealing how a particular coach prioritizes training. My desert island workout has always been an easy choice: TempoRun. In my opinion, training at and right around lactate threshold is the highest priority for endurance athletes because performance at lactate threshold is the most trainable aspect of endurance physiology (providing the greatest potential for improvement) and the one most directly correlated with success in endurance events.

With so many variables affecting performance in ultradistance events, why prioritize cardiovascular fitness above all else? Because fitness makes everything easier. It enables you to sustain a given pace while utilizing less of your total capacity.

As I will describe in Chapter 4, which examines common limiting factors for performance, an athlete combats several sources of fatigue during a race. Your muscles, digestive processes, and thermoregulatory system are constantly competing for your body's resources. Fitness reduces the cardiovascular stress of locomotion, freeing up more of your body's resources for other functions.

I take this emphasis on cardiovascular fitness even further by focusing on the workouts and techniques that deliver the greatest cardiovascular adaptation. There are many ways to create workload, and the easiest thing a coach can do is smash an athlete with a ton of work. I don't like wasting time with workouts that are difficult (i.e., those that create a lot of fatigue) but deliver only minor adaptations. That is why you will see only a handful of workouts discussed in this book. It is also why the long- and short-range planning processes discussed in Chapters 8 and 9 focus on one energy system at a time. It is why I prefer to assign uphill interval work (enhances cardiovascular adaptation), limit downhill-specific sessions (produces little cardiovascular adaptation), demonize fat adaptation (limits cardiovascular adaptation), shy away from strength training (produces little cardiovascular adaptation), and concentrate training load on one energy system at a time (enhances cardiovascular adaptation).

CLIMBING AND DESCENDING COME SECOND

The amount of climbing and descending in an ultramarathon varies wildly from race to race. A 100-mile ultramarathon might have 50,000 feet of elevation change and individual climbs that last an hour or more. These variations cause big changes in the way athletes run (and walk), including the locomotive biomechanics that change as you go from climbing a 5 percent grade to climbing a 25 percent grade. After your cardiovascular fitness, preparing for the climbing and descending in your particular event is the next most important adaptation you should focus on. However, as you will see in Chapter 8, "Organizing Your Training," even though this is a high priority throughout your training, it becomes even more important as your race draws near.

THE QUESTION OF DOWNHILL REPEATS

Downhill running is important in ultrarunning. As the old adage goes: What goes up must come down. Add to that the fact that between uphill and downhill running, downhill is much sexier. Go ahead, check out YouTube and gawk at the Salomon videos of young, fearless athletes bombing down ridiculously steep, off-trail, technical terrain at preposterously high velocities. It is tempting to lace up some body armor, point downhill and let it fly. From a purely practical standpoint, there are two fundamental aspects to improving your downhill running prowess in an ultramarathon setting. The first is the speed you can run downhill; the second (which is more important to ultrarunning) is repeatability. Can you run downhill at the same speed mile after mile after mile? You can improve both of these things, but before jumping in headfirst and barreling down the next descent, consider how much of an impact this has in making you a better ultrarunner.

Many coaches and athletes advocate specific downhill and quad-banging sessions to properly prepare for downhill running. Others emphasize strength training to "season" the quads. I dislike both of those approaches, and I don't advocate either one of them. Make no mistake: You can become a better and more consistent downhill runner if you do specific, hard downhill sessions. But these improvements come at too high a cost, and you are sacrificing one benefit for another. Yes, your quads might improve. You might become a faster downhill runner. You might be able to better tolerate more vertical feet of descending. But you do so at the expense of improving something else, namely, your cardiovascular fitness. I will always take 1 percent improvement on the ups (related to cardiovascular fitness) versus 1 percent improvement on the downs. Why? Simple math. In any ultramarathon race you are going uphill for a far greater proportion of time than you are going downhill. Sometimes, the ratio is as much as 2 to 1. You will gain more time by being a faster climber than you will gain   >

being faster downhill. Or, put another way, even with training, you don't descend fast enough to overcome the time you lose by going slower uphill. Add to that the fact that the risk of injury, both acute and overuse, is far greater from high-velocity downhill running than from uphill running. Yes, you should practice downhill running, but not at the expense of improving climbing performance and certainly not to the extent that you are doing specific downhill sessions.

Practically speaking, the best high-performance ultramarathon training will incorporate running and hiking on the specific grades that the athlete will experience during the race. In a perfect scenario, I have athletes actually get out on the racecourses in the weeks leading up to their events. In these cases, grade specificity is easy to accomplish. But most athletes do the majority of their training on their local trails and therefore can only use the grades that are available. So how do you train for 12 percent grades when you don't have hills of that particular grade in your area?

Aside from the ideal scenario of training on the actual racecourse, the best way to prepare for the amount of climbing and descending in your race is to find the average elevation change per mile and train on trails that mimic that general average. Let's use the Hardrock 100 as an example. Colorado's San Juan Mountains, where the race takes place, serve up 67,984 feet of elevation change (gain + loss) over the 100 mountainous miles, for an average elevation change of 679 feet per mile (67,984 feet of change / 100 miles), or 6,790 feet of elevation change in a 10-mile run. In training for this event, I constantly emphasize the importance of trying to match the average elevation change of the Hardrock course, particularly as the race draws closer. The reason this is effective, despite not exactly matching the grades you'll face in the race, is that athletes with generally varied terrain to work with will achieve a distribution of grades similar to their goal race when they are climbing and descending enough to achieve the average elevation change of their race. There are certainly exceptions, like Kaci Lickteig, who runs in Nebraska

///// *KACI LICKTEIG* I AM VERTICALLY DEPRIVED

My name is Kaci Lickteig, and I am vertically deprived. Yes, I am short, but that's not what I am talking about. I train in Omaha, Nebraska. My version of a hill is the one on Pacific Street, which gains a total of 91 feet in 0.3 mile, according to Strava. In an average week, if I get 3,000 feet of elevation gain and loss around the roads and trails of Omaha, it's a good week. That means it takes me nearly seven weeks and 700 miles to accumulate the climbing and descending that I will go through during the Western States 100-Mile Endurance Run. But I fear not. I focus on how fit I can be on race day. I do this so that when I am faced with the vertical challenge in front of me during the race, I do so on an established base of cardiovascular fitness. I have confidence that my fitness means more than accumulating the vertical. Yes, I wish I could climb mountains and descend sweet singletrack every day. But the hill on Pacific Street and the fitness I can gain are my reality, and they continue to carry me up and over many tall mountains.

/////

and has very limited access to hills and even less access to varied grades. Athletes without access to hills for training need to place even more emphasis on the already high priority of cardiovascular fitness.

NEXT, INCORPORATE YOUR NUTRITION PLAN

Ultramarathon events are tricky. Part of that difficulty comes from the sheer energy output required to cover 50 or 100 miles on foot. Consuming calories is a necessity, and even with all the food you'll eat during an ultramarathon, you will still finish with a massive caloric deficit. However, filling the nutrition gap is not as simple as popping more gels or gorging on some pumpkin pie at an aid station. As I'll explain in detail in Chapter 4, "Failure Points and How to Fix Them," and Chapter 10, "Fueling and Hydrating for the Long Haul," you can't simply take a marathon fueling plan and extend it. Marathon fueling plans assume you are well fed going into the race and that you will be able to eat another meal soon after a 3- to 4-hour race. A 100-miler can take runners 13 to more than 30 hours to complete. A 50-miler can take 5 to 16 hours. Even if the hourly caloric intake is similar to what you might consume during a shorter run, the overall volume of food you have to consume during an ultramarathon is uncommonly high. You don't normally ask your body to process that much food in 5 to 30 hours, so you have to train it to be able to take it all in. Even more important, you have to adapt to eating this quantity of food while dealing with the up-and-down jostling required of running and without developing gastrointestinal distress. All of this can be trained, and it's important to do so because GI distress is the leading reason—before injuries or exhaustion—that athletes fail to finish 100-mile running races (Hoffman and Fogard 2011).

AFTER THAT, DO LONG RUNS

If you have maximized your cardiovascular fitness, run on terrain similar to the race, and dialed in your nutrition plan, I consider that a win. Many people obsess over the length of their longest training run, but even if your longest run is far less than half of your race distance, I'll take it. Long runs are great, but physiologically the adaptations that result from very, very long runs occur over the course of several months and years, not one run. Believe me, I would love it if every athlete I coach could put in a 100K before a 100-miler or a 50K before a 50-miler. But even when this is logistically possible, it's not always the best thing for the athlete, particularly if he or she still has room to make cardiovascular fitness improvements. Very long runs are hard on the body. They take time and energy to complete. Most important, they take a lot of time to recover from. Cardiovascular fitness, grade specificity, and a nutritional game plan are must-haves; I view superlong runs as "nice to have." Bottom line, your longest runs are most helpful for dialing in your habits and your nutrition and hydration strategies, and for developing the toughness discussed earlier in this chapter. If you can, you should absolutely do long runs, even up to 75 percent of the race distance or time. But these should be a priority only after you have maximized your fitness, trained for the grade, and established your nutritional game plan.

FINALLY, INCORPORATE OTHER STIMULI

Dean Golich, our resident sports scientist at CTS, has coached Olympic and world championship medalists along with professional hockey players, NASCAR drivers, and a host of other high-performance athletes. One of the things that makes Dean such a successful coach is that he knows when to incorporate other stimuli such as altitude training, strength training, and heat acclimatization, and also when not to. "Win two world championships, *then* think about using an altitude tent" is a phrase he is famous for saying in high-level coaching conferences. It's not that he dislikes altitude training or altitude tents. He uses both with his high-performance athletes. His point is that you can't take your focus off the fundamental aspects of training to chase marginal gains. Even athletes at the highest levels of sport focus on—and improve—their basic, boring, fundamental skills and energy systems year after year, even after winning one (or two) world championships. That doesn't mean you shouldn't incorporate heat acclimatization or altitude training; it just means you need to be careful not to make them a higher priority than they deserve.

These prioritized adaptations set the fundamental framework for how athletes should focus their training and preparation throughout the year. You will see these ideas manifest themselves in the daily workouts and long-range and short-range planning processes described in Chapters 7, 8, and 9 of this book. If you can keep these priorities in mind, they keep your training from "going down the rabbit hole." They prevent you from getting off track with activities that keep you busy but don't do enough—or anything—to improve your ultrarunning performance. As such, they also serve as a guide to what not to do. I would never advocate heat acclimatization for an athlete who still needs to prepare for elevation change in his or her event. Nor would I have an athlete focus on training for a specific amount of vertical gain and loss in lieu of fitness. There will always be something else you *can* do. The key to preparing for ultramarathons is choosing the training activities that matter the most and that you *should* do.

WHAT ABOUT CROSSTRAINING?

There are numerous activities you might choose to augment your ultrarunning training: strength training, Pilates, yoga, CrossFit, and stretching, to name a few. Most of these activities have merit for improving one's quality of life. However, very few, if any, have merit for acutely improving ultrarunning performance. The reason is precisely related to the prioritized adaptations mentioned earlier. From an ultrarunning performance perspective, the activity that will improve your performance the most is running, period. As will be discussed in the next chapter, your ultrarunning training needs to be specific to the demands of the event you are training for. This means incorporating the necessary vertical gain and loss and the terrain specificity of the event, as well as actually running (and hiking if that is what the event will call for). Sounds simple, but many people miss this point. They sweat it out in a Bikram yoga class when they could be resting. They pump iron when they could be running a few more intervals. If there is room in the day and energy in the tank to do other activities, quite frankly it would be in the best interest of your ultrarunning performance to simply rest (so that you can work harder in the next workout) or increase your workload in lieu of adding another activity.

Doing some of these nonrunning activities certainly has merit in your athletic life. If you want to build some bigger muscles, relax and meditate in a yoga class to achieve balance, or enjoy the camaraderie of a pickup basketball game, go for it. Will those activities make you a better overall athlete? Absolutely. Will they make you a better ultrarunner? Probably not, particularly if you do them at the expense of your run-specific training.

CHAPTER 3

THE PHYSIOLOGY OF BUILDING A BETTER ENGINE

The human body is an absolutely incredible machine. You take in food, an all-encompassing term that covers everything from fresh berries to a Big Mac, and within minutes convert it (or at least some of it) into usable energy. When it comes to accessing that energy, you are able to go from the sedentary state of reading this book to sprinting (if necessary) at a moment's notice. And as you run longer or change your pace, your body seamlessly adjusts how it produces energy based on how quickly you are demanding it and the energy sources available. To do this, the human body has three primary energy systems that power all activities: the immediate energy system (adenosine triphosphate [ATP] and creatine phosphate [CP]), the aerobic system, and the glycolytic (anaerobic) system. All three energy systems produce ATP, which releases energy when one of its three phosphate bonds is broken. The resulting adenosine diphosphate is then resynthesized to ATP so it can be broken again, and again, and again. All three energy systems are always working; there is no on-off switch, and at any given time the amount of energy produced by each system is based on demand. These three energy systems are fundamental to endurance training, and although you don't need a physiology degree to be a good ultrarunner, it is nonetheless helpful to understand the systems you're training.

THE IMMEDIATE ENERGY SYSTEM: ATP/CP

The ATP/CP system supports high-power efforts that last less than about 10 seconds. You use it when you have to jump out of the way of a speeding bus, and from an athletic standpoint it's most important in power sports like football. In endurance running, this system is used mostly for explosive movements like jumping across a creek or bounding up a series of boulders. During those few seconds, you demand energy faster than either the glycolytic or aerobic energy system can deliver it. The ATP/CP system is immediate because the ATP part is the energy-yielding molecule produced by the other systems. The very limited supply that is stored in your muscles can provide energy without the more than 20 steps required to produce ATP through the aerobic system. Endurance athletes don't rely heavily on this system, and it is typically adequately developed through normal training.

THE AEROBIC SYSTEM

The aerobic system, which is the body's primary producer of energy, is an utterly amazing machine. It can burn carbohydrate, fat, and protein simultaneously and can regulate the mixture it burns based on fuel availability and energy demand. It's a flex-fuel engine that's remarkably clean and efficient; when the aerobic system is done with a molecule of sugar, the only waste products are water and carbon dioxide. In comparison, the glycolytic system (discussed in more detail later) produces energy faster, but it can only utilize carbohydrate, produces less ATP from every molecule of sugar it processes, and produces lactate as a by-product.

The rock stars of the aerobic system are little things called mitochondria. These organelles are a muscle cell's power plants: Fuel and oxygen go in, and energy comes out. For an endurance athlete, the primary goal of training is to increase the amount of oxygen the body can deliver and process. One of the biggest keys to building this oxygen-processing capacity is increasing mitochondrial density, or the size and number of mitochondria in muscle cells. As you run, having more and bigger power plants running at full capacity gives you the ability to produce more energy aerobically every minute.

When training increases the speed at which you can run aerobically, you can maintain a faster pace before reaching the point where you're demanding energy faster than the aerobic engine can deliver it, the intensity otherwise known as lactate threshold. But increasing your pace at lactate threshold is only part of the equation. With specific training at intensities near your lactate threshold, you can also increase the amount of time you will be able to run at and slightly above and below threshold.

THE GLYCOLYTIC ENERGY SYSTEM

There's been a lot of confusion about the glycolytic system, mainly because of semantics. This is the system people often refer to as "anaerobic," which literally means "without oxygen." This terminology causes confusion because it implies that the body has stopped using oxygen to produce energy, which is not the case. As exercise intensity increases, you reach a point at which your demand for energy matches your aerobic engine's ability to produce it in working muscles. Then you decide to push the pace or hit a hill. Your energy demand increases, and in order for your mitochondria to continue producing enough energy, your body uses a metabolic shortcut called anaerobic glycolysis. Although the actual process involves many chemical reactions, to put it more simply, glycolysis rapidly delivers the ATP necessary to meet your increased energy demand by converting glucose (sugar) into lactate to keep other energy-producing reactions moving.

Lactate is a partially utilized carbohydrate that eventually will build up in your muscles. The molecule is created as a normal step of metabolism and is constantly being recycled back into usable energy. As exercise intensity increases, you reach a point where lactate removal or processing can no longer keep up with production. A disproportionate amount of lactate builds up in the muscle and blood, and this accumulation is what we look for when we're determining an athlete's lactate threshold.

What ultimately happens to these lactate leftovers? Lactate has gotten a bad rap for years. It has been blamed for the burning sensation in your muscles when you surge above your sustainable pace. It has been blamed for delayed-onset muscle soreness. People have tried to massage it away, flush it out, and buffer it. But the best way to get rid of lactate is to reintegrate it back into normal aerobic metabolism to complete the process of breaking it down into energy, water, and carbon dioxide. Increasing the amount of lactate you can process per minute so you can exercise at a higher intensity level before lactate accumulates significantly in your blood is one of the primary goals of endurance training. This training adaptation also enables you to recover from hard efforts more quickly because deriving energy from glycolysis is like buying energy on credit. You're getting the currency you need as you need it, but you don't have unlimited credit, and sooner rather than later you're going to have to pay back every cent you borrowed. What's more, you have to cut back on spending while you're paying it back, which means you have to slow down. As an endurance athlete, one of the key adaptations you're seeking is an improvement in your ability to get that lactate integrated back into the normal process of aerobic energy production so it can be oxidized completely. The faster you can process lactate, the more work you can perform before lactate levels in your muscles and blood start to rise. Or, in the financial analogy, a stronger aerobic system puts more cash (aerobic metabolism) in your pocket so you're not so quick to use credit.

VO₂MAX

Lactate threshold is the point at which your demand for energy outstrips the aerobic system's ability to deliver it, but lactate threshold doesn't define the maximum amount of oxygen your body can use. When your exercise intensity reaches its absolute peak, and your body is pulling in and utilizing as much oxygen as it possibly can, you're at VO_2max. This is your maximum aerobic capacity, which is one of the most important indicators of your potential as an endurance athlete.

An exceedingly high VO_2max doesn't automatically guarantee you'll become a champion; it just means you have a big engine. To make a comparison to car engines, some people are born with 8 cylinders, whereas others have 4 (and extremely gifted athletes are born with 12). A finely tuned 4-cylinder Honda can go faster than a poorly maintained V-8 Corvette, and 12-cylinder supercars can beat everything, but they can be finicky and difficult to control. You have to have a big engine to be an elite athlete, but no matter what size engine you start with, you can optimize your performance with effective training.

It takes a great effort to reach intensities near your VO_2max, and during VO_2max-specific workouts you generate an enormous amount of lactate and burn calories tremendously fast. But the reward is worth the effort, because increasing your pace at VO_2max gives you speed. Ultradistance athletes sometimes suffer from a one-pace mentality. When your goal is to keep moving for 15 to 30 hours, it seems to make the most sense to use primarily endurance and some lactate threshold workouts to get to the fitness level necessary to sustain that effort. It's the sustainable aspect that keeps too many athletes from venturing into more threshold and ultimately VO_2max training. The perception is that the sport is all about making steady forward progress, that one only needs endurance, and that somehow speed comes naturally from greater endurance.

Speed does not come from endurance. If you can sustainably run a 9-minute mile pace now, running more 9-minute miles will not give you the ability to sustain an 8-minute pace. Your body adapts to the stress it experiences, and if you continue running 9-minute miles, it will adapt to make that pace more and more sustainable, but your body won't become able to sustain a pace faster than that unless you give it a reason.

In contrast, speed can enhance endurance performance. One of my colleagues, Nick White, coached triathlete Craig Alexander as he was making his transition from half-Ironman to Ironman triathlons. At the shorter distances, Craig's speed had already made him a world champion, and the question was whether he had the endurance to be in contention for victory in longer races. In the three years Nick worked with him, Craig Alexander finished second in his debut appearance at the Ironman World Championships in Kona, Hawaii, and won the next two. One of the takeaways from that experience was the importance that speed—and training for speed—played in preparing for longer endurance events. During a coaching roundtable at CTS, I remember Nick saying, "Craig had an advantage when he moved up to the Ironman distance; he already had the speed of an Olympic and

70.3 competitor. Building the endurance for Ironman is a cinch when you already have the speed."

Speed comes from training efforts at and above lactate threshold. It may not seem like an ultrarunner has much need for speed, but when you look at performance data from races, it is clear that successful athletes at the front and the back of the pack all can put out powerful efforts lasting from just a few minutes to 20 to 30 minutes. These efforts are necessary for success in ultrarunning events, whether success means standing on the podium or crossing the finish line within the final time cut.

More than just giving you the ability to pick up the pace, the true value of high-intensity training is that VO_2max training further improves your ability to tolerate lactate threshold intensity. That means VO_2max training is complementary to your interval work at and just below lactate threshold; it provides a boost to the lactate threshold work you're already doing, which leads to greater gains in your maximum sustainable pace.

THE ENDURANCE STRING THEORY

Delineating the various ways your body can produce energy is both a blessing and a curse. On the positive side, knowing how each system works gives us the information necessary to design training that makes it produce energy more quickly and sustainably. On the downside, the same information has inadvertently led people to believe that these systems operate independently of each other. Sports scientists, coaches, and even the folks who made your heart rate monitor watch have told you that training in "zone something-or-other" will target your glycolytic energy system and increase your pace at lactate threshold. And although that is true, the glycolytic system isn't the only one doing the work at that intensity, nor is it the only one that will reap a training benefit.

You are always producing energy through all possible pathways, but your demand for energy determines the relative contribution from each. At low to moderate intensities, the vast majority of your energy comes from the aerobic engine (mitochondria breaking down primarily fat and carbohydrate). As your intensity level rises above about 60 percent of VO_2max, the contribution from the glycolytic system starts to increase, and then it really ramps up quickly once you reach lactate threshold. Because glycolysis burns only carbohydrate, the overall percentage of energy coming from carbohydrate rises dramatically as your intensity increases from lactate threshold to VO_2max. You're still burning a lot of fat, however, because your mitochondria are also still chugging along as fast as they can.

Rather than seeing your various energy pathways as separate and distinct, it's better to think of them as segments of one continuous string, arranged based on the amount of energy derived from each. At one end is a large segment representing the aerobic system, which theoretically could power your muscles at a moderate intensity level forever if it had sufficient oxygen and fuel. After that is the glycolytic system, which can do a lot of work but can run at full tilt for only a limited time before you will have to reduce your exercise intensity. Finally, there is the segment for VO_2max, which is the maximum amount of work you can do but represents an intensity that is sustainable for only a few minutes. We can put the small but powerful contribution from the immediate energy system (ATP/CP) in this region too, since it powers maximal efforts that are only a few seconds long. Improving fitness in one system is like lifting the string in that region—all other areas of the string rise too. The extents of these ancillary improvements vary, based on the system you initially targeted. For instance, targeting VO_2max has a greater lifting effect on lactate threshold fitness and aerobic metabolism than training at aerobic intensities has on lifting lactate threshold or VO_2max. All of the systems are interconnected, and how you focus your training affects the amount of work you can do not only with the system you're focusing on but with all the others as well.

FUNDAMENTAL PRINCIPLES OF TRAINING

Just as all endurance athletes work to improve the same basic physical systems, training progress is governed by a common set of principles. When you distill the world's most successful training programs, across all sports, you arrive at five distinct principles of training:

1. Overload and recovery
2. Progression
3. Individuality
4. Specificity
5. Systematic approach

OVERLOAD AND RECOVERY

The human body is designed to respond to overload, and as long as you overload a system in the body properly and allow it time to adapt, that system will grow stronger and be ready for the same stress in the future. All forms of physical training are based on the body's ability to adapt to stress (or overload). To achieve positive training effects, this principle must be applied both to individual training sessions and to entire periods of your training. For instance, a lactate threshold interval workout must be difficult enough and long enough to stress your glycolytic energy system, but lactate threshold workouts must also be scheduled into a block of training so that the training loads from individual workouts accumulate and lead to more significant adaptations.

Many novice athletes start out with haphazard or scattered training, but they nevertheless make steady gains because they are beginners. Just the act of training leads to significant improvement when you're starting out. But that progress stalls relatively quickly because you reach the point where the stimulus applied to each individual system is not high enough or consistent enough to lead to further adaptation. Focusing your training on one area for a number of weeks, as you can do with a block of lactate threshold training, targets your workload and training time on overloading that one system. This becomes even more important for ultraendurance athletes because you are already adapted to a high overall workload. To make progress in any one aspect of fitness, you not only have to focus on it but also have to reduce focus on other areas during the same period.

On the other end of the spectrum, there's recovery. Recovery is not merely the absence of workouts but rather a crucial component of training. Days off should not be viewed as missed opportunities to get in another run. In reality, the periods between your workouts are when the really important stuff happens in your body. When you're in the middle of a training run, you're not improving your fitness; you're just applying stress and accumulating fatigue. But when you back off, sleep, hydrate, and provide your body with adequate and proper nutrition, that's when your fitness improves. So, the next time your type A buddy who's trained every day of the past four years chastises you for sitting on the couch or going for a walk with the dog instead of a 60-minute run, just smile and tell him you're busy adapting.

Gains are made when you allow enough time for your body to recover and adapt to the stresses you have applied. This is why recovery cannot be separated from training. Recovery is part of your training, and thinking of it that way helps you remain as committed to recovering as you are to working out.

PROGRESSION

Training must progressively move forward. To enjoy continued gains in performance, you have to increase training loads as you adapt. Time and intensity are the two most significant variables you can use to adjust your workload. For instance, you can increase the number of hours you devote to training (volume), or increase the overall intensity of your workouts by making the intervals more intense. You can use time and intensity to manipulate training a hundred different ways, but the end result must be that you're generating a training stimulus great enough to make your muscles, connective tissue, and aerobic engine adapt. Just as important, once you adapt and grow stronger, you have to manipulate the time and intensity variables again so that you further increase the workload to generate another training stimulus. In other words, it will take a bigger workload to overload a stronger system.

Interestingly, some of the most compelling evidence supporting the effectiveness of interval training relates to the principle of progression. Neither training time nor intensity is limitless, even for professional athletes. There are only

24 hours in the day, and the human body can only be pushed so hard. Professional athletes—across the range of endurance sports—are pretty much maxed out in terms of the annual hours they can accumulate while still performing at a high level. Indeed, studies have shown that for highly trained athletes, even if they could add more training volume, it wouldn't lead to additional improvements in VO_2max, power at lactate threshold, or mitochondrial density (Laursen and Jenkins 2002). With volume effectively maxed out and therefore not a limiting factor for improvement, you can really observe the impact of increasing an athlete's workload with interval training.

At the 100-mile distance, ultrarunners spend the vast majority of their time well below lactate threshold pace and almost no time at intensities approaching VO_2max. Yet I incorporate high-intensity intervals into training programs for

SEQUENCE OF TRAINING

Progression should not be interpreted to mean "faster" as it specifically relates to a chronology of moving through the year. Yes, your specific aerobic, lactate threshold, and VO_2 paces should get faster. However, that does not mean that the sequence of training has to move from lower-intensity aerobic training to medium-intensity lactate threshold training and finally to higher-intensity VO_2max training. Rather, progression should be thought of as occurring within each energy system so that the system gets stronger and needs a bigger stimulus (volume and intensity) in order to adapt.

Starting off with low intensity and moving to higher intensities is a stereotypical—and flawed—way of organizing training, particularly for ultrarunners. As will be discussed in Chapter 8, "Organizing Your Training: The Long-Range Plan," an ultrarunner's training does not have to move through this order of low to medium to high intensity. Rather, it should move from developing the least-specific aspects of your ultramarathon physiology to the most specific.

Dylan Bowman, Dakota Jones, Kaci Lickteig, and every other ultrarunner I work with. They do a lot of interval work above lactate threshold because no amount of moderate-intensity training volume will be enough to generate the cardiovascular fitness necessary to stay in contention at the front of the pack. To make the additional progress that's necessary for success at the highest levels of the sport, elites have to incorporate high-intensity intervals into their training.

Most amateur athletes are not maxed out in terms of training volume, but you may be maxed out in terms of the time you can devote to training. Dakota Jones arranges his entire life around his training, but for almost everyone lining up at an ultramarathon, running is a priority that has to be balanced with—and almost always comes after—many other priorities. The other commitments in your life mean you have to do what you can in the time you have. To achieve progression within the weekly training hours you have available, you have to manipulate the type and number of intervals, as well as interval duration and the recovery between efforts.

INDIVIDUALITY

The individuality principle simply states that the training program that works for you, right down to the individual workouts and interval intensities, has to be based on your physiological and personal needs. Training is not a one-size-fits-all product. All parts of your program—the total mileage, the number and type of intervals, and even the terrain—must be personalized. That doesn't mean that you can't train with your friends or training partners; it just means that while you're with them, you have to stay true to your own program.

The individuality principle is another reason there are no full-length training plans in this book. As I'll say many times throughout the book, ultrarunning is not just a longer marathon. If I were writing a marathon running or Olympic-distance triathlon training book, I'd include training plans because a generalized training plan can work for events of those lengths. Whenever I have tried to write generalized training plans for ultrarunning events, they just don't work. Popular running magazines offer numerous 12- to 20-week marathon training plans. A training plan for Western States 100-Mile Endurance Run, Hardrock, Wasatch Front 100 Mile Endurance Run, and similar races would have to be 30 weeks, minimum. With a time frame that long, a prewritten training plan is bound to under- or overestimate an individual runner's response to training and his or her ability to stick to the schedule. It will end up being way too hard and will run you into the ground, or way too easy and will not adequately prepare you for the demands of the event.

Ideally, every athlete would work with a coach and get a training program built from scratch, but personal coaching is not an option for everyone. The workouts and concepts in this book are rooted in the principles I use to coach my athletes, and you'll be able to apply the individuality principle to them when you establish your personal training program and fit the workouts into your busy work and family schedules.

SPECIFICITY

Your training must resemble the activity you want to perform. In a broad sense, this means that if you want to be a runner, you should spend the vast majority of your training time running. In a narrower sense, it means you have to determine the exact demands of the activity you wish to perform and tailor your training to address those demands, particularly as any critical races draw near. Conversely, it also means that your training is going to prepare you optimally for specific events and activities.

The importance of specificity becomes clear when you look at how competitive ultrarunning has evolved over the past decade. The speed at the front of the pack has increased dramatically, so much so that running a course record pace from a decade ago might only put you in the top 10 now. Is this because today's runners are that much more talented than runners from 10 years ago? Are they running more miles than athletes did 10 years ago? Are the shoes that much better? Are the energy bars that much better? No, none of the above. Athletes at the top of the sport are getting faster because their training has become more specific to the unique demands of the events they are training for. And the more we have learned about tailoring training to those demands, the more athletes of all ability levels can benefit from the same knowledge.

SYSTEMATIC APPROACH

When it comes to achieving high-performance fitness, you need a training program that integrates and addresses all the principles of training. A systematic approach to training integrates all the crucial components: overload and recovery, progression, individuality, and specificity. Focusing on any one of the principles while neglecting others will take your training off course.

Ultrarunners devote a lot of time to training, so it is unfortunate when I see athletes wasting much of that time with ineffective workouts and poorly planned programs. Workouts that are neither hard enough to contribute to positive adaptations nor easy enough to provide active recovery just contribute to fatigue. Scattered training plans that jump from this energy system to that one and then another before any system has time to develop make athletes work hard without creating progress.

In order to leverage the benefits of each of the previous four principles of training, they need to be combined into a systematic approach to improvement. Appropriate levels of overload and recovery must be established based on your individual needs and manipulated so that you achieve progression. And a training program doesn't do you much good unless it prepares you for the specific and unique demands of your goal event.

You can apply any of the previous four principles individually, but you're not likely to be satisfied with the results. A common failure of training results from achieving mastery of overload and recovery and progression while completely neglecting individuality and specificity. I see this most often with the data junkies, the athletes so focused on numbers, graphs, and training logs that all they care about is the trend of the data, even if it's leading them away from the fitness they need to perform at their best in their goal event!

Another problematic scenario is created by neglecting individuality and progression. This is typically an issue for social runners, athletes who value the social environment of the running community so highly that they substitute socializing for progression and individuality, which causes their training progress to stall or even collapse. These athletes are essentially going through the motions or treading water. That can be OK for short periods because social runners maintain a base level of sport-specific fitness and stay fully engaged in the community. Preparing for an ultramarathon requires a lot of focus for a significant period of time, and that level of focus may not be sustainable year after year. I would much rather see runners reduce their focus on individuality and progression for a while and focus on staying active in the running community, rather than drop out or burn out completely. In this situation, they feel less pressure to keep pushing their fitness upward but still experience the satisfaction of training and being an active athlete.

Some people seem to be able to remain superfit regardless of what they do or how much they do. Some stay thin regardless of what they eat. These people are the fortunate anomalies. Most athletes, even those of you who like to think of yourselves as rebels, thrive with structure and benefit significantly from approaching training systematically. As you plan your training and get ready for your ultramarathon, remember that with limited training time, every hour and every interval counts, and all workouts are connected through the principles of training.

CHAPTER 4

FAILURE POINTS AND HOW TO FIX THEM

$$\text{Velocity} = \frac{F \times VO_2 max}{Cr}$$

This simple and elegant equation is traditionally used to determine running velocity in endurance even ts. It states that velocity is determined by how big your aerobic engine is ($VO_2 max$), the fraction of it that you are utilizing (F), and the oxygen cost it takes for you to run a given distance (cost of running [Cr]). It explains why a runner with a bigger aerobic engine can run faster than one with a smaller engine. It explains why the cost of running is important, particularly if you have maximized your aerobic engine. Innumerable hours of scientific research have been dedicated to studying how these three simple variables are affected by body weight, temperature, shoe mass, genetics, elastic energy return, flexibility, running cadence, stride length, training, gender, age, biomechanics, and many other factors. The equation is extremely versatile, allowing us to predict and explain performance in endurance events from 5Ks to marathons (Di Prampero 1992). Furthermore, training for running events ranging from the 5K to the marathon has been rooted in optimizing these three variables. Improve your $VO_2 max$ and the fraction that you can utilize and you will run faster. Reduce your cost of running and you can run faster still. In order to improve over distances from a 5K to a marathon, this is the basic proposition: velocity equals the fraction of $VO_2 max$

utilized divided by the cost of running. But beyond the marathon distance, the equation starts to break down. Ultrarunning is not a marathon. It's not even a long marathon. It's a different sport altogether, and the variables associated with it mean that performance can no longer be determined solely by oxygen consumption and the cost of running.

THE SCIENCE OF ULTRARUNNING

While other endurance sports such as triathlon, marathoning, and cycling have an abundance of scientific research to draw upon, ultrarunning has very little. In the ultrarunning world only a few researchers (most notably Martin Hoffman and Guillaume Millet) have attempted to delve into the nuances of how ultramarathon runners work and what ultimately affects their performance. It's a difficult proposition for a researcher. Finding subjects who are willing to run on a treadmill for the necessary durations is understandably challenging. And because of the remote nature of most ultras, fieldwork and race-day biological assessments are difficult to attain. Taking post-race measurements involves poking and prodding athletes who in many cases have just finished the most difficult race of their lives. With all these variables, the scope of what can be studied is somewhat limited.

Much of the research that has been conducted is based on pre- and post-race questionnaires. Why did you drop out of the race? What was your biggest issue? How many miles was your longest training run? While the answers to these questions offer a glimpse into a runner's trials and tribulations during an ultramarathon, their usefulness is limited. They are the runner's own interpretations of what happened, not necessarily clear explanations for *why* it happened. Take, for example, a commonly cited reason for underperformance in an ultramarathon: nausea. "I had a queasy stomach" and "I couldn't tolerate any food" are certainly important sentiments to capture, but then what do you do about them? Very little research exists into *why* that nausea happened in the first place in an ultramarathon setting. Did you take in too much food? Not enough fluids? Too much of a particular carbohydrate? Is the gut actually damaged and leaking endotoxins into the bloodstream? Did your vision become altered late in a race, causing disequilibrium and nausea? We know that nausea is in fact an issue, but no one knows for sure what the key triggers for nausea are in an ultramarathon setting. Make no mistake: We're getting closer and closer to finding helpful answers for this and many other questions. But you would be hard-pressed to find a singular "aha" discovery that would prevent nausea from happening in every case.

So what do we really know about the science of ultrarunning? In 2011, Martin Hoffman and Kevin Fogard published an article titled "Factors Related to Successful Completion of a 161-km Ultramarathon." Their study explored the characteristics and issues that affected the performance of runners during the 2009 Western States 100-Mile Endurance Run and 2009 Vermont 100 Mile Endurance Run via pre- and post-race questionnaires. One of the more interesting tables in their article outlined the main problems self-reported by both finishers and non-finishers (Table 4.1).

Through this lens, we can look at many of the failure points and limiting factors of performance and what the science has to say about them. Nausea, blisters, exhaustion, and muscle pain/cramping top the list of ailments runners mentioned

TABLE 4.1   Comparison of Problems That Impacted Race Performance

PROBLEM	FINISHERS (%)	NONFINISHERS (%)
Blisters or "hot spots" on feet	40.1	17.3
Nausea and/or vomiting	36.8	39.6
Muscle pain	36.5	20.1
Exhaustion	23.1	13.7
Inadequately heat acclimatized	21.0	28.1
Inadequately trained	13.5	15.1
Muscle cramping	11.4	15.8
Injury during the race	9.0	10.1
Ongoing injury	7.5	15.8
Illness before the race	6.0	5.0
Started out too fast	5.1	6.5
Vision problems	2.1	3.6
Difficulty making cutoff times	1.8	27.3
Other, not categorized	11.7	26.6

Source: Adapted from Hoffman and Fogard 2011.

as limiting their performance. Surprisingly, in another part of Hoffman and Fogard's study, being inadequately trained was the least cited reason (at 0.7 percent) for dropping out among nonfinishers (Table 4.2) and represented only 13 to 15 percent of the complaints among both groups as a reason for limiting performance (Table 4.1). For me, this data point is crucial.

I would argue that if you are nauseated, are unable to make the cutoff times, and have muscle pain that is forcing you to drop out

TABLE **4.2**	Main Reason Given by Nonfinishers for Dropping Out
PROBLEM	**%**
Nausea and/or vomiting	23.0
Unable to make cutoff times	18.7
Other, not categorized	12.2
Ongoing injury	7.9
Injury during the race	7.2
Inadequately heat acclimatized	7.2
Blisters or "hot spots" on feet	5.8
Muscle cramping	5.0
Muscle pain	4.3
Exhaustion	3.6
Illness before the race	2.9
Vision problems	0.7
Started out too fast	0.7
Inadequately trained	0.7

Source: Hoffman and Fogard 2011.

or causing you significant issues, above all else, *you are inadequately trained*. A successful training process for an ultramarathon addresses all those issues. Any ultramarathon will still be hard, and even the most well prepared ultramarathon runners encounter these issues, but training either alleviates or completely fixes these complaints. The striking fact is that while runners often are able to identify the acute causes of their discomfort, they usually do not correlate those sensations with being inadequately trained. This is important because it means runners are focusing on the symptoms and not the root cause of the problem: training.

Using nausea as an example, you absolutely can and should train to have a stronger stomach, and I'm not talking about six-pack abs. Your digestive system is a combination of muscular and cellular machinery, and it adapts to stress just like the heart and skeletal muscles. That being the case, you can train your guts and digestive machinery to absorb calories from carbohydrate faster, to digest food more rapidly, and to resist damage caused by bacteria (Carrio et al. 1989; Harris, Lindeman, and Martin 1991; Cox et al. 2010; Jeukendrup and McLaughlin 2011). Furthermore, as part of the training process, you can and should use different types of calories to see what does and does not work for you. Nausea is particularly accentuated in ultramarathon running because the event is long enough for consistently poor nutritional choices to significantly affect performance. You can eat poorly and hang on long enough to finish a 4-hour marathon. But add another 20 hours of running, and those mistakes catch up to you. Training for the gastrointestinal stress of racing will produce a positive adaptation, just as interval work will improve your cardiovascular system. If you are too nauseated to continue, quite frankly you are inadequately trained for that stressor of an ultramarathon! Blisters, dead legs, muscle pain, and all the remaining items on the list are similar. They are all stressors in an ultramarathon, and they can all be trained. The key is that you have to know what the science says in these areas in order to know how to train them. So, using Hoffman and Fogard's list, let's take a look at these limiting factors for performance, what the science says about them, and how to properly train for them.

LIMITING FACTORS

"What does success look like to you?" I routinely ask this of all of my athletes, whether they are just starting out, are trying to finish their first ultra, or are elite athletes trying to win races. This question allows me to get a comprehensive view of what they are trying to accomplish. Inevitably an athlete's answer includes some outcome goals ("I want to finish Leadville in under 30 hours") and some process goals ("I want to be able to actually run at the end of the race"). As a coach, I learn a whole lot more from "I want to be able to run at the end of a 100-miler" than from "I want to finish the Leadville Trail 100 in under 30 hours." Why? Because when it comes to the outcome goal, determining the range of performances an athlete is capable of is a matter of simple math. How he or she becomes the most adept at achieving that goal is a much bigger—and more vexing—question. By asking what success looks like, I get the color and context of the entire athlete, not just the end goal.

In my experience, most ultramarathon athletes, even the elites, *find success through a lack of failure* on race day. They achieve their goals, win races, and get those coveted belt buckles not because they ran one section very well but because they prevented the negative. They prevented time spent at 0 miles per hour. They prevented themselves from becoming a nauseous, sore, blistered, battered, and stumbling mess. They continued to be able to eat, drink, and locomote down the trail, even if it was not very fast. Because so many things can go wrong, and the penalties for failure are high, "success by lack of failure" is a key element in successful ultramarathon running. These failure points are somewhat universal, as indicated by Hoffman and Fogard's research, and help define the limiting factors for ultrarunning. The very small exception is elite athletes competing in 50Ks and 50-mile distances and flat 100Ks. This is because the finish line for the elite athletes in those races often comes before the failure points discussed in this chapter have a chance to impact performance.

All reasonably healthy individuals can locomote at the necessary speed to beat the cutoffs for any ultramarathon. I say this not as an opinion but as a biomechanical fact. The preferred walking speed for the average human is around a 19-minute mile (Levine and Norenzayan 1999; Browning and Kram 2005; Mohler et al. 2007). With a little effort, one can easily achieve 18-minute miles, which is a pace that would yield a 30-hour 100-mile finish.

As of this writing, Timothy Olson holds the course record for the Western States 100 at 14:46:44. This time works out to about 8:50/mile. When we tested Timothy in our lab, his lactate threshold pace was under 6:00/mile. At a pace slower than 6:00/mile, his aerobic system can keep up with his energy demand, delivering oxygen to his muscles at a rate that is sustainable with few negative by-products. Having coached Timothy since he set that record, I can attest that on any given day, an 8:50/mile pace is not challenging for his cardiovascular system, even on terrain similar to that of Western States. Yet if you look at his Cal Street section (from mile 62 to mile 78), you will see that he ran for 16 miles with a net elevation loss at a pace of nearly 9:00/mile. From the standpoint of cardiovascular fitness, that 9:00/mile pace, which is more than 50 percent slower than his lactate threshold pace, was easy. It was essentially a normal recovery-run pace for him.

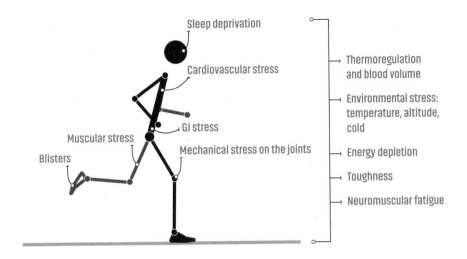

FIGURE **4.1** *Ultramarathon race stressors*
Source: *Illustrated by Charlie Layton.*

So why, on race day, 62 miles into a record-setting performance, couldn't Timothy run faster than his normal recovery-run pace? The answer lies in the fact that there are many stressors on race day, and success in an ultramarathon has far more to do with your ability to cope with the sum total of those stressors than with just the capacity of your cardiovascular system.

Figure 4.1 illustrates the major limiting factors experienced by ultrarunners. They are not all equally limiting, but they all play some part in any ultramarathon. Your goal is to arrive at the starting line as a 100 percent ready athlete, meaning your training has fully prepared you to handle all the various stressors of the event.

This sounds like a simple task. However, distinguishing fact from fiction in today's world makes finding good information on how to train for these limiting factors problematic. Particularly because of the proliferation of social media, readily accessible information, and worldwide connectivity, there is more information than ever about how to prepare for any endurance sport. The minute another study comes out, the popular press jumps on any new and unique angle. The 140-character version is posted on Twitter; the highlights of the article are "shared" and "liked" on Facebook; athletes read said interpretation of the study and chase it accordingly. How can you not? You might read, "Study shows that breathing through the left nostril improves endurance performance by 12 percent" and think, then why the heck do I need a right nostril in the first place? Some of the research is better than the rest, some is outdated, and some is very good, but how do you wade through it all? One of the failings of popular media is that they can always find some research to support an idea on how to improve endurance performance. Additionally, like any other area of science, sports science is constantly evolving. What we knew to be true several years ago may no longer be considered true now or in the future. With this limitation in mind, I developed my training strategy for ultramarathoners by combining research specifically done with ultramarathoners, research in other endurance disciplines that can be authentically applied to ultrarunning, and practical coaching experience. Academics and journalists would lay out all the studies, strategies, and philosophies side by side and leave you to figure out what to do with them. That's like having a doctor hand you textbooks when you go into the office feeling like death warmed over. When you're sick, you want to know what to do to get better. As an athlete you want to know how to use the best science has to offer to improve your performance. I'm going to do both—explain the science and show you how to practically use it to optimize your performance.

HYDRATION, SODIUM, AND THERMOREGULATION

Although an ultramarathoner will face many stressors on race day, much of the associated duress is fundamentally determined by two very simple physiological factors: hydration status and fuel availability. Of the two, hydration status is far more important. The fact of the matter is, fueling errors are easy to fix, but your hydration status (more specifically, a drop in blood volume) is not. You can pop a gel, drink a Coke, or eat some noodles and within minutes add fuel to the fire. Your body's process for this is simple: Eat, get sugar into your bloodstream, and deliver it to your muscles and brain. Even if you eat the "wrong" thing, you will still, eventually, get sugar into your body relatively quickly. If you screw up your hydration status, the fix is not so simple. Compared with fixing a bonk, the remedy involves the far more complex mechanisms of hormonal regulation and electro-chemical gradients. In addition to sounding more complicated than "eat sugar and let it digest," these mechanisms of regulating blood volume are indeed slower. They take hours to rectify if disturbed, and the series of steps an athlete may need to take is often complicated. More important, the penalty for screwing up your hydration (and therefore blood volume) is far more severe than bonking. If you bonk, you simply slow down and eat. At the worst, you get a little disoriented. A drop in blood volume can be much more catastrophic (Table 4.3). I'm not trying to scare anyone off from running an ultra, but if you screw up your hydration enough, you could end up in the hospital or even die. The magnitude of the "penalty for failure" in this respect is precisely why hydration, sodium, and thermoregulation are the most important nutritional aspects to understand while preparing for an ultra.

Over the past several years, it seems like more sports science research has been done in the area of hydration and sodium consumption than in any other. This makes sense, given the aforementioned importance and the overall complex-ity of the issue (not to mention the financial incentive for for-profit companies to demonstrate the efficacy of their drinks). In ultramarathoning, sodium supple-mentation has gone from being demonized to in vogue and back again. Even the most basic measurements, such as an ultrarunner's body weight, cause confusion. For many years, high-profile races such as the Western States 100 and Wasatch Front 100 used body weight to determine if a runner was fit to continue. While that practice is no longer followed at those races, the fact that one of the simplest

TABLE 4.3	Effects of Increasing Dehydration on Physical Performance
BODY WATER LOSS (%)	EFFECTS
0.5	Increased strain on the heart
1	Reduced aerobic endurance
3	Reduced muscular endurance
4	Reduced muscle strength; reduced fine motor skills; heat cramps
5	Heat exhaustion; cramping; fatigue; reduced mental capacity
6	Physical exhaustion; heatstroke; coma

Source: Adapted from Casa 1999; Casa et al. 2000; and Sawka 2007.

tools available, one that physicians have used for hundreds of years, was deemed essential and then disappeared in the matter of a few years emphasizes how complicated the practice of monitoring hydration can be.

The current battle between "drink early and often" versus "drink only in response to thirst" only adds more confusion for ultrarunners. It is important to realize that in the context of hydration, water, sodium, and carbohydrate need to be considered simultaneously. These components are intertwined, with one always affecting the others. Therefore, the recommendation for when to drink always needs to begin with the answer to an earlier question: What should you drink? While some physiological aspects of fluid and sodium balance are still debatable, research has provided athletes with key recommendations for maintaining hydration and sodium balance and ultimately performing better. This is such a large topic that rather than getting bogged down in it here, I have covered it in greater detail in Chapter 10, "Fueling and Hydrating for the Long Haul."

FUELING AND GI DISTRESS

For several years on April Fools' Day, GU Energy Labs designed elaborate pranks that revolved around a nutrition "breakthrough." One year it was the flavor of their gels. Their lineup of "savory" flavors like Pimento Loafer, Lard Dart, and Savory Sardine was simultaneously funny and vomit-inducing. One memorable prank, though, struck a particular chord: DermaCharge, a gel that you smeared on your skin that delivered energy and electrolytes. The gag was hilarious, complete with scents of Tenacious Tomato, Sultry Cucumber, Intense Butter, and Furious Avocado, and, of course, photos of a fitness model smearing the goop on his six-pack abs. I got a good laugh out of it, but that day the questions I received by e-mail ranged from "What do you think of this? Is it going to work?" to "How come you never mentioned this to me?" Some athletes were actually upset that they learned about this breakthrough news from social media, not from their beloved coach. At first I was stunned at how easily the wool had been pulled over their eyes. I mean, come on, a goop that you rub on your skin that smells like butter and delivers carbohydrate? Really? Besides the lesson to be wary of marketing, however, their reactions reemphasized an important point: Athletes are always looking for a better way to fuel. If one thing is drilled into ultramarathon runners' heads more than any other concept, it is that you must fuel in order to be successful. Even for my athletes, who have worked considerably on their nutrition strategies to minimize the stomach distress referenced in Hoffman and Fogard's research, any conceivable way to take in calories without eating sounded too good to pass up, even if it was as silly as rubbing avocado-scented goop on their bellies.

What the Science Says

At a fundamental level, digestion is a relatively simple process. You mechanically break down the food by chewing it in your mouth and churning it in your stomach. Then, your stomach and intestines chemically break it down further. Finally, the intestines absorb the nutrients from the broken-down food across the intestinal walls. The key is that there is both a mechanical and a chemical process in play in order to properly digest and absorb foodstuffs. Both phases of this process are central to an understanding of fueling and nausea.

Your Stomach and Intestines Are Made of Muscle Too!

When you eat a gel, cookie, or anything else at the aid station table, you must first mechanically break it down in your mouth and stomach. That foodstuff is then passed to the small intenstines, where most of the nutrient absorption takes place. Because your stomach and intestines are muscular organs, they require blood flow to do their job, like any other muscle in your body. The problem is, blood flow is a hot commodity when you are running. Your total blood volume is limited, and blood is needed to deliver oxygen to your working muscles (including your stomach and intestines) and deliver nutrients, as well as to move to the surface of your skin to dissipate heat. This creates a fierce competition between the aforementioned processes of digestion, oxygen/nutrient transport, and cooling. And guess which competitor wins? Ding, ding, ding! If it has to, your body prioritizes cooling over delivering oxygen to working muscles (thankfully so, I might add). When this happens, there is less blood flow to the stomach and intestines, movement of food through the gut slows or stops, and pretty soon you start experiencing gastrointestinal distress. In this way, training to become more fit increases your body's ability to process food during an event, as training increases your overall heat tolerance and reduces the required blood flow to the skeletal muscles at the same pace, both of which free up the blood to be sent to the gut.

The number one recommendation when you have a queasy stomach is to "slow down and cool off." Besides being easy to remember and implement, this advice is effective because both actions redistribute blood flow from other areas back to the stomach. Slowing down reduces the oxygen and nutrient demand from your working skeletal muscles, which reduces the need for blood flow, thereby freeing up blood for digestion. Cooling off does the same, reducing your body's need to send blood to the skin in order to cool. You get the greatest bang for your buck by doing both because slowing down also reduces the heat generated by skeletal muscles and helps you cool down more quickly.

Damage to the Gut

In addition to competition for blood flow, damage to the gut occurs during any endurance running activity as a by-product of digestion, blood flow reduction, and constant jostling up and down (Papaioannides et al. 1984; Heer et al. 1987; Øktedalen et al. 1992; Lucas and Schroy 1998). Recently, researchers at Monash University studied the naturally present bacteria (endotoxins) that leak into the bloodstream as a result of this damage. They found that most individuals participating in an ultramarathon had markers in their bloodstream equivalent to those found in hospital patients with sepsis (Gill et al. 2015). This means the gut is so damaged that it leaks endotoxins and triggers an immune response on the scale of a life-threatening infection. Although the researchers concluded that the damage was significant and that the gut was impaired, little evidence was presented as to how to alleviate or avoid the condition. The one correlating factor suggested by the research team was that the individuals who had simply trained more exhibited less damage (http://monash.edu/news/show/extreme-exercise-linked-to-blood-poisoning). Further research is needed to better understand why this extreme

TO EAT ON THE UPHILLS OR DOWNHILLS?

When and what you are doing while you eat can affect food tolerance and cal-orie absorption. The less jostling you are experiencing and the more blood flow you have available, the better you will tolerate food. Furthermore, eating smaller portions of food means less blood flow is required by the gut for digestion, and you will have less stuff bouncing around in your stomach that could potentially damage it. So, when considering taking in your next cookie, pretzel, or gel, think first about the ideal time to eat it. Smaller, more frequent portions of calories are always better because they digest more easily. If you do have to take in a bigger caloric punch, do it when you have the greatest blood flow available and the least jostling—in other words, during a slower uphill hike. More specifically, you want as much of that food as possible digested and into your bloodstream by the time you return to higher intensity or more jostling. Depending on the length of the climb, try to finish eating at least 10 minutes before the summit. Taking in your bigger calories during the slower, less intense portions of any ultra will help stave off the gut distress that can be caused by reduced blood flow and damage to the gut.

amount of damage to the gut occurs, but the current takeaway suggested by the research team is simple: Better training equals less damage to the gut.

BLISTERS

My first ultramarathon experience was as a crew member for Dean Karnazes during the Badwater Ultramarathon. Talk about jumping into the deep end. I was extremely nervous and legitimately underqualified. Assisting a well-known athlete in a big, demanding race in a completely foreign environment was way over my head. Before the race, I did copious amounts of research on the course: what to expect, the limiting factors for performance, and how the race worked (Badwater is unique in that the crew can accompany the runner nearly the entire way). Through that research, two things stuck out: Death Valley would be hot as hell (duh), and the runners end up with mangled feet. I immediately made three purchases: an ice bandana, a prepackaged blister kit, and the book *Fixing Your Feet* by John Vonhof. When I opened up the package and started rifling through the contents of the blister kit, I had no clue how all the powders, lubricants, tapes, adhesives, and bandages worked. So I read and I practiced. I would read through a section of my new book, contort my legs to gain access to my foot, apply some concoction of adhesive and tape, and then go run to test out the technique. Every day, I tried something different. As the race neared, I was obsessed. To put some of these newfound techniques to the ultimate test, and to mirror the conditions of the race—where you are constantly pouring cold water over yourself and your runner—I routinely soaked my laced-up feet with the garden hose before setting out on a run.

As it turns out, I got to use my newfound skills in the wee hours of the morning in Death Valley, as Dean managed to get a blister smack-dab on the ball of his right foot. Somehow, my tape job held up for the remaining 40 miles of the race. After Dean's race and our celebratory dinner were over, we staggered into the Dow Villa Motel in Lone Pine, California. The motel is on the racecourse (mile 122) and is used as a medical checkpoint and communications hub for the event. A constant stream of runners ran (or staggered) right in front of the motel throughout the night, illuminated by a union of streetlights, headlamps, multicolored safety lights, and reflective vests. Curious and hopped up on far too much caffeine, I stayed awake all night watching the battered runners gradually make their way down the course. Most of them looked awful, limping and moving very slowly through the darkness. They were dealing with a variety of issues: tired legs, fried brains, hyponatremia, bonking, hallucinations, you name it. However, one prevailing issue bound them together as brothers and sisters of this race: Collectively, their feet were destroyed. Runner after runner stopped at the motel to get their feet patched up, sometimes by professionals and sometimes by their crews. Some foot issues were relatively benign. Most were dreadful. All night and into the next day, the runners came in, got patched up, and left ready to tackle the final 13 miles of the race.

Upon returning home, I decided to reinforce my blister prevention and treatment arsenal and purchased a red plastic toolbox from the Home Depot. I filled the box with an array of products to help repair feet when they become battered, bruised, bloodied, and blistered. Admittedly, the toolbox is a bit makeshift, somewhere between the basic necessities and a full-blown medical kit, but it was mine, and I knew how to use every product in it. Nearly a decade later, I still have this same box. I bring it with me whenever I attend an ultramarathon as a coach or as an athlete. Often it remains idle. At other races it is a lifeline for athletes. I take comfort in knowing that if athletes do run into trouble with their feet, I have some level of skill to patch them up and get them on their way.

Hoffman and Fogard's survey of participants in the Western States 100 and Vermont 100 demonstrates that blisters remain a prevalent issue and do limit performance. Quite simply, your feet propel you forward. When your foot is damaged, it affects the entire kinetic chain from the ankle to the knee and through the hip. You might be able to limp through for a while on a sore foot, but chances are that the change in biomechanics will eventually catch up with you and compound the issues you face. In many cases, it's not the blister that leads to the DNF. The blister just starts the process by changing the way you run, and over time those changes lead to other biomechanical problems, slowing you down, knocking you off your nutritional strategy, exposing you to the elements longer, and so forth. This does not have to be the case. Blisters can be largely prevented through training, prevention, a little treatment know-how, and better race-day management. Treatment is relatively easy, requiring a few basic products and skills to fix the majority of issues. It takes practice, but it's worth it.

Preventing and Treating Blisters

Whenever you stress an organ or a structure in your body beyond its capabilities, you cause damage. Ultramarathons normally represent a longer, more difficult run than your day-to-day training, complicated by the fact most ultramarathon events occur in areas away from your home training grounds. The trail surface, camber, dirt, dust, and debris your feet encounter are undoubtedly different during the race than at home. Furthermore, your biomechanics are different depending on the properties of the trails, placing stresses on different areas of the skin of the foot. Therefore, the shoe/sock/powder/tape/lubricant/insole combination that worked in training may not always work during the race. Just as training on flat ground will not completely prepare you for a mountainous ultra, training on your home trails might not fully prepare your feet for the rigors of race day. Therefore, a combination of education, preventive measures, and wound care skills offers the most comprehensive way to ensure that your hard-earned training does not come undone by the unraveling of your feet on race day.

What the Science Says

What runners commonly refer to as a blister is clinically termed a *friction blister* because friction is the primary culprit. Although heat and moisture are contributing factors, friction and the underlying shear forces are what ultimately cause the dreaded blister (Figure 4.2). As I will discuss later in this chapter, with each and every foot strike, you apply shear forces parallel to the surface of the ground in both the anterior-posterior (forward-backward) and the mediolateral (side-to-side) direction. At foot strike, the ground pushes backward on your shoe, your insole pushes backward on your sock, and your sock pushes backward on your skin. As you push off the ground, these forces between your skin and sock, sock and insole, and shoe and ground all reverse direction. The problem is that the surface of your skin is pliable (after all, it is called soft tissue). As your body applies these shear forces, your soft tissue (skin on the feet) moves more than your skeletal system (rigid bone). This out-of-sync movement between your skeleton, soft tissue, sock/shoe, and shoe/ground is what ultimately causes the frictional force that leads to a blister. Your shoe and sock move against your outer layer of skin (epidermis) more than your outer layer of skin moves against your inner layer of skin (dermis). As the bump and grind between these two skin layers continues, the layers eventually separate. Once this separation occurs, fluid fills the void due to hydrostatic pressure. The result is a fluid sac between

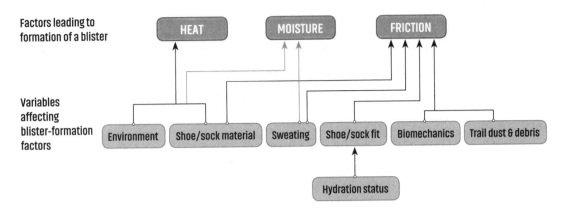

FIGURE **4.2** *Heat + moisture + friction = blister*

the newly separated layers of skin bordered by yet-to-be separated layers along the edges.

The addition of heat and moisture exacerbates blister formation. Heat accelerates the blistering process primarily by loosening the bond between the dermis and epidermis. Research has demonstrated that an increase in skin temperature of 4°C will accelerate blister formation by 50 percent (Kiistala 1972b). Increases in foot skin temperature, heat from the environment, increases in metabolic response, and heat from frictional forces all add to the heat within your shoes. Furthermore, the warmer your feet are, the more they sweat. The more your feet sweat, the more saturated your socks, shoes, and skin become. Dumping water on your head, running through a river crossing, and running in the rain all accomplish the same feat (excuse the pun). They increase the moisture in your shoe, in your sock, and on the skin of your foot. This moisture further increases the frictional forces between your foot and sock with every foot strike, adding to blister susceptibility (Naylor 1955). Furthermore, the moisture weakens the outer layer of skin, making it more prone to injury.

While heat, trauma, and moisture are attacking your skin from the outside, on the inside your hydration status can also make you more susceptible to blisters. If a runner becomes even slightly hyponatremic (having low blood sodium), one of the body's protective mechanisms—long before blood sodium levels are dangerously low—is to pull water out of the plasma into the extracellular space, thus increasing the concentration of sodium in the blood. As a simple by-product of gravity, this fluid in the extracellular space pools in the extremities, commonly resulting in puffy hands or feet. Unlike your hands, your feet are subject to the rigors of propelling you forward. The increased fluid in the extracellular space in the skin of your feet accelerates the blistering process. It causes your feet to get bigger, turning your once perfectly broken-in shoes into a friction-laden trap. It also loosens the skin layers, as fluid is more easily pushed between the dermis and epidermis.

Training, Gear, and Protection

Each of the three aforementioned blister factors of friction, heat, and moisture can be alleviated with the right combination (in order of priority) of training, gear (shoes and socks), race-day preventive measures, and finally, treatment.

How training influences blister formation. Training is the first level of prevention in blister formation. Your skin adapts to stress just like any other organ in your body. Many studies, primarily involving the military, have demonstrated that gradual exposure to frictional forces on the foot (through hikes and marches) decreases the skin's susceptibility to blisters (Allan 1964; Hodges, DuClos, and Schnitzer 1975; Knapik et al. 1995). As you train, your epidermal skin cells become thicker and in theory more cohesive, making them more resistant to blistering. How does this happen? As you run, you slough off skin cells faster than normal. These are rapidly replaced by new skin cells, but these young cells don't get the chance to differentiate into layer-specific cells (epidermis, dermis) before they are stressed by another run (S. H. Kim et al. 2010). When this happens frequently over a relatively short time, it results in overthickened skin (i.e., the callus).

How shoe and sock choice influences blister formation. Your shoe and sock combination is the next level of blister prevention. With respect to blister prevention, your shoe/sock combination should serve the dual purposes of reducing frictional forces between your skin/sock and sock/shoe and managing moisture transfer from your foot into the air. Some socks that segregate the toes (toe socks) also aim to reduce

SHAVE DOWN YOUR CALLUSES

Should you keep your calluses or shave them down? Proponents of keeping the callus say the extrathick skin is less prone to damage and therefore acts as a protective layer. Although there is some truth to this, the far greater risk is that the callus will continue to grow and become an anomaly in the foot/shoe interface (i.e., it sticks out). Remember that a blister forms when an outer layer of skin moves out of sync with an inner layer of skin. A callus can act as the outer layer and still separate from the inner layer of dermis, leading to a blister *under* your callus! When this happens you generally lose the entire callus, which defeats the purpose of building up this protective layer of extrathick skin. Because allowing calluses to become overly thick greatly increases the likelihood of forming a blister *under* the callus, I encourage athletes to keep calluses shaved down to maintain a smoother, more uniform skin surface. That doesn't mean remove calluses entirely. Use a pumice stone or metal callus shaver and file down the callus so that it is flush with the surrounding skin. Shaving them is a matter of maintenance, not removal.

the skin-to-skin friction between the toes. Overwhelming research has shown that a well-fitting wicking sock offers the best blister prevention strategy (Herring and Richie 1990; Knapik et al. 1995, 1996). Fortunately, most sock companies are now wise to this idea and are moving away from thicker, bulkier, and less wicking socks for runners and ultrarunners. Shoe companies are following suit. Materials for shoes are constantly becoming more pliant and breathable, and shoes are available in a wider variety of shapes and sizes. Perhaps blister prevention is not the shoe manufacturers' end goal, but the improvements in materials and fit do help.

Your shoe/sock combination should be tested in training, and shoe trials should be completed early in the season. It is important to figure out what works and what doesn't far out from your event so you can ramp up your training without fear of damaging your feet. Along these lines, once you find the combination that works for you, I recommend investing in enough shoes and socks to get you through the entire season. Ultrarunners burn through shoes and socks, and designs or availability can change unexpectedly. You don't want to be searching for new shoes or having to switch to a new model or design in the middle of the season when your training workload is very high.

Race-day preventive measures. One lesson I've learned from racing and crewing ultramarathons, and from watching the parade of mangled feet at Badwater, is that athletes use an incredibly wide range of techniques to prevent blisters on race day. Some use tape, some use lubricants, others use powders. The more creative ultrarunners will use elaborate combinations and concoctions, sometimes taking hours to apply. In many cases, two runners will use techniques with opposing goals (keep the skin from moving versus encourage the skin to move with less friction), and both techniques may (or may not) work. This reinforces the "find what works for you" advice from the bible of blister prevention and treatment, *Fixing Your Feet*, which makes the point by providing numerous personal N of 1 anecdotes from athletes. From a scientific standpoint, this advice rings true. In fact, there is little scientific evidence that any of the aforementioned strategies work. Furthermore, there is conflicting research indicating that some preventive measures actually exacerbate the problem by adding moisture and thus increase skin friction (Figure 4.3; Allan and Macmillan 1963; Allan 1964; Quinn 1967; Nacht et al. 1981; Knapik et al. 1995; Reynolds et al. 1995; Knapik, Reynolds, and Barson 1998).

This is an area where less is more. The prevention strategies we know work are training (conditioning the feet to handle the stresses of long miles) and an effective shoe/sock combination. These should always be your starting points. Adding other techniques like tape, lubricant, powder, or antiperspirant increases complexity, adds more variables to any training or race-day situation, and might exacerbate the problem. Nonetheless, many athletes desperately continue to go far beyond training and shoe/sock choices to solve recurrent skin issues with their feet. Even for these athletes, it is worth the effort to find a minimal solution.

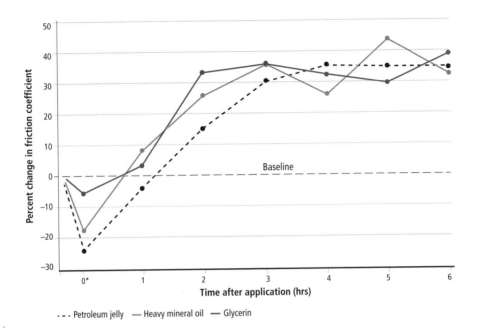

FIGURE **4.3** *Graph showing an initial decrease, then increase, in friction of common lubricants when used on the skin*

*Immediately after application

Source: Nacht et al. 1981.

It is also important to realize there is no combination of equipment or amount of training that will entirely eliminate the risk of developing blisters during training or on race day. You can minimize these risks as much as possible, but you also have to learn to patch and repair a blister in the field when things go wrong.

Blister patch and repair. If you do get a blister (or the precursor, which is referred to as a "hot spot"), you have a decision to make: You can save some time and continue running, or stop and lose some time treating your feet. In making this decision, you need to balance your race-day goals, performance expectations, safety, and race situation. Generally speaking, the more time you have left to run and the bigger the problem could become, the more it is worth your while to take a few minutes and fix what is wrong. Don't let little problems become big problems.

My advice is to always err on the side of caution and fix problems early, particularly at the 100K and 100-mile distances, where there is a lot of ground to cover.

If you are in a situation where you choose not to stop and fix a blister, or you are many miles from the next aid station and you have no products to treat the blister, it is time to suck it up. Blisters hurt because the foot is highly innervated, and runners tend to find relief by changing their gait or foot-strike pattern. While this is a logical strategy ("I have pain there, I am going to try to avoid it"), the ramifications of changing your gait too much can have consequences up the kinetic chain. Your foot, ankle, knee, and hip are all connected and constantly affect one another. Although I am an advocate for manipulating gait and biomechanics in an effort to combat muscular fatigue (see the next section), I do not advocate doing so in the context of a blister. In this case it's time to be tough and keep your gait as normal as possible. Running with your normal gait may make the blister worse, but that's still only one problem, and one you can treat and get under control. Changing your gait to "run around a blister" can lead to pain or injuries you can't effectively treat and control while continuing to race. That said, you might have to tough it out and run on a blister on race day, but it's not a strategy to rely on. Blisters can and should be prevented and treated.

Blisters come in a variety of shapes, sizes, and levels of discomfort. Treatments also come in many shapes and forms. Unless you are a medical professional with many years of blister management experience, a simple solution is always best. I have found success with the following nine-step plan:

1. Clean the surface of the blister and the surrounding skin. If an alcohol pad or disinfectant is available, use it. If not, it is still usually best to proceed to step 2. You are less prone to infection if you can properly manage the blister while it is small and treatable. Large broken blisters will become more prone to infection more readily than small broken blisters because there is more opportunity to become infected through the larger area of damaged and exposed skin.

2. Puncture the blister with a needle, sharp scissors, or scalpel. Take care to puncture the blister enough to allow fluid to drain but not so much that the

blister roof becomes detached. If you are using a needle (safety pins from a race number also work well), put three to four holes in the blister so that it will drain. Ideally, place the punctures such that fluid can continue to drain while you keep on running.

3. Squeeze the fluid out of the blister.

4. Clean and dry the surface of the blister and the surrounding skin. You are now prepping the skin to apply a patch, so ensure that it is dry and free of debris. You can choose to add a very small dab of lubricant to the blister roof. This is to prevent the patch from sticking to the blister roof when you eventually peel the tape off.

5. Size up the area you are going to patch, and cut a piece of tape or bandage to cover the blister. The patch should be large enough so that it can stick to the surrounding skin. If the blister is on a toe, this might mean wrapping the entire toe. If you do have to wrap a toe, it's usually best to wrap the adjacent toes also so that the tape does not rub directly on adjacent skin.

6. Apply a tape adhesive such as tincture of benzoin to the area surrounding the blister. Although the tape has its own adhesive backing, using an additional tape adhesive will ensure a better stick.

7. Place the tape down on the skin from one edge of the tape to the other. Be careful to avoid folds and creases. If you do get a fold or a crease, start over.

8. Lightly press down on the patch to ensure the adhesive completely sticks to the skin.

9. Put your socks on, lace up your shoes, and run!

If you are particularly blister prone, practice various techniques at home. Cutting and placing the patch on the surface of the skin can be the most frustrating part of the process during a race. The tape is sticky and adheres to itself and to your fingers. You're in a hurry. You're sweaty and dirty. And you're working in a dirty, dusty environment. Finding a routine and learning some simple skills goes a long way to making the process smoother and faster in race conditions. As with any other skill, practice makes perfect!

WHAT A BLISTER KIT SHOULD CONTAIN

This small assortment of products will be enough to fix minor and moderate blisters out in the field and keep you moving. It is manageable for your crew to carry or to pack in a drop bag. It is neither a substitute for a full medical kit nor what you would use to treat skin injuries after a race.

- Adhesive felt sheet or moleskin
- Needles or small scalpel (size 11)
- Alcohol pads or Betadine swabs
- Gloves
- Kinesio Tex Gold tape, Elastikon tape, or Leukotape (to patch or prevent)
- Scissors
- Adhesive such as tincture of benzoin
- Lubricant such as Body Glide or BlisterShield
- Gauze pads

MUSCULAR BREAKDOWN AND FATIGUE

The overall concept of muscular breakdown and fatigue incorporates several areas of physiology. Physical trauma to the muscle, depleted energy stores, neuromuscular dysfunction, central versus peripheral fatigue, and myriad other phenomena fall under this umbrella. To avoid re-creating a muscle physiology textbook, I will focus specifically on the aspects of ultramarathoning that lead to muscular breakdown and fatigue.

Ultramarathons and Muscular Breakdown

It is well documented that a significant amount of muscular breakdown occurs during an ultramarathon. Researchers have studied the blood parameters that indicate muscular trauma, particularly creatine kinase (CK), from finishers in Spartathlon, the Ultra-Trail du Mont-Blanc, and the Western States 100, among others. With respect to muscular breakdown, all the research comes to the same conclusions: There's a lot of it in ultrarunning, and there's tremendous variability among individuals. Blood markers for CK after an ultramarathon range from relatively normal to more than 100 times normal values (Fallon et al. 1999; Overgaard et al. 2002; Guillaume Millet et al. 2011; Kim, Lee, and Kim 2007). That's a lot of muscular tissue turnover. This is all obvious to ultrarunners, even if they've never heard of CK or any of the other biochemical markers associated with pain, fatigue, and muscular breakdown because they run slower at the end of a race.

Although it's clear that muscular breakdown and fatigue are significant, there's so much individual variability that it is difficult to determine ways to prevent them (Figure 4.4). Correlations between muscular fatigue and training components such as volume and vertical are scant. The same goes for correlations between any race-day phenomenon (nutrition, pacing, hydration) and muscular fatigue or damage. Whenever this is the case, it is important to rely on best practices and research in other areas to help guide training principles. With that as an introduction, a quick biomechanics lesson is in order.

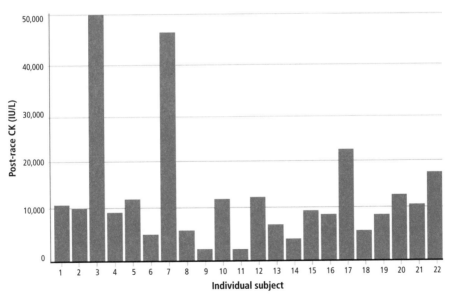

FIGURE **4.4** *Post-race creatine kinase (CK) levels in Ultra-Trail du Mont-Blanc finishers*

Source: Guillaume Millet et al. 2011.

STEP VERSUS STRIDE

For years the words "step" and "stride" have been used interchangeably (and thus incorrectly) in the popular literature. For the purposes of this book and to be accurate, I am going to use these terms correctly. A step is defined as one foot strike to the opposite foot strike, in terms of either length or time (i.e., your left foot hitting the ground to your right foot hitting the ground). A stride is defined as one foot strike to the same foot striking the ground (i.e., the distance or time from your left foot hitting the ground to your left foot hitting the ground again). Therefore, your stride length will be double your step length, because two steps essentially equal one stride.

- Step length: the distance between the initial contact of one foot and the initial contact of the opposite foot
- Step rate: the total number of right and left foot strikes per minute
- Stride length: the distance between the initial contact of one foot and the next initial contact of the same foot
- Stride frequency: the total number of the same foot strikes per minute (i.e., the total number of right foot strikes per minute)

Source: Illustrated by Charlie Layton.

During the course of running, your muscles can only pull. That phrase has been drilled into the young brain of every undergraduate who has taken a biomechanics class. Your muscles can only pull, or contract, to move your limbs. They cannot push. When muscles pull, you generate positive force. This positive force is what pushes you off the ground and propels you forward. However, during the course of a step on level ground, you need to generate an equal amount of negative force (or counterproductive force) as your foot initially hits the ground and your body is lowered. During this initial phase of foot strike, many of your muscles are actively being lengthened, or pulling against a force in the opposite direction. Make no mistake: They are still pulling; they are just doing so against a larger force and are therefore lengthened. This active lengthening is what is oxymoronically referred to as an eccentric contraction. This is unavoidable, whether one is running or walking (Enoka 2008; DeVita, Helseth, and Hortobagyi 2007). Whenever an eccentric contraction happens, a certain amount of muscular breakdown occurs. The amount of breakdown varies with the individual and with velocity, force, and the total repetitions that need to be produced (Tiidus and Ianuzzo 1982; Chapman et al. 2006; Nosaka and Clarkson 1996). That's all fine and dandy to know, but what do you do about it?

How to Combat Muscular Breakdown

Eccentric contractions and the muscular breakdown associated with them have long been villains in the coaching and training world. The victims are your muscles, which lose their ability to function when you have stronger, more frequent, and a higher total number of eccentric contractions (Ebbeling and Clarkson 1989; Eston, Mickleborough, and Baltzopoulos 1995; Proske and Morgan 2001; Proske and Allen 2005; Chapman et al. 2006). By its very nature, an ultramarathon creates these conditions because of the hundreds of thousands of steps and associated eccentric contractions required to reach the finish line. Adapting your physiology and finding strategies to handle this huge stress can be a big advantage. Failing to do so can result in a catastrophe—so much so that ultrarunners have contrived

ARE WOMEN MORE FATIGUE-RESISTANT THAN MEN?

Are women better at ultra distance events than men? Every year, some ultramarathons are won outright by women. Adding fuel to the fire are anecdotal tales from expedition-length adventure racers about the women commonly outperforming the men on mixed teams late in the race. Many in the ultrarunning world have speculated that women are more psychologically and physically suited for ultramarathons than men, and scientists and researchers have debated whether women should or should not be able to outperform men in ultrarunning, noting the statistical performance differences between men and women at different distances. Early in this statistical debate, it was theorized that women could, in fact, outperform men as the distance increased (Bam et al. 1997). Later statistical analyses, however, contradicted those initial theories (Peter et al. 2014; Zingg et al. 2014). Bringing this argument full circle, recent research into the difference in fatigue resistance between men and women might now actually begin to turn the initial statistical speculations into physiological reality.

Yes, women might be able to outperform men in ultramarathon events. Researchers examined different variables related to fatigue for male and female finishers of the 2012 version of the Ultra-Trail du Mont-Blanc (that year's race was shortened to 100K due to inclement weather). What did they find? While both men and women demonstrated similar amounts of central fatigue and muscular damage and inflammation (creatine kinase, C-reactive protein, and myoglobin levels), they differed in the amount of peripheral fatigue (fatigue within the muscle itself) measured after the race. The 100K race negatively affected men more than women specifically in the amount of voluntary force produced in the knee extensor, and the evoked mechanical response in the plantar flexor (Temesi et al. 2015). Simply stated, within these muscle groups, women fatigued less than men after 100K of mountainous running. Does that translate to women being better ultramarathon runners than men? At this point, no. But the door is certainly open!

numerous techniques to solve the problem. Equipment such as trekking poles and highly cushioned shoes has been used to minimize the damage. Additionally, (flawed) training techniques such as strength training and downhill repeats have been utilized by ultrarunners to combat this phenomenon. While many of these efforts deserve credit for trying, problems arise when you look at the science and the practicality of directing a lot of time and effort specifically to this problem.

While the science is not crystal clear on this aspect of performance, most research points to the rationale that a little eccentric training will go a long way in preventing muscular breakdown and that those adaptations last a long time (Clarkson, Nosaka, and Braun 1992; Nosaka et al. 2001). What is not clear is what the curve of diminishing returns looks like in this area and how we should determine the optimal amount of eccentric training. Additionally, some academic research has suggested that downhill running prowess has more to do with movement coordination than with oxygen consumption or force toleration (Minetti et al. 2002). Thus, training to run downhills harder (at higher cardiovascular intensity levels and higher forces) might not have as much of an effect as training to run downhills with better technique.

SHOULD I CHANGE MY STRIDE?

Emerging research has suggested that one way to cope with the massive amount of muscular breakdown is to vary your stride throughout the course of the race (Giandolini et al. 2015). If you are a heel striker, you would intentionally run with a forefoot strike periodically and vice versa. The theory is that the slight changes in biomechanical patterns will spread the work and subsequent damage out among different muscle groups. In trail running, with its varied terrain, this happens to a certain extent naturally. But in events where the terrain is more benign, consciously altering your gait could prove to be a useful tool to help prevent muscular breakdown.

In contrast, we know a lot more about the recovery from large bouts of eccentric training and associated muscular breakdown, and we can use that information to evaluate and compare eccentric training with other training components. The more you descend, the longer recovery times you will need. Additionally, the faster you descend (the higher forces you apply), the longer recovery times you will need. Foot for foot of elevation change, it will take longer to recover from descending than from ascending, even though ascending requires more energy to perform and a longer time to complete. From a practical standpoint we need to look at this from a cost-benefit ratio. It doesn't take a lot of descending to achieve the desired adaptation, and more descending requires disproportionately long recovery periods. It is for these reasons (and a couple more I will explain in the next chapter) that my philosophy for coping with muscular fatigue and breakdown revolves around a singular strategy: Match the grade and speed of your training to what you will experience during the race. This concept is examined further in Chapter 5, "The Four Disciplines of Ultrarunning."

RESEARCHERS WANT YOU!

There is a lack of comprehensive research in ultramarathoning. There are bits and pieces of scientific literature dedicated to how the body reacts after 26.2 miles, but these bits and pieces are just that. This does not have to be the case! You can help. I encourage you to participate in the research being done in ultramarathon running. Some of this is done at races, and some is conducted in the lab. If you run across a researcher asking for subjects, please consider participating. Your involvement increases our understanding of the discipline. It might even help to save a life.

CHAPTER 5

THE FOUR DISCIPLINES OF ULTRARUNNING

Many ultramarathons are run over challenging terrain. Some courses have massive amounts of elevation gain, with average grades of more than 10 percent. Most ultramarathons contain a mixture of level running, uphill running, downhill running, and walking (which ultrarunners affectionately refer to as power-hiking). It does not take a rocket scientist to know that flat, level running, uphill running, downhill running, and power-hiking are fundamentally different. Much as a swimmer can train for different strokes, these can be viewed as four different disciplines runners can train for, each with its own set of specificities. If you know some key biomechanical differences among these forms of locomotion, you can better tailor your training for any event. Looking at them side by side will make it easier to see why I prefer uphill interval work, avoid downhill intervals, and recommend trying to match the average grade and locomotive specificity in training to the course you will be running.

BIOMECHANICAL DIFFERENCES

The best way to differentiate among the four disciplines of ultrarunning is along two facets:

- Differences in ground reaction forces
- How muscles and joint angles propel you forward or slow you down

MAY THE (GROUND REACTION) FORCE BE WITH YOU!

Each time your foot hits the ground, the ground pushes back with an equal amount of force. Biomechanists refer to these forces as your *ground reaction forces* (GRFs). With every step taken while running on a flat, level surface, you strike the ground with a force of about 2.5 to 3 times your body weight in the vertical plane (Cavanagh and Lafortune 1980; Kram et al. 1998; Yack et al. 1998; Chang 2000). Running faster increases these forces (Munro, Miller, and Fuglevand 1987; Nilsson and Thorstensson 1989; Hamill and Knutzen 2006). As you run uphill or downhill, these forces change yet again in both magnitude and pattern for the vertical (normal) plane (Gottschal and Kram 2005b). As indicated in Figure 5.1, peak vertical forces for running uphill and downhill *at the same speed* are only slightly different, with forces for downhill being slightly greater (Gottschal and Kram 2005b). But in the real world you go downhill a lot faster than you go uphill, right? *At the same effort level, running downhill produces much larger forces than flat, level running or uphill running because you are running faster* (Figure 5.2).

Walking is a whole different kettle of fish. As can be seen in Figure 5.2, the forces in walking (or power-hiking in the context of ultrarunning) are utterly

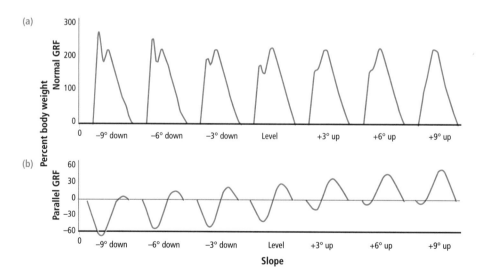

FIGURE **5.1** *Normal (a) and parallel (b) ground reaction forces versus time traces for a typical subject (73 kg) running at 3 m/s on different slopes*

Source: Gottschall and Kram 2005b.

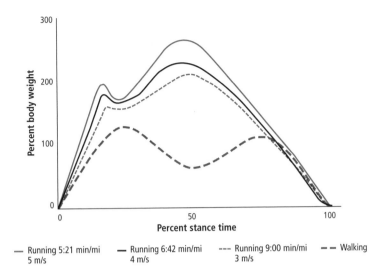

FIGURE **5.2** *Vertical (normal) ground reaction force (GRF) for running at different speeds and walking. The running GRF increases with speed, and the walking GRF is noticeably less.*

Source: Adapted from Nilsson and Thorstensson 1989; Keller et al. 1996; Gottschal and Kram 2005b; Browning and Kram 2007; Grabowski and Kram 2008.

benign compared with those in running. The force patterns do not resemble running in the slightest, and peak GRFs are much lower at 1.2 times body weight (Margaria 1976; Browning and Kram 2007).

These differences in GRFs represent one way the four disciplines of ultrarunning are indeed different. Within each discipline, you strike the ground with a different pattern and peak force.

MUSCLES AND JOINT SEGMENT ANGLES

Just as GRFs differ across the four disciplines, the way your muscles and joints are used also varies. Scientists measure this activity in two ways. First they look at the muscles' electromyography (EMG), which is their electrical excitation. The more forceful the muscular contraction, the higher the EMG reading. The second way to measure how your muscles and joints operate is to look at your limbs under a high-speed three-dimensional video and measure the joint segment angles. This latter analysis provides a physical look at how the limbs move through three-dimensional space and therefore provides clues as to how the underlying musculature is working.

With both of these types of analyses, pictures are worth thousands of words. You certainly do not need to know the minutiae of EMG data and high-speed video analysis to interpret the results. I present Figures 5.3 and 5.4 simply to show that there are obvious and noticeable differences in the data patterns created by each of the four disciplines, which demonstrates that you utilize muscles differently for each discipline.

Figure 5.3 summarizes the results of a study in which researchers placed subjects on a treadmill and had them walk, increased the treadmill speed to a run, and then decreased the speed back to a walk. The researchers then analyzed the resulting EMG data and lower limb angles at these different speeds. Obviously, lower limb angles changed from walking to running. Additionally, nearly all the lower leg muscles exhibited more electrical excitation during running versus walking (see Figure 5.3A). This should come as no surprise because running generally

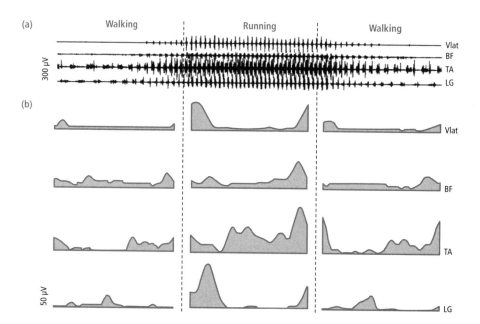

FIGURE **5.3** *(a) EMG activity for various muscles in walking, running, and returning to walking. The higher the EMG amplitude, the greater the muscle activation. (b) EMG patterns for various muscles while walking, running, and returning to walking. The patterns of activation are different for walking, running, and then returning to a walk.*

Note: Vlat = vastus lateralis; BF = biceps femoris; TA = tibialis anterior; LG = gastrocnemius lateralis.

Source: Cappellini et al. 2006.

requires more muscular force than walking. A more important finding as it pertains to ultrarunning is that the actual pattern of muscular activation changed significantly when the athlete went from walking to running and from running back to walking (see Figure 5.3B). So not only was there a change in electrical excitation, but there was also a shift in the pattern of how muscles worked together to complete the task.

Similarly, on a whole-body level, joint segment angles can tell the story of the interplay between flat, level walking, flat running, uphill running, and downhill running. Figure 5.4 visually summarizes how the hip, knee, and ankle angles change during these different disciplines.

As can be seen from the force EMG and joint segment data, the four disciplines of ultrarunning serve up different biomechanical stressors. While the cardiovascular system links them all together, the patterns of movement are distinctive enough that I consider them akin to separate sports and hence address them individually in training.

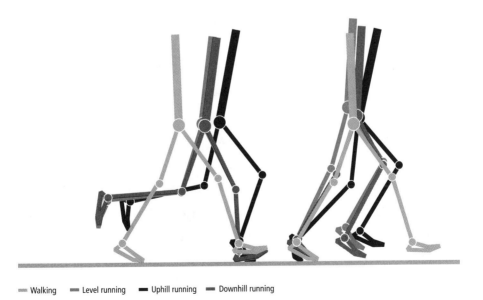

▭ Walking   ▭ Level running   ▬ Uphill running   ▬ Downhill running

FIGURE **5.4** *The hip, knee, and foot are all in different positions when walking or running on level ground, running uphill, and running downhill.*

Source: Adapted from Yokozawa 2006; Guo et al. 2006; and Hicheur et al. 2006.

SHOULD I RUN OR POWER-HIKE THAT HILL?

Chances are, if you are asking that question, you should power-hike. At slower speeds, walking is a more economical form of locomotion than running. It is only when you speed up to near the 12-min/mi range on level ground that walking is less economical (Falls and Humphrey 1976; Margaria 1976; Glass and Dwyer 2007). The practical decision to run or power-hike has to do with both the situation you are in and the difference in energy costs between the two forms of locomotion. While most elite runners, particularly at the 50K and 50-mile distance, will choose to run anything they can in order to finish faster, they knowingly do so at the expense of economy and have to spike their efforts up the steepest climbs in order to continue running instead of slowing down to a power-hike. At shorter ultra distances, this strategy can work because winning a race is a good trade-off as long as the increase in effort is reasonable. However, most ultrarunners are not in that position. Most want to finish as fast as they can, but prioritizing economy and effort level over short-term speed, specifically when choosing whether to walk or run, will almost always end up saving the average ultrarunner time. For the average ultrarunner—and definitely anyone flirting with cutoff times—running when you should be power-hiking burns a lot of energy and takes a toll on your system. Any time you gain in the effort will likely be lost (plus additional time) when you are forced to slow down.

Now, what speed you should choose for power-hiking is a more complicated question due to individual variability, course specificity, terrain technicality, and fatigue. The preferred walk-to-run transition speed is around 2.1 meters per second or 12:46 min/mi on flat ground (Beuter and Lalonde 1988; Hreljac 1993; Diedrich and Warren 1995). This means that if you begin walking and gradually increase your speed, you will naturally transition from a walk to a run at about this pace. The scientific explanations vary, but one thing is certain: At speeds slower than the preferred walk-to-run transition point, *on level ground*, it is energetically optimal to walk (Falls and Humphrey 1976; Margaria 1976; Dwyer 2007). This means running at a 12- to 13-min/mi pace requires more cardiovascular effort and more energy than walking at a 12- to 13-min/mi pace. This balance changes with increases in grade and differences in surface. Generally speaking, the speed at which you should transition slows down as the surface gets more technical and the grades get steeper. To put it in practical terms, if you are running on any normal climb (4 to 15 percent grade) around 18- to 19-min/mi or slower, it's in your best interest to drop to a power-hike, even at the expense of a few extra seconds at the top. You will be far more economical, and the required effort is substantially lower. As a bonus, you can take the opportunity to take in a few calories.

To illustrate this concept, I put one of my athletes on a treadmill at a pace that was in between a walk and a run for her (see figure): an 18-min/mi pace at a 13 percent grade. I had her alternate running and walking for 3 minutes at a time to demonstrate to her the difference in cardiovascular effort required between the two forms of locomotion. The results are easy to see. Running requires a higher heart rate and thus a greater cardiovascular effort than walking at the same speed.

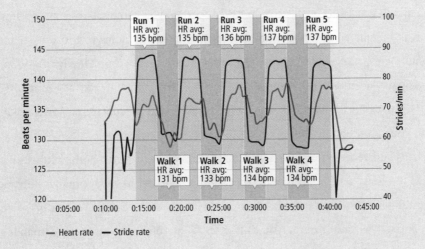

HOW TO TRAIN FOR THE FOUR DISCIPLINES

Knowing that each of the four disciplines of ultrarunning is unique and requires specific training, you can now put that knowledge into action in your day-to-day training. The simplest way to do this is to determine your event's average elevation change per mile and then try to re-create that elevation change over the course of a week's worth of training, particularly in the last several weeks before an event. (See Chapter 8, "Organizing Your Training: The Long-Range Plan," on why this latter point is particularly important.)

The average elevation change per mile is determined using this simple calculation:

total elevation change in feet/total miles

For example, the Western States 100-Mile Endurance Run boasts an elevation gain of 18,090 feet and an elevation loss of 22,970 feet over 100.2 miles. Therefore, the average elevation change per mile for the course is the following:

(18,090 + 22,970)/100.2 = 410 feet of elevation change/mile

Granted, this is the average for the entire course, including the steepest of climbs, level terrain, and varying descents. There are obviously sections that are more or less steep. However, if you attempt to match this average elevation change per mile in a week's worth of training, you'll be on the right path.

If you want to take this concept even further, you can break the course down into the major climbs and descents, find the average grades of those particular components, and search out local trails that are analogous. Finally, if you can anticipate the amount of power-hiking you will do during the race (as a function of the steepness of the climbs), you can incorporate that percentage of power-hiking into your training.

If you live near the course itself, consider yourself lucky. Some ultrarunners have the exact terrain and grade specificity they need to be optimally prepared. Most do not. But, with some background research on the course you are preparing for and a little simple math, you can better tailor your training to the demands of the event and more specifically prepare yourself for the four disciplines.

Flat running, uphill running, power-hiking, and some downhill running can all be done as specific workouts. At CTS we use a specific nomenclature for workouts, and I will use that throughout the book. TempoRuns (TR), SteadyStateRuns (SSR), and RunningIntervals (RI) are all specific workouts that can be done at a variety of grades depending on the goals for the phase (see Chapter 8, "Organizing Your Training: The Long-Range Plan"). When building fitness early in the season, it is preferable to do these intervals uphill to maximize their aerobic benefit. Later in the year, during training for the specific demands of the event, a mixture of uphill, downhill, and flats can be used.

WEEKLY SUMMARY

The following list shows weekly statistics from Dylan Bowman's final training phase leading up to the 2014 Western States 100. Note that the elevation change per week is simlar to that of the Western States racecourse (410 feet of elevation change per mile).

May 12–18
Total miles: 89
Total elevation change: 36,756 ft
Elevation change/mi: 413 ft

May 19–25
Total miles: 79
Total elevation change: 33,254 ft
Elevation change/mi: 421 ft

May 26–June 1
Total miles: 107
Total elevation change: 45,098 ft
Elevation change/mi: 421 ft

June 2–June 8
Total miles: 91
Total elevation change: 34,580 ft
Elevation change/mi: 380 ft

June 9–June 15
Total miles: 80
Total elevation change: 28,372 ft   Elevation change/mi: 354 ft

SHOULD I USE POLES?

The use of poles in ultramarathons has become increasingly popular. Once largely confined to European races, ultrarunning-specific trekking poles can now be seen in nearly every mountainous ultra in the United States. Advancements in materials and construction have helped to make poles lighter and easier to carry and stow. Poles can be used to aid in propulsion and stability and to help spread out the total load of running uphill and downhill. The use of poles is always a personal choice: Consider these factors before deciding to use or not use poles in your ultra:

- Generally speaking, the more you are going to power-hike and the greater the amount of vertical change on the course, the more aid you will get from using poles.

- You must train with poles for at least four weeks leading up to the race. This is to acquire the necessary skill, strength, and stamina in your arms to use the poles effectively. It will also give you time to decide if you want to use the poles only when moving uphill or in both the uphill and downhill portions.

- The use of poles in many instances will be less economical and thus will require more energy. Training consistently with poles can improve your economy.

- You can use your poles for stability (uphill and downhill), for propulsion (uphill only), and as a means of coping with the forces associated with downhill running. You will get the most benefit if you learn to use them for all three.

- Find the right pole size. Your elbow should be bent at a 90-degree or slightly greater angle when your elbows are at your sides and the poles are touching the ground. You should be able to grasp the handle grip higher or lower, depending on the situation.

- If using your poles for propulsion, align and time the pole strike with your foot strike, step for step. This will maximize the work done by the upper body.

THE ROLE OF BODY WEIGHT IN ULTRARUNNING

Conventional wisdom tells us that it is easier to move a smaller mass than a larger one, especially over long distances. There are three important facts of physiology that support that conventional wisdom:

1. The energy cost of running can be calculated as 1 calorie per kilogram per kilometer on flat ground (Margaria et al. 1963).
2. An athlete's VO_2max is expressed as milliliters per kilogram per minute.
3. Your running GRFs are typically expressed as a function of your mass (e.g., 2.5 to 3 times your body weight).

These facts would seem to indicate that lighter is always better, since being lighter would simultaneously reduce the caloric expenditure of transporting your body

WHAT'S SO GREAT ABOUT UPHILL INTERVALS?

Roughly 80 percent of all the intervals I prescribe are uphill. Why?

- Uphill running elicits a higher cardiovascular response than does flat, level running. This is precisely why most standardized running VO_2max tests will increase in grade in order to measure maximal oxygen consumption.
- Uphill running is a hedge against injury. It slows you down, therefore decreasing the peak GRFs on every foot strike.
- More time is spent climbing versus descending in ultrarunning. If you can get 1 percent improvement on the uphills, it's worth more time on race day than a 1 percent improvement on the downhills.
- A little downhill work goes a long way and the effects last a long time, so the focus needs to be on the uphills (see "How to Combat Muscular Breakdown" in Chapter 4).

down the trail, increase your VO_2max, and reduce the necessary biomechanical forces. However, the issue of body weight and running performance is more complicated than that, especially for ultrarunning. While being excessively heavy is not advantageous, there is a benefit to carrying some additional muscle, and being too lean can be problematic.

BODY WEIGHT AND ENERGY COST

The interesting thing about the energy expenditure of running is that for the average midpack runner on flat ground, the calories burned per kilometer are independent of speed. When you run faster, you burn more calories per minute, but you also cover distance more quickly, so the overall caloric expenditure per kilometer stays relatively constant. Similarly, when you run slower, you're burning fewer calories per minute because you're running at a lower percentage of your VO_2max, but it takes more minutes to run that same kilometer. However, regardless of your speed, it will require less energy to propel a smaller mass down the trail.

What happens to the energy cost of running when you lose weight? For each 1 percent reduction in body weight, you reduce the energy cost of running by 1 percent. So, for a 70-kg (154-pound) runner, losing 0.7 kg (1.54 pounds) reduces the energy cost of running by 1 percent. Put another way, a 70-kg runner expends 70 calories to run a kilometer on flat ground. If that runner reduces his or her weight to 65 kg, there's a savings of 5 calories/kilometer. That might not seem like an energy savings worth the effort of losing 5 kg, but think about the impact over the duration of an ultramarathon. For 160 kilometers (100 miles), that 5-kg weight loss translates to an 800-calorie savings.

BODY WEIGHT AND RESISTANCE TO FATIGUE

When you look at athletes who are successful at shorter distances such as 5K, 10K, half-marathon, and marathon races, there's no doubt that lighter is faster. The top athletes in these disciplines have slight builds and are extremely lean. The top athletes in ultrarunning have more muscular builds. We already know that a lot more muscle damage is incurred during an ultramarathon than during a marathon, and one theory is that athletes with more muscle mass are better able to spread the damage across more muscle tissue so they can continue to move forward. Athletes with less muscle tissue may be at a disadvantage because they have less capacity to cope with the stress of muscle breakdown at longer distances.

There's a balance point, though, to the advantage of having more muscle to work with and the disadvantage of having to carry more weight. Carrying more weight gives you the capacity to cope with more muscle damage, but it also increases the amount of muscle breakdown you experience because of the greater eccentric work required of the muscles.

BODY WEIGHT AND VO₂MAX

All right. Based on everything mentioned earlier, you want to be light to reduce the energy cost of running, but you need to have some muscle mass to cope with the damage caused by ultradistance running—just not too much muscle mass because then you increase GRF, which in turn increases muscle damage. Now let's add one more variable: VO_2max.

The maximum amount of oxygen your body can take in, transport, and utilize per minute is dependent on your weight. When we say a 70-kilogram elite ultra-runner has a VO_2max of 65 ml/kg/min, it means he or she can consume 65 ml of oxygen for each kilogram of body weight in a minute. Put another way, this athlete has an absolute VO_2max of 4,550 ml or 4.55 L of oxygen per minute (65 ml/kg/min × 70 kg). When you reduce body weight to 65 kg, absolute VO_2max stays relatively constant, but relative VO_2max goes up to 70 ml/kg/min. This is important because even though you are taking in the same amount of oxygen, you are now delivering it to a smaller body, which means there's more oxygen available for working muscles!

Absolute VO_2max is trainable, and focused interval work (namely, Running-Intervals) can increase this performance ceiling. That can get you from 4.55 L/min to, let's say, 5 L/min (an increase of approximately 10 percent). If you can do that and stay at 70 kg, your relative VO_2max goes from 65 ml/kg/min to 71 ml/kg/min. If you can both increase absolute VO_2max to 5 L/min *and* reduce mass to 65 kg, you end up with a relative VO_2max of 76 ml/kg/min, a 17 percent increase!

What does all this mean for a midpack ultrarunner? Using the same math as in the earlier example but starting with an absolute VO_2max of 3.5 L/min, a 70-kg runner has a relative VO_2max of 50 ml/kg/min. Increasing absolute VO_2max by 11 percent to 3.89 L/min with no change in weight moves relative VO_2max to 55 ml/kg/min. Losing 5 kg of body weight increases it further to just shy of 60 ml/kg/min. While each of these changes individually would be substantial, they are a great example of how one can move from an average runner to having physiological traits similar to those of the top athletes in the sport. Increasing VO_2max, even if you accomplish the increase only through weight loss, impacts performance at all levels of intensity. Not only does being lighter make more oxygen available to working muscles at the very highest intensity you can achieve, but your aerobic pace and your lactate threshold pace are now faster as well. Furthermore, with a higher VO_2max, running at any pace will take less out of you. All paces will be more sustainable for longer periods, and you will be able to recover from efforts above lactate threshold more quickly.

WEIGHT MANAGEMENT FOR THE ULTRARUNNER

A look at the bigger picture shows that body weight is not as crucial a component or predictor of race-day performance in ultrarunning as it is in marathon running. Researchers have studied whether certain anthropometric measurements increase or decrease a runner's chances of finishing an ultramarathon or affect finishing times. In some studies, higher body-fat percentage didn't correlate with slower finishing times, but higher body mass and larger upper-arm circumference did. Having a larger calf or thigh circumference, though, didn't lead to slower finishing times (Knechtle et al. 2009). There are many variables to be considered, but the data suggest that carrying a lot of upper-body muscle isn't helpful for ultrarunners—especially when it contributes to a higher overall body mass—but carrying more muscle mass in the legs can correlate with faster finishing times (Knechtle, Rosemann, and Lepers 2010). It is worth noting, however, that training volume and finishing times at the marathon distance were better predictors of ultrarunning performance than any body measurement (Knechtle et al. 2009; Knechtle, Rosemann, and Lepers 2010), which is why I prefer to focus on training first, with weight management as a secondary issue. Even with elite-level ultrarunners, I focus on cardiovascular development and the limiting factors for performance outlined in Chapter 4. Weight management tends to take care of itself as a result of increased training volume and intensity. For midpack and novice ultrarunners, weight management is still less of a concern than other limiting factors for performance; if anything, excessive weight loss is a greater concern.

Being too lean can absolutely hinder performance. When you are losing weight because you are not sufficiently supporting your training workload with calories and nutrients, you will lose both fat and lean muscle mass. Because some of this muscle mass is important for coping with the metabolic stress of running long distances, losing weight by losing muscle is problematic. Athletes who are too lean cannot train as effectively because they cannot recover from hard efforts as quickly. Being too lean also puts additional stress on the immune system, leaving some athletes more susceptible to illness. When I encounter a lean runner who is not responding positively to training, is struggling to finish races, and is constantly dealing with small colds, gastrointestinal bugs, and nagging injuries, the first thing I look at is the athlete's nutrition program. It is likely the athlete is not consuming enough calories to support his or her training workload.

THE TECHNOLOGY OF ULTRARUNNING

I killed a lot of trees when I first started coaching. Throughout the course of a workday, I received numerous faxes and e-mail attachments of training files from my athletes. I printed out every single one of them, and then I'd pore over each file, examining the critical data. Highlights of yellow, orange, and pink would adorn the sheets, denoting intervals, critical heart rate values, and anything else I found significant. I'd fill the margins with notes from conversations and debriefs on each workout from the athlete. Finally, I'd place the sheets of paper in individually labeled folders, one for each athlete.

At the conclusion of a training phase, I'd spread the contents of an athlete's folder out on a table. My preferred canvas for this exercise was a large, round table in our conference room, but that seldom gave me enough space. Papers were every-where—on the table, floor, and chairs and in the adjoining rooms; no horizontal surface was safe. Once the documents were strewn about to my liking, I'd try to make sense of it all. Was the athlete improving? Was he or she hitting the correct intensities? Was it time for rest? The colors, highlights, notes, and scribbles all provided clues; the conclusions, however, I had to determine myself. As rudimentary as this system of paper, pen, and colors was, it did its job, and I could get a good fix on what was going on with the athlete. It was not perfect, but it was all I had.

Over time, training-related technology and software improved and have now become quite sophisticated. Sheets of paper collected in file folders gave way to electronic storage and access. The device manufacturers, motivated to differentiate their products from the rest, all created ways of organizing and making sense of the information collected from their widgets. Each system had its own spin. Some were very good at taking individual files and breaking them down. Others were better at aggregating many files to identify trends. All were helpful to coaches trying to understand it all.

As heart rate training gave way to power-based training (in cycling) and GPS-based training (in running), some of our previously unidentified training flaws started to show. The software developed by device manufacturers and third-party platforms helped to reveal these flaws. We could now see pace and power decoupled from heart rate (renowned endurance coach Joe Friel developed a name for this phenomenon: aerobic decoupling and efficiency factor). We could quantify and aggregate training load and see how various loads affected performance. Myriad other insights ensued, none of which would have been possible from staring at 8½ × 11 sheets of paper, no matter how much highlighter I used.

As a coach working with endurance athletes, I took to this evolution, which helped me gain insight into how my athletes were training. In road running, triathlon, and cycling, the data acquired in the field could be meaningfully interpreted in order to analyze and adapt training for athletes. I had tangible quantifications of workload, and improvement could be easily identified. I wish I could say the same kind of data existed for trail ultrarunners.

In ultrarunning, particularly trail ultrarunning, the proposition is tricky. The tangible quantification of workload and work rate that exists in road running and cycling becomes inconsistent and blurry for runners training on mixed surfaces. Improvement markers are also difficult to come by, particularly in mountainous areas where the properties of the trail surface can change from one run to the next or even during a single run.

Nonetheless, when I started working with ultrarunners, I realized I needed to solve the same problems I always had. I needed a way to quantify workloads and work rates, and to compare one workout to the next. I needed a way to determine if an athlete had improved. Harking back to my earlier experiences with folders and highlighted sheets of paper, I hacked together a way to use the available data and tools to better coach ultrarunners. Is it perfect? Hell, no. Does it do the job? You bet. Technology and software will continue to evolve. In the meantime, people still have to run and train, and I—and you—have to figure out ways to make sense of it all.

TOOLS TO TRACK YOUR TRAINING

The primary tracking devices for recording day-to-day ultrarunning performance are GPS monitors. Several manufacturers produce them, and ultrarunners have to pick the features and price point that best suit their needs. This technology is constantly evolving, so rather than focus on specific brands and the differences between them, I will focus on the key features to look for to track your training.

GPS ACCURACY

Much of what you can do to train for the specificity of any particular ultra is rooted in the exercise of matching the grades and surfaces you train on to what you will experience on race day. This being the case, GPS and altitude accuracy are important considerations in choosing a watch. The quality of GPS data is fundamentally determined by the strength of the satellite signal, how many satellites are acquired, the position of the antenna within the watch, and how frequently the satellite information is collected. Most of the traditional watch manufacturers do a great job with this aspect, and there are few notable differences among high-quality watches.

BATTERY LIFE

Battery life on many GPS watches hinges on the quality and size of the battery and the amount and quality of data samples collected. Many of the device manufacturers are becoming wise to the fact that athletes are going longer. They engineer their watches and batteries to last as long as possible and provide a reasonable footprint for the watch to wrap around your wrist. Battery technology is improving all the time, stretching the life span of what a watch can record in a single session. Taking battery life a step further, device manufacturers also provide options for athletes to manipulate the GPS recording variables of the watch. This saves battery life by recording data at less frequent intervals or by manipulating how the GPS signal is acquired. The watch then uses non-GPS movement data to fill in the gaps to determine speed when GPS position is not being recorded. Some GPS devices come with this as the only recording option to minimize the size and bring the watch down to a less expensive price point. It is a classic compromise that prioritizes the battery life (and sometimes price point) over the accuracy of the data collected.

As another approach, some manufacturers give athletes the ability to improve GPS quality by utilizing GLONASS satellite capabilities and other GPS signal-strengthening tools. This decreases the battery life for any one particular workout but improves the accuracy of the data collected.

As a coach, I prefer to have the highest-quality data possible. In analyzing files, it makes a difference looking at information that was collected every second versus information that was collected every several seconds, particularly when evaluating intervals that are just a few minutes in length. From a practical standpoint, interval recording options of one second are necessary for any trail-running GPS watch. Furthermore, because trail running is done where terrain and trees can interfere with satellite signals, a premium must be placed on acquiring the most precise position possible at all times. While the option of sparing battery life at the expense of lower-quality data is a good one particularly for longer races, in day-to-day training it is best to stick to the highest-quality data and most frequent data collection rate possible.

LOGGING YOUR TRAINING

Choosing the right device will start you on the right path to correctly monitoring and tracking your training. The next step in this process is to home in on the software that is going to harness the data and give you actionable information you can use to better guide and focus your training. As a coach, I have thousands of hours of practice aggregating and tracking training information. I don't ask my athletes, and I would not ask you, to delve that deeply into the data. However, with a few key insights into how concepts like total workload, work rate, fitness, and fatigue work, you can utilize the information collected by your GPS watch, as well as personal feedback, to better monitor your training.

THE TOOLS OF STRAVA AND TRAININGPEAKS

While each device manufacturer has developed its own software to harness data, the trend over the past several years is that third-party platforms simply do a better job in this role. Garmin, for example, makes numerous GPS devices (and even cameras) for use in running, golf, boating, driving, aviation, and other activities. Suunto and Polar and other GPS device manufacturers similarly make a range of different products. All of these manufacturers are experts in making devices that can capture information on a miniature computer (a watch in a running application). Meanwhile, software-specific companies focus solely on taking the data acquired from a training device and presenting actionable information. They are experts in taking information from the tiny computers and making sense out of it for athletes and coaches. So, it is not surprising that the better platforms for monitoring and tracking training come from the software-specific manufacturers. Recently, two have emerged as the go-to platforms for endurance athletes: Strava and TrainingPeaks.

Comparing Workload and Work Rate

An inability to determine total workload (kilojoules) and work rate (power) is one of the long-standing challenges in coaching trail ultrarunners. While volume quantifies the *amount* of training (in time or miles), and intensity describes the *effort* of training, total workload and work rate are more useful in determining how much training stress an athlete incurs.

According to simple Newtonian physics, work is a product of force and distance. A bigger force applied over a longer distance leads to more work done. In level running, the amount of work performed is a function of your weight (remember ground reaction forces from Chapter 5; they are a function of body weight) and how far you ran (distance). Therefore, for level running, workload can be well represented by how many miles you ran and how much you weigh. A heavier runner will have a higher total workload than a lighter runner who covers the same number of miles.

Work rate is the total amount of work done divided by the time it took to perform it. In level running, running a mile takes approximately the same *amount* of work regardless of how long it takes to run it. You can see this manifested in caloric expenditure equations (total calories = 1 calorie per kilogram per kilometer); caloric expenditure is a function of distance and weight, not speed. Your work *rate*, however, is dependent on speed. The faster you run any given distance, the higher your work rate. For flat running, work rate can be represented by pace and weight. Similarly, a heavier runner will have a higher work rate than a lighter runner at the same speed.

For a runner who is training primarily on the flats, workload can be represented by miles and work rate by pace. These two values can even be compared among different runners who have the same mass. In cycling, work rate and workload can actually be measured by power meters. At the time of this writing, nothing analogous is available in trail running, but power-measuring technology for runners is in development. The differences in trail surface and elevation gain and loss make capturing workload and work rate problematic at best. There are tools out there that trail runners and ultrarunners can use, but to properly evaluate training, it is important to know the basis for and limitations of such tools.

Normalized Graded Pace and Grade Adjusted Pace

Both Strava and TrainingPeaks have developed algorithms to convert running on uphills and downhills to flat, level running (Table 6.1). TrainingPeaks' Normalized Graded Pace (NGP) and Strava's Grade Adjusted Pace (GAP) take your running and "normalize" it as if you were running on flat, level ground. For example, if you are running up a 6.0 percent climb at a 12:00 min/mi pace, your NGP would be 9:21. In other words, running 12:00 min/mi on a 6.0 percent uphill is comparable to running 9:21 min/mi on the flats. This gives athletes the ability to compare paces on different climbs and descents with the equivalent pace for flat, level running.

TABLE **6.1**	Examples of NGP and GAP at Different Paces and Grades													
PACE PER MILE	**GRADE**													
	−10%		−6%		−2%		0%		2%		6%		10%	
	NGP	GAP	NGP	GAP	NGP	GAP	NGP	GAP	NGP	GAP	NGP	GAP	NGP	GAP
8:00	15:18	11:27	11:13	10:05	8:51	8:40	8:00	8:00	7:19	7:22	6:14	6:16	5:26	5:21
10:00	19:07	14:19	14:00	12:37	11:04	10:50	10:00	10:00	9:09	9:13	7:48	7:50	6:47	6:42
12:00	22:56	17:11	16:48	15:08	13:17	13:00	12:00	12:00	10:59	11:04	9:21	9:24	8:08	8:02

Both of these algorithms do a decent job of comparing the respective paces (and therefore work rates) of climbing and flat, level running when performed on similar surfaces and at normal gradients. You can go out and do intervals on flat sections and climbs, compare the efforts, and determine which effort was harder or easier. However, there are two glaring flaws in utilizing these algorithms for trail runners.

Flaw 1: When the surface is different. Neither GAP nor NGP has the ability to account for the difference in work associated with running on different surfaces. You intuitively know that running through sand is more difficult than running on a track. Similarly, running over technical terrain requires more effort than running over smooth terrain. However, the paces and calculated GAP and NGP will not account for the difference in those surfaces.

Flaw 2: Descents. The calculations for GAP and NGP use the difference in energy cost between uphill, downhill, and level running to arrive at the equivalent pace for level terrain. While on flat ground, your pace is directly related to work rate. Your cardiovascular system has to work harder in order to go faster, which means a higher pace requires a higher work rate. But remember that for downhill running in particular, energy cost tells only part of the story. For downhill running, other factors outside of the energetic cost combine to significantly affect the overall training stress. These include changes in foot speed, coordination, and musculo-skeletal stress, all of which are different in downhill running than in level or uphill running. Neither GAP nor NGP takes these additional stresses into account, and as a result they underestimate the overall stress of downhill running. In a single or shorter run, that may not be a big issue. For ultrarunners, however, it represents a greater flaw as you try to sum up cumulative training stress during a very long run or over a longer period of training.

Total Training Stress

Total workload and *relative* work rate can be used to quantify the amount of training stress for any particular run. This is important because it gives an apples-to-apples comparison of how stressful different runs were. Hilly, undulating runs with wild differences in pace can be compared with flat runs with little deviation in pace on the basis of their total amount of stress. Similarly, interval workouts can be compared to EnduranceRuns. These values are referred to as Running Training Stress Score (rTSS) in TrainingPeaks and Suffer Score in Strava. Both scores are trying to do the same thing, but by markedly different methods.

Both rTSS and Suffer Score take your lactate threshold intensity (defined by pace or heart rate) and the time you spend at your relative intensities (endurance, lactate threshold, VO_2max) to score each workout using a point-based system. Strava uses heart rate, your lactate threshold heart rate, and the time spent in various heart rate ranges to assign an overall score to the run. The resultant points are cleverly referred to as your Suffer Score for the run. The higher the score, the more stressful the run. The flaw in this method is that heart rate (for reasons that will be discussed in Chapter 7, "Train Smarter, Not More: Key Workouts") is not a very good training tool for ultrarunning. So let's move on.

On the TrainingPeaks platform, total training stress (rTSS) is quantified using total time and NGP compared with your lactate threshold pace. Once again, the higher the score, the more stressful the run. The algorithm is calibrated using a 60-minute run at lactate threshold to equal 100 points. Recovery runs will be less than 100 points, and longer endurance runs will typically be more than 100 points. This gives you a basis to determine how stressful a short, high-intensity run is compared with a longer, lower-intensity run (see Table 6.2 for examples).

TABLE **6.2**	rTSS Values for Different Types of Runs	
TYPE OF RUN	**rTSS POINTS**
60-min RecoveryRun	50–80
90-min EnduranceRun with 3 × 10 min. TempoRun	100–150
90-min EnduranceRun with 6 × 3 min. RunningIntervals	100–150
2.5-hr EnduranceRun	150–200
50-mile race	400–600

Aggregating Total Training Stress

Within TrainingPeaks, your rTSS can be aggregated and trended over time. This provides one of the more valuable pieces of feedback when analyzing training load. Acute Training Load (ATL) and Chronic Training Load (CTL) provide snapshots of the long-term (>7 days) aggregate training load.

Acute Training Load is a 7-day weighted average of the rTSS for each particular day. Chronic Training Load is the same thing but over a 42-day period (the time frame for CTL and ATL can be customized). By looking at both of these numbers over time, one obtains a big-picture view of historical training that provides clues as to when an athlete is the most fit (highest CTL), most fatigued (highest ATL), and most ready for performance (positive difference between CTL and ATL). TrainingPeaks provides useful charting capabilities of these metrics that athletes can use simply by uploading their training files on a day-to-day basis.

Figure 6.1 is an analysis of Dylan Bowman's 2014 season. You can see his CTL was highest just before his critical races (Western States 100-Mile Endurance Run and North Face Endurance Challenge, San Francisco), indicating that he was at his peak fitness for those races. You can also see the consistency with which he built his training load over the course of the season, as indicated by the ramping gray area.

Beware the flaws. Unfortunately, the flaws with rTSS, ATL, and CTL mirror those with NGP (as NGP is used in the equations). Changes in surface and large amounts of descending make it difficult to compare one run with the next. However, if your training generally contains the same trail surface and climbing and descending

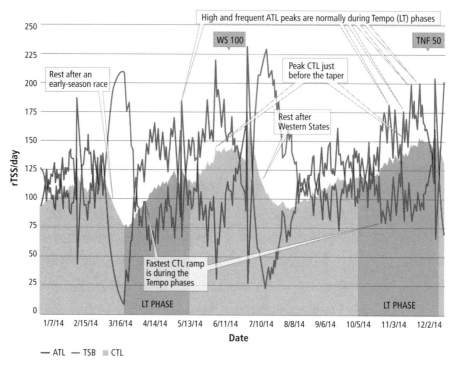

FIGURE **6.1** *Analysis of Dylan Bowman's 2014 season. The CTL (gray-shaded area) is highest just before Dylan's A races, the Western States 100 and the North Face Endurance Challenge, San Francisco (TNF50). This indicates that he was most fit just before those races. His CTL also ramps up fastest during his tempo phases, denoting that they are generally the most stressful phases.*

from day to day, rTSS, ATL, and CTL can give you a ballpark idea of how hard or easy one run is compared with the next and how these training loads stack up over time. Figure 6.2, which presents the rTSS for an athlete who ran down Pikes Peak, illustrates some of the flaws associated with using this value. The route is 12.2 miles, with more than 7,000 feet of loss. A 12-mile run with that much descending would be difficult for any runner; just ask the hundreds who do the Pikes Peak Marathon every year. However, the rTSS for this section is just 58.2 points, equivalent to a normal RecoveryRun.

Monitoring Improvement

How do you know you if are becoming more fit? In the road-running world, your day-to-day paces and workouts can provide answers to this question. In trail running,

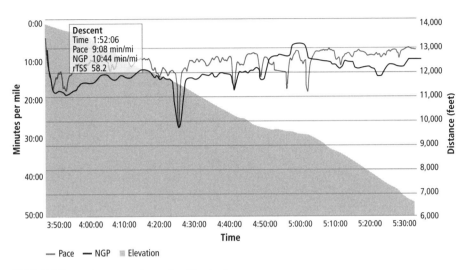

Descent
Time 1:52:06
Pace 9:08 min/mi
NGP 10:44 min/mi
rTSS 58.2

FIGURE **6.2** *rTSS for a runner descending Pikes Peak*

the process is similar, though the answer requires more investigation, particularly if you are doing your specific interval work on trails (as you should be).

Both Strava and TrainingPeaks provide tools to help you understand how your fitness is trending. These tools do not provide stoplight answers that turn green when things are good, red when they are bad, and yellow for somewhere in between. Rather, they provide general trends you can interpret to see if your training is on the right track and if you are making improvements over a period of weeks or months.

Strava segments. One of the great and convenient features of Strava is segment tracking. Strava segments are marked-out sections of road and trail created by users. You can even create your own segments for sections of trail you commonly use for specific interval work. Every time you run across that section of trail, your segment time is recorded for everyone to see (you can change this setting if you wish to keep your run private). Results are racked and stacked on a leaderboard, and you can see where your time fits in with the rest of the pack or in relation to your previous runs. While you should not be trying to set a PR every time, the general trend line can provide clues to how your fitness is trending, particularly if the segment of trail is one you use frequently for training (Figure 6.3). The great thing about these segments (other than being addictive) is that they are automatically

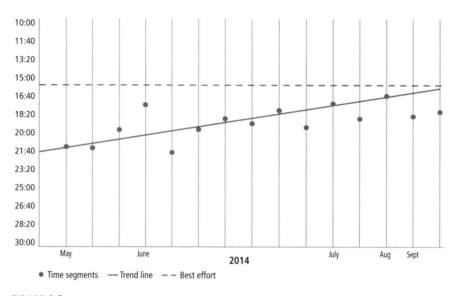

FIGURE **6.3** *Strava segments with the trend line generally getting better over time*

calculated and tabulated once you have uploaded your run. No need to print out pages and mark them up with a highlighter.

NGP between efforts. TrainingPeaks provides fitness tracking via the capability to break down files and create laps once the file is uploaded. In this way, after doing specific workouts, you can come back to the file and analyze the NGP of the specific segments. You can use these data to gauge the quality of your workouts from interval to interval (Figure 6.4) and by looking at different intervals across several days or weeks.

EMERGING TECHNOLOGY

The hallelujah moment may be coming for trail running! We may soon be able to measure workload and work rate. Manufacturers are developing devices that can measure force at the foot and therefore calculate workload and work rate (or watts). Others, notably Stryd, are working on devices that calculate (not directly measure) workload and work rate based on the movement of a runner's center of mass (Figure 6.5). As of this writing, both technologies are promising, but they are

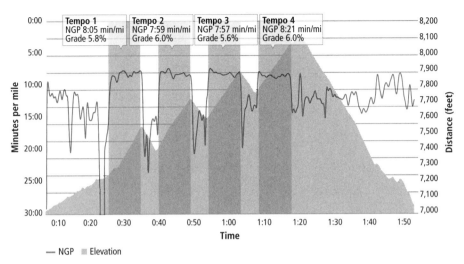

FIGURE **6.4** *A 4 × 10 Tempo workout from Missy Gosney. Note that each of the repeats is at a consistent NGP. This is a well-paced workout.*

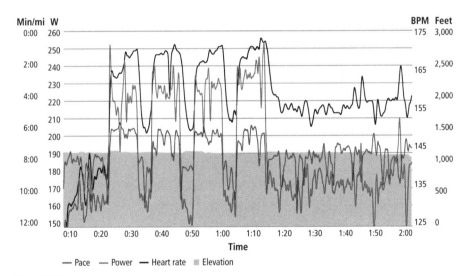

FIGURE **6.5** *A Tempo workout from Kaci Lickteig using a Stryd running power meter*

not ready for prime time. If further refined, they could once again change the way we see trail running and ultrarunning and how we train.

WHAT THE COACH USES

I will let you in on a secret. Very little, if any, of this information is actionable by itself. In all my years as a coach, I cannot recall a time when I have taken one piece of such information and used it to decide what an athlete should do. Rather, action is determined by the aggregate of the information, combined with feedback from the athlete. From a practical standpoint, I utilize the following system to drive the creation of and adjustments to an athlete's training. I encourage you to do something similar.

- Use TrainingPeaks to schedule workouts (see the short-range plan as described in Chapter 9).
- Use NGP, rTSS, and Strava segments to evaluate and compare workouts.
- Use rTSS/CTL/ATL to track training load.
- Use feedback from the athlete to further gauge fitness, fatigue, and motivation.
- Use knowledge and experience to synthesize the information and drive action.

NO MAGIC BULLET

Unfortunately for trail runners, there is no magic bullet for tracking workload or work rate or for monitoring progress. There is an amalgam of approaches you can use to get a better handle on these aspects, but no single one will give you a definitive answer. I wish it were that simple. In reality, it never will be. Even when better tools emerge, coaches and athletes will continue to take their training and analysis beyond the realm of what the data will provide. Soon enough, running workload and work rate will become the norm. These will replace pace, NGP, and GAP just as those metrics have largely replaced the heart rate monitor. Even when that happens, don't expect to see stoplight answers. The training picture will never be green or red; nor will it be encapsulated by my quiver of highlighters. Instead, it will be a blur of many different colors, altogether subject to interpretation. As technology progresses, expect to be able to train more precisely and with greater knowledge. But don't expect the information to do the training for you.

Many of the training file graphs produced throughout this book were done through TrainingPeaks' WKO4 software. I would like to thank Frank Pipp and Mike Bonenberger at Training Peaks for their assistance.

CHAPTER 7

TRAIN SMARTER, NOT MORE: KEY WORKOUTS

It's not that athletes were training incorrectly at the beginning of ultrarunning; it's that there wasn't really any specific training going on at all. Fit and very hardy individuals took on outlandish challenges and managed to finish them. More people became interested in these modern-day feats of endurance, and events became more organized and recognized. Through a lot of hard work and dedication from men and women we now know as icons of the sport, the events grew and course records were established, and a little bit of money came into the sport in the form of sponsorship and prize money. As the winning times in the big ultramarathons started dropping, the sport developed beyond the point where "go run more" was a viable training strategy.

Ultrarunning isn't the only sport to experience this evolution. In fact, it's an evolution common to many sports. Triathlon, for instance, originated in 1977 in Mission Bay, California (the first Ironman in Kona occurred in 1978), and in the early years the sport's top athletes were the ones who could endure the greatest workload. The sports science that had previously shaped the accepted practices in triathlon's component disciplines—swimming, cycling, and running—didn't catch up to the unique demands of triathlon until several years later. Training techniques, equipment technology, and nutritional strategies all evolved—and continue to evolve—and course records continue to be broken.

One of the milestones for any sport occurs when training becomes organized and sport-specific, when "go run more" is replaced by specific kinds of running activities, separated by rest and organized into a schedule. Consider the concept of periodization, which has been around in various rudimentary forms for thousands of years. The modern and almost universally accepted version of periodization—systematically changing the focus and workload of training to maximize the positive impact of overload and recovery on training adaptations—was constructed by Tudor Bompa and other Eastern bloc coaches in order to win Olympic medals in the 1950s, when the Olympics were as much about the battle of East versus West as they were about athletic achievement.

Before Bompa, German scientist Woldemar Gerschler took the relatively informal but highly effective training practices of Swedish running coaches and in the 1930s refined them into what you and I recognize today as interval training. At the time, the Swedes were using changes in terrain to interject periods of intensity and recovery into their longer runs. They referred to the practice as "fartlek" running, which is still widely used. But Gerschler eliminated the unpredictability of fartlek training by adding structure—in the form of precise times, distances, and paces—so he could quantify both the work being done and the recovery being taken between efforts. But neither Bompa nor Gerschler had you in mind when they were pushing the boundaries of sports science. Bompa had to earn Olympic medals to show the world the power of the Soviet system, and Gerschler was working to find a way to help his athletes—including eventual record holder Roger Bannister—break the coveted 4-minute barrier in the 1-mile run. But the science they discovered changed the face of endurance training for athletes at all levels.

Interval training is effective for improving performance because it enables you to accumulate time at specific intensities, and it is time at intensity that creates the stimulus necessary to achieve positive adaptations. The interval workouts described in this chapter are designed to apply the principles of training—overload and recovery, progression, individuality, specificity, and a systematic approach (discussed in Chapter 3)—to individual training sessions. These workouts are in turn governed by five components of training: intensity, volume, frequency/repetition, environment, and stride rate. By manipulating these components, you can create a workout to target just about any physiological demand found in sport.

THE FIVE WORKOUT COMPONENTS

When you get ready to head out for your training sessions, you can use the following variables to address the five principles of training:

1. Intensity
2. Volume
3. Frequency/repetition
4. Environment (terrain, surface, and amount of vertical relief)
5. Running cadence/stride rate

You can change the goal of a workout by changing one of its components. The clearest example of this is found in changing the intensity. Two 10-minute intervals can target completely different energy systems if you simply change your pace. You can maintain a pace at the high end of your aerobic intensity to develop greater aerobic endurance, or you can run at your lactate threshold pace to increase your ability to produce and process lactate. You can also manipulate the environment for your workout—running uphill versus running on flat ground—to change its purpose.

INTENSITY

Intensity is a measure of how hard you are working, and the impact of a workout is directly related to the intensity at which you are working. Measuring intensity is notoriously difficult in running, particularly trail running. Unlike cycling, where athletes can utilize power meters to directly measure workload, or road running, where runners can generally use pace, trail runners can at best observe the body's response to workload in the form of rating of perceived exertion (RPE). New technologies may soon enable us to measure power or normalized pace in running, but until then the best measurement tool we have is RPE.

VOLUME

Volume is the total amount of exercise you're doing in a single workout, a week of training, a month, a year, or a career. The most important concept related to interval training volume is volume-at-intensity. One of the purposes of intervals is to break hard efforts into smaller bites so you can accumulate more time at a specific intensity than you would be able to sustain in one longer effort. For instance, if the goal of a workout is to spend 60 minutes at lactate threshold pace, but currently you can sustain that pace for only 10 minutes, you can organize the workout into six 10-minute intervals, separated by recovery periods. By the end of the workout, you have run at your lactate threshold pace for 60 minutes and generated a training stimulus that will increase the amount of time you can stay at your threshold pace in a single effort. You can also schedule two or three of these workouts in a single week and accumulate up to 180 minutes of volume-at-intensity targeted at your lactate threshold pace.

To properly quantify volume, you have two choices: miles or time. Volume in an ultrarunning and trail running setting is best prescribed by time. This is because a 2-hour run on the flats is more equivalent to a 2-hour run on varied terrain than a 10-mile run on the flats is to a 10-mile run on varied terrain. When you view volume as a volume of time (rather than as a volume of distance), you can more accurately quantify training.

FREQUENCY AND REPETITION

Frequency is the number of times a workout is performed in a given training period, whereas repetition is the number of times an exercise is repeated in a single session. Frequency and repetition are used to ensure the quality of your training sessions. Intervals are effective only if they are performed at the prescribed intensity, volume, frequency, and repetition based on your current fitness. It is the correct combination of all these variables that leads to the most effective training, not the dominance of any of the variables over the others.

Let's say your lactate threshold pace is 9:00 min/mi, and you can sustain that pace for 20 minutes. You might be able to run 8:45 pace for 3 minutes during a RunningInterval workout (defined later in this chapter), which targets pace at VO$_2$max. There's no point in trying to complete a 20-minute RunningInterval because your pace would fall so dramatically after the first 3 to 5 minutes that the rest of the effort would no longer be at VO$_2$max. It would feel ridiculously hard, but once your pace drops, that effort is no longer addressing the goal of a RunningInterval. In contrast, if you do seven 3-minute RunningIntervals at 8:45, separated by 3 minutes of easy running at a recovery pace, you'll accumulate 21 minutes at 8:45 pace.

Frequency gives you another way to accumulate workload, by repeating individual interval sessions during a given week, month, or even year. For instance, a week with two RunningInterval workouts like the one just described means 42 minutes at 8:45 pace. The harder the intervals, the more recovery you need before you'll be ready to complete another high-quality training session. In any effective training program, workouts are spaced out to provide adequate recovery between sessions. I will discuss the relationship between interval workouts and recovery days later in this chapter.

ENVIRONMENT

You can use environmental factors to manipulate your workouts. In some cases you can increase or decrease the workload of particular efforts, as with performing intervals while going uphill. As discussed previously, I prefer certain intervals, especially RunningIntervals, to be done uphill to maximize the aerobic benefit and to be more specific to the race, particularly if the goal race is hilly. Running your intervals on hills can also be useful for overcoming flagging motivation. Sometimes it can be difficult to push yourself through maximum-intensity intervals on flat ground, but a hill adds resistance and a visible challenge, which can be the little something extra you need to make your workout more effective.

Environment has a big impact on specificity in all sports. The surface you run on can make a difference in your pace and in the amount of stress you apply to your body. Ultramarathons almost always have a mixture of surfaces, including trails of varying technical difficulty, dirt roads, and some pavement. Training is not just about developing energy systems; it's also about preparing the musculature, joints, bones, and connective tissues for the challenges of competition.

You can use treadmills to your advantage in training. The suspension found in treadmills means that treadmill running typically has less impact on your feet and legs than running outdoors—even less than running on some trails. For athletes who have a history of foot or knee problems, running on a treadmill may enable you to complete more running time without pain. Running on the treadmill can also make interval training more convenient because you can program in the appropriate paces and durations and let the treadmill adjust your pace and hold it steady for the duration of the interval. This is often helpful for athletes who have trouble motivating themselves to maintain a fast enough pace on their own for difficult intervals. In the end, you'll have to find that motivation to push yourself if you want to succeed on race day, but if you sometimes need the treadmill to provide that motivation, that's OK. Regardless of whether or not you will use a treadmill for interval workouts, EnduranceRuns, or RecoveryRuns, you can set the incline at various degrees depending on your goals.

RUNNING CADENCE AND STRIDE RATE

Decades ago, Cavanaugh and Williams (1981) showed that runners naturally gravitate toward the stride length that is most economical for them in terms of oxygen consumption. Numerous other investigations on running economy have reached similar conclusions. Over time, however, your running stride will most likely get longer as you become a more experienced endurance athlete. Not only are you running faster, but your muscles and joints adapt to a greater range of motion for running faster, and you gain the muscle power and aerobic capacity to propel yourself farther with each stride. Interestingly, once you're a reasonably proficient runner, your biomechanics don't change all that much as you get progressively faster. The maximum angle between your front and back leg doesn't increase much to produce a longer stride; the fact that you're propelling yourself forward with more force and have greater forward momentum means that you travel farther during the airborne portion of your stride.

For an ultrarunner, there are advantages to developing the ability to run at different stride lengths and rates. It may seem counterintuitive to purposely change your stride, given that you have gravitated toward the one that is optimal for you, but this makes sense in ultrarunning because changing your stride and foot strike patterns changes the ways you are stressing your body. A faster stride rate with a shorter stride length, even if it is not your naturally chosen stride, changes the stresses on the muscles and ligaments in your legs. This shortened, rapid stride can be useful for maintaining a solid pace while sparing your legs for harder terrain in later miles.

Stride length and frequency can also be manipulated during drills to prepare you for harder work in interval sessions. For instance, during a warm-up, a series of 20-second RunningStrides (drills from a standing start, focusing on a constant 20-second acceleration) help to develop the neuromuscular pattern for higher-speed running before you have the fitness necessary to maintain those higher speeds. Similarly, when used during a warm-up before a hard interval workout, RunningStrides get your body ready for the neuromuscular pattern and force production you'll be using during the intervals.

MEASURING AND PERSONALIZING TRAINING INTENSITY

If you are going to use interval training to accumulate time at intensity and target specific areas of your fitness, you need a way to figure out how hard you are working. In some sports this is simple. Ultrarunners don't have it so easy. For a long time, runners have tried to use heart rate to gauge intensity, creating intensity ranges based on percentages of lactate threshold heart rate or the average heart rate recorded during a 5K time trial. Others have used pace ranges based on time trials or goal race paces, or a combination of heart rate and pace ranges. Prescribing intensity based on either heart rate or pace is notoriously difficult in ultrarunning, and after trying all manner of methods, I found the greatest success in a remarkably simple, nontechnical, yet scientifically accurate method: rating of perceived exertion (RPE).

WHY HEART RATE IS NOT A GOOD TRAINING TOOL FOR ULTRARUNNING

The heart rate value you see on a watch is a measurement of your body's response to exercise. It's not a direct measure of the work being done; instead, the work is being done primarily by muscles, which in turn demand more oxygen from the cardiovascular system. Because that oxygen is delivered via red blood cells, heart rate increases as demand for oxygen rises. It's an indirect observation of what's happening at the muscular level, but in the absence of a direct way to measure workload, heart rate can provide valuable information. Research has shown con-clusively that there's a strong correlation between heart rate response and changes in an athlete's workload, and that research allowed sports scientists and coaches to start creating heart rate training zones back in the 1980s. But as sports science has evolved over the past 30-plus years, we have learned that many factors affect an athlete's heart rate, and those factors reveal that heart rate response is not reliable and predictable enough to be an effective training tool.

Factors Affecting Heart Rate

Core temperature. As your core temperature increases, heart rate at a given exercise intensity will increase. Your circulatory system carries heat from your core to your extremities to aid with conductive and radiant cooling.

Caffeine and other stimulants. When you consume caffeine, either from your morning cup of coffee or from a caffeinated gel during a training session or race, your heart rate increases.

Excitation/nervousness. A race is an exciting event (or at least it should be if you have the right emotional engagement), and that causes an adrenal response that increases your heart rate. Other emotional responses, including frustration, anger, and anxiety, can also affect heart rate.

Hydration status. Although heart rate changes due to hydration status are often coupled with or concurrent with impacts from core temperature, your heart rate can increase from dehydration with or without a rise in core temperature. As your blood volume diminishes, your heart needs to beat faster to deliver the same amount of oxygen per minute.

Elevation. Most athletes train within a small range of elevations in their local area, but goal races may feature dramatically different elevation profiles. Heart rate and respiration rate increase at elevation, starting at about 5,000 feet above sea level, because the reduced partial pressure of oxygen in the air you're breathing means there are fewer oxygen molecules in each lungful of air.

Fatigue. While many of the factors that impact heart rate act to increase it, fatigue often suppresses it. When you are fatigued, your heart rate response to increasing energy demand is slower and blunted. A tired athlete will see heart rate climb more slowly at the beginning of an interval or hard effort and will struggle to achieve the heart rate normally associated with a given intensity level.

Of all the factors that affect heart rate, fatigue can get an athlete in the most trouble. When heart rate response is exaggerated and heart rates are higher than expected, athletes who are training or competing by heart rate tend to slow down. If your ranges say to run at 150 beats per minute (bpm) to sustain a pace at the high end of your aerobic system without exceeding your lactate threshold, but your heart rate response is being boosted by 5 to 8 bpm due to elevated core temperature and caffeine, running at 150 bpm will result in a slower actual pace. But when fatigue suppresses heart rate, you may push even harder in an effort to achieve your goal intensity of 150 bpm. Figure 7.1 is from an athlete in a 100K race. The first three climbs of the race were paced perfectly at similar Normalized Graded Pace. However, the heart rate on the first climb is markedly higher due to the athlete's initial freshness and adrenaline rush of the start of the race. The heart rate on the third climb is suppressed because of the accumulated fatigue. Had the athlete

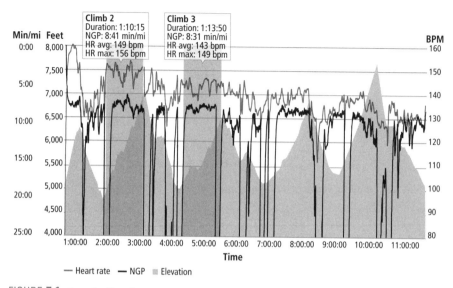

FIGURE **7.1** *Example of how fatigue affects heart rate. Heart rate (orange line) starts high due to freshness and then drops as fatigue sets in, even though NGP remains roughly the same for the first three climbs.*

tried to target a specific heart rate on the first climb, she would have been much too slow. Had she tried to match her heart rate from the first two climbs on the third climb, she would have run far too hard, particularly that early in the race.

There are two problems with pushing harder in response to a suppressed heart rate response. The first is that a suppressed heart rate at a given effort level or pace doesn't always mean you aren't performing as much work. Athletes who are fatigued can often perform the same workout two days in a row but experience suppressed heart rate response the second day. Figure 7.2 shows a runner performing TempoRuns on back-to-back days. On the second day, the athlete is able to perform the workout at a similar NGP but at a generally lower maximum and average heart rate due to the accumulated fatigue. This phenomenon plays into the second problem caused by suppressed heart rates. If you are gauging the success of your workout by your ability to run at a specific heart rate—or within a small heart rate range—and that heart rate is difficult to achieve because of fatigue, you may just push yourself harder to achieve the heart rate number you want to see. The effort feels harder than it should, but you push through anyway. If you are truly fatigued, you're just digging the hole deeper.

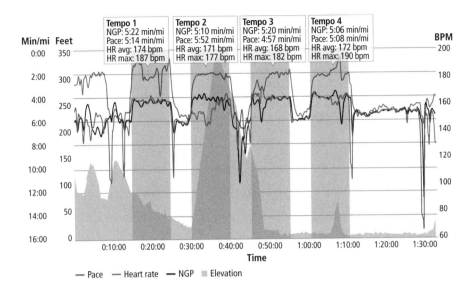

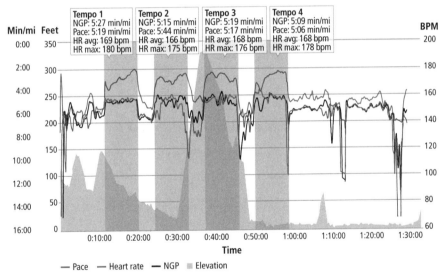

FIGURE **7.2** *Two consecutive days of TempoRuns. While the normalized paces are similar, the heart rate is generally depressed on the second day. Had the athlete been training using heart rate, he either would not have been able to do the workout or would have pushed too hard.*

Cardiac Drift

One of the greatest disadvantages of using heart rate alone to gauge training intensity is "cardiac drift." Because up to 75 percent of the energy produced in muscles is lost as heat, your body has to work to dissipate that heat to keep your core temperature from rising out of control. As you exercise—especially at higher intensities—your body uses your skin much like your car uses its radiator. Heart rate increases not only to deliver oxygen to working muscles but also to direct blood to the skin so it can supply fluid for sweat and cool off through convection (provided that the ambient temperature is lower than your core temperature). The sweat is released onto the skin so it can evaporate, which carries much of this excess heat away from the body. Much of the fluid that appears as sweat on your skin was most recently part of your bloodstream. As you lose blood plasma volume to produce sweat, your heart has to pump even faster to continue delivering the same amount of oxygen to working muscles. As a result, your heart rate will increase slightly as exercise duration increases, even if you maintain the same level of effort. The impact of cardiac drift will be lower if you are able to stay well hydrated; you're replacing the fluid lost by sweating and helping to maintain a higher overall blood volume. However, no matter how diligent you are about consuming fluids, some level of cardiac drift is unavoidable during intense endurance exercise.

You can see the impact of cardiac drift in Figure 7.3. In this heart rate file from a lactate threshold interval workout, the athlete performs three intervals at roughly the same pace, but his heart rate gets progressively higher for each effort. When athletes train by heart rate alone, they are instructed to maintain the same heart rate range for each interval. Ideally this would result in efforts of equal intensity,

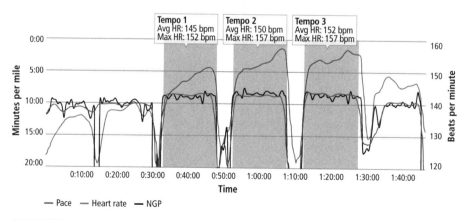

FIGURE **7.3**   *Impact of cardiac drift during a 3 × 10-minute TempoRun workout, where the heart rate increases throughout each interval and from interval to interval*

but as a result of cardiac drift, the first interval is actually completed at a faster pace than the subsequent ones. To the athlete, heart rate seems right on target, but he or she doesn't realize that workload is actually falling, and as a result, the workout loses some of its potential effectiveness.

WHY ULTRARUNNERS SHOULD EMBRACE PERCEIVED EXERTION

As much as I embrace the role of technology in enhancing the precision of training, there's an incredibly simple measure of workload that continues to hold its own against new gadgets and software applications. Rating of perceived exertion is the ultimate in simplicity: It is nothing more than a scale of how hard you feel you are exercising. There's not one single piece of data collected, and you don't need any special equipment. All you need is a numerical scale.

In the physiology lab, I use the Borg Scale, which ranges from 6 to 20 (with 6 being no exertion at all and 20 being a maximum effort). Why 6 to 20? Borg's research has shown that there's a high correlation between the number an athlete chooses during exercise, multiplied by 10, and his or her actual heart rate at that time. In other words, if you're on a treadmill during a lactate threshold test and tell me that you feel like you're at 16, there is a pretty good chance your heart rate is around 160 bpm. This isn't absolutely true of all athletes, but you'd be surprised at how accurate the 6 to 20 scale tends to be.

Outside the lab, however, the Borg Scale isn't as helpful for athletes, most of whom find it easier to relate to a simpler 1 to 10 scale (with 1 being no exertion at all and 10 being a maximum effort). Using this scale, an endurance or "forever" pace would be a 5 or 6, a challenging aerobic pace would be a 7, lactate threshold work occurs at about 8 or 9 (lactate threshold intervals on climbs are a solid 9), and VO_2 intervals are the only efforts that reach 10. Just as the Borg Scale multiplies the perceived exertion number by 10 to correlate with heart rate, the number chosen on the 1 to 10 scale, multiplied by 10, seems to correlate closely to the percentage of VO_2max that an athlete is currently maintaining.

With GPS-equipped heart rate monitors providing more detailed pacing information for runners, some athletes are tempted to relegate RPE to the trash bin of sports science history, but RPE remains critically important because it provides valuable context for the data files from a heart rate monitor or GPS watch. When you're fresh, 9:00 min/mi may feel like a moderate pace, but when you're fatigued, you may feel like you're having to work harder than normal to run that same 9-minute mile. It turns out that RPE is a great early-warning device for recognizing fatigue: Your body is telling you it can still do the job but that the effort to complete it is greater.

In addition, RPE can indicate progress. For example, at the beginning of the season, a 10-mile run at 9:00 min/mi pace may feel strenuous enough to rate a 7 or even an 8. Later in the season, when your fitness has improved, running that same course at that same pace may take less out of you and feel more like a 6. To reach an RPE of 7 to 8, you may now need to hasten your pace to 8:30 min/mi.

Although many of my athletes have access to the best training technologies and gadgets on the market, I base the vast majority of their training on perceived exertion. The main reason is because everything else is irrelevant during an actual competition. When you are scrambling up a 25 percent grade in a cold thunderstorm at 10,000 feet above sea level, 65 miles into a 100-mile ultramarathon, what heart rate would define lactate threshold pace? What minute-per-mile pace should a midpack ultrarunner aim for in that scenario?

Your brain is the most valuable tool you have for monitoring and evaluating your intensity, and it's the only training tool yet designed that can determine the correct interval and racing intensities for an ultrarunner. Your job as an athlete is not to find the gadget that will give you the information you seek but, rather, to master the ability to gauge intensity and workload by perceived exertion. It's the only information you need, which is good, because it's also the only accurate information you have.

To use perceived exertion to accurately gauge your workload, you need a good understanding of what you're trying to accomplish at each intensity level, the impact that intensity level has on your body, and the ways you can detect or interpret those impacts.

RPE AND BREATHING RATE

Your respiration rate is highly attuned to the amount of carbon dioxide in your blood. Interestingly, in normal conditions at rest, your involuntary respiration rate is more controlled by the carbon dioxide you're trying to get rid of than the oxygen you need to survive. As your energy demand increases and your muscles break down fuel for energy, the carbon dioxide levels in your blood increase. To keep carbon dioxide levels from rising too much, heart rate and breathing rate increase so more venous blood passes through the lungs each minute. There, pressure gradients transport carbon dioxide out of the blood and oxygen into it, and you exhale the carbon dioxide. Table 7.1 shows how different types of workouts affect RPE and breathing rate. (See also "RPE and the Talk Test," page 138.)

Because exercise increases both your oxygen demand and your production of carbon dioxide, it makes intuitive sense that increasing exercise intensity leads to faster and deeper breathing. It's so intuitive that it's largely ignored, but you can monitor your breathing as a gauge of intensity. At a recovery pace (RPE 4 or 5), you should be breathing only a bit faster and deeper than when you walk at a brisk pace. If have just finished an interval, your breathing will of course be much faster and should come down to this level during your recovery period. The exception is

TABLE 7.1   Workouts, RPE, and Breathing Rate

WORKOUT	TARGETED INTENSITY LEVEL	RPE (1–10 SCALE)	BREATHING RATE	TALKING ABILITY
RecoveryRun	Recovery	4 or 5	Comfortable breathing, barely above walking rate	Story time!
EnduranceRun	Endurance	5 or 6	Rhythmic, moderate-depth breathing; not labored	Comfortable conversation
SteadyStateRun	High-end aerobic	7	Deep and labored breathing	2–3 sentences
TempoRun	Lactate threshold	8 or 9	Deep and labored, faster than at high-end aerobic	5- to 7-word sentence
RunningIntervals	VO$_2$max	10	Short and rapid	Single word, probably 4 letters

during high-intensity interval workouts, where the recovery periods are purposely too short to allow full recovery.

The amount of carbon dioxide you produce in response to energy expenditure does not increase linearly, and this is the phenomenon athletes need to pay attention to. You produce more carbon dioxide when you burn more carbohydrate for energy, and a higher percentage of your energy comes from carbohydrate as your exercise intensity increases because glycolysis (the partial breakdown of carbohydrate that provides energy quickly but also results in lactate production) breaks down only carbohydrate, not fat. At rest you normally exhale less carbon dioxide than you inhale oxygen. This respiratory exchange ratio (RER) is indicative of the fuels you are burning; an RER (volume of CO_2 expired/volume of O_2 inspired) of 0.7 to 0.85 is normal at rest or low activity levels and is associated with burning a mixture of fuels. With more intense exercise, RER rises as you start exhaling more

RPE AND THE TALK TEST

How fast you're breathing impacts how easily and comfortably you can speak. I call recovery pace "story time" because you should be able to tell your training partner all about last weekend's epic adventure without pausing. When you bring the pace up to endurance or "forever" speed, you should be able to have a comfortable conversation, but you're probably not talking very long before having to pause. At the high end of your aerobic range, your ability to converse will dwindle to two or three sentences before you need to focus full-time on breathing. When you are running at or near your lactate threshold pace, you should only be able to say one complete sentence, maybe five to seven words. If someone tells you they are running at lactate threshold yet they are carrying on a normal conversation, they are lying to you (or they don't know any better). Finally, there's no talking at VO_2max, unless you count four-letter expletives and grunts.

WHAT ABOUT LACTATE THRESHOLD AND VO₂MAX TESTING?

We have a great physiology lab in our Colorado Springs training center, and most of the elite athletes—and many other runners—I coach have been in the lab for lactate threshold and VO$_2$max testing. I mostly use the tests as benchmarks to establish baseline physiological values for an athlete and then build a profile of her progress through subsequent testing. On a practical level, however, I don't use the test results to create training intensity ranges for ultrarunning athletes, as I do for athletes training for other endurance events. I think the most valuable thing an ultrarunner can learn from testing, and the most valuable thing I've learned from testing many ultrarunners, is that more than other endurance athletes I've tested, ultrarunners have lactate threshold values that represent a higher percentage of their overall VO$_2$max. In other words, a cyclist might come into the lab, and his lactate threshold power is 78 percent of his power at VO$_2$max. An elite cyclist might increase that to about 85 percent. Most marathon runners are similar. But an ultrarunner will frequently record a lactate threshold value at 95 to 97 percent of VO$_2$max! What does that mean? For the most part it means ultrarunners have traditionally done a poor job of training to improve VO$_2$max and a good job of developing their physiology at lower intensities. Their training has improved performance at aerobic and lactate threshold intensities but has not had much effect on their maximum capacity to take in and deliver oxygen to working muscles. Normally, I'd say having a lactate threshold at 95 to 97 percent of VO$_2$max is great, but in the context of ultrarunners, what it actually shows is where most ultrarunners are underdeveloped. VO$_2$max is your maximum potential—the ceiling or roof of the building. If you want to fit more stuff in the building (more endurance, greater performance capacity), then raise the roof!

carbon dioxide; RER approaches and can exceed 1.0 as the rate of carbohydrate utilization increases from glycolysis.

Because higher levels of carbon dioxide drive you to breathe faster and deeper to get rid of it, and a dramatic increase in carbohydrate utilization leads to a big increase in carbon dioxide levels in the blood, your breathing rate can give you a good (not perfect) indication of when you have reached lactate threshold.

As you progress from recovery to an endurance or "forever" pace (RPE 5 or 6), your breathing becomes deep and rhythmic; it is faster than at recovery pace but not labored. When you step up the intensity to target the high end of your aerobic range (RPE 7), your breathing will remain deep, but you should start to feel that you are laboring to breathe fast enough. The next intensity level is the tricky one: lactate threshold (RPE 8 or 9).

The easiest way to use your breathing to find lactate threshold is to go beyond it. When you exceed lactate threshold intensity, your breathing will go from deep, labored, and in control to short and rapid. The intensity or pace you want to hold during a lactate threshold interval is below the point at which your breathing shifts from controlled to short and rapid. In contrast, when you are doing VO_2max intervals (RPE 10), you want to exceed this ventilatory threshold; your breathing should be short and rapid.

KEY RUNNING WORKOUTS

Workouts such as endurance, tempo, and steady state are used by many coaches and athletes. All too often, these words can be confusing and fail to precisely describe the workout in question. At CTS we use these words as well, but with very specific definitions so that our coaches can communicate with each other and with their athletes consistently and precisely. Throughout this book, I use the following terminology to describe workouts and their associated intensities.

RECOVERYRUN (RR)

To be effective, a RecoveryRun needs to be very easy. All you're trying to do is loosen up your legs and increase circulation and respiration with some mild activity. Your recovery runs should be no more than 60 minutes; the typical dura-tion I prescribe is about 40 minutes. Perceived exertion for a RecoveryRun is about a 4 or 5, so it's not a leisurely walk, but it should be substantially easier than an EnduranceRun. The frequency for RecoveryRuns depends on your training sched-ule, since this workout needs to be balanced with your harder training sessions, but I frequently have athletes run two or three of them in a week.

ENDURANCERUN (ER)

You're going to spend much of your running time in the EnduranceRun inten-sity range. This is the moderate-intensity running time surrounding your focused interval sets, as well as the "forever" intensity for your EnduranceRuns that contain no specific intervals. Perceived exertion for this intensity is 5 or 6 and will naturally vary with uphills and downhills. EnduranceRun durations range from 30 min-utes to more than 6 hours. A typical workout would be a 2-hour EnduranceRun. When you are running at this intensity, however, it is important to slow down when you begin going uphill. It can be easy for your intensity level to creep up into SteadyStateRun or lactate threshold territory, and then you are adding training stress and using energy you may need and want later.

STEADYSTATERUN (SSR)

A SteadyStateRun workout pushes you to a challenging aerobic pace but keeps you below your lactate threshold intensity and pace. This intensity plays a very important role in developing a stronger aerobic engine because you are maintaining an effort level greater than your normal "forever" pace. You are generating more lactate and working to process it. SSR intervals should be long and as continuous as possible, with individual intervals ranging from 20 to 60 minutes and total time at intensity for a single workout ranging from 30 minutes to 2 hours. A typical SSR workout might be two 30-minute SSR intervals separated by 5 minutes of easy recovery with light jogging or hiking. The RPE for SSR is 7, and as with EnduranceRun workouts, you need to be careful not to let your intensity level creep up toward lactate thresh-old territory on hills. The important distinction between SSR and EnduranceRun is that the duration defines the intensity of the effort. EnduranceRun is at an intensity you could maintain from start to finish of a medium or long training run, whereas SSR is at an intensity you cannot sustain as long.

TEMPORUN (TR)

TempoRun intervals are a crucial workout for making you a faster and stronger runner. The pace and intensity for these intervals are strenuous, and you will be running slightly below or at your lactate threshold intensity. It has long been said that you can't become a faster runner without first running faster in training, and that's exactly what these intervals do. They help to drive the process of increasing the size and density of mitochondria in your muscles, improving your ability to process and utilize lactate. TempoRuns also increase your ability to manage core temperature. TempoRun intervals should be run at an RPE of 8 or 9, and at this intensity you will only be able to run intervals of 8 to 20 minutes. Recovery periods between intervals should be half the duration of the interval, meaning a 2-to-1 recovery ratio, or 6 minutes of recovery between 12-minute intervals. Total time-at-intensity in a single TempoRun workout should range from 30 to 60 minutes. Again, it's the duration of the interval, the number of intervals, and the amount of rest that help define the intensity. The maximum amount of accumulated time for these intervals—in a single workout—is 1 hour; be careful not to exceed it. When you try to do too much at this intensity, you will naturally slow down, and the effort you are doing will be compromised.

RUNNINGINTERVALS (RI)

RunningIntervals are VO_2max efforts lasting 1 to 3 minutes. The RPE for these efforts is 10. Because of the high intensity of these workouts, it is a good idea to warm up with 15–30 minutes of EnduranceRun and 6 to 8 RunningStrides (see sidebar on page 143) of 20 seconds each. As you start the interval, accelerate over 15 to 20 seconds to the highest intensity you can sustain for the remainder of the interval. The recovery periods between RunningInterval efforts are purposely too short to allow for full recovery because part of the training stimulus comes from

RUNNINGSTRIDES

RunningStrides (commonly called "strides," "stride-outs," or "striders") are short, high-intensity intervals intended to gradually get the body used to operating at a high intensity. They are typically between 10K and 5K race pace for the 20 seconds. Rest between each RunningStride is 1 minute.

starting the next high-intensity effort before you're completely recovered from the previous one. During the recovery periods, slow to a jog, or you can slow to a hike if you need to, but keep moving.

Some athletes get confused by what "RPE of 10/10" means for RunningIntervals. When I say "as hard as you can go for the duration of the interval," I'm acknowledging that there's a difference between the maximum pace you can sustain for 1 minute and the maximum you can sustain for 2 minutes or 3 minutes. A maximal 3-minute interval will be slower than a maximal 2-minute effort. One mistake some athletes make is to start a VO_2max interval like a sprint. To reach VO_2max, you have to max out your cardiovascular system, and that doesn't happen the instant you leave the starting line. If you start a 3-minute VO_2max interval with a 100-meter sprint, your skeletal muscles will fatigue so rapidly that you won't be able to maintain an effort hard enough to continue ramping up your cardiovascular system. That's why it's better to work your way into the effort by accelerating over the first 15–20 seconds of the interval to the fastest pace you can maintain through the end of it. Will you slow down in the final 30–45 seconds of a VO_2max interval? Yes, and that's OK. When these efforts are done correctly, you are running at a pace you can barely sustain for the duration of the interval, and slowing down slightly in the final 30 seconds of the effort is a sign that you've pushed yourself appropriately.

Although these intervals can be completed on any terrain or on a treadmill, I recommend doing them uphill if possible. The incline is helpful for increasing the workload and enabling you to reach VO_2max intensity more consistently. The total

TABLE **7.2**		Summary of the Five Key Running Workouts				
	RPE	**TYPICAL INTERVAL TIME**	**TOTAL TIME-AT-INTENSITY**	**WORK: REST**	**TYPICAL WORKOUT**	**FREQUENCY PER WEEK**
RecoveryRun (RR)	4 or 5	NA	20–60 min	NA	40-min RR	2–3
EnduranceRun (ER)	5 or 6	NA	30 min– 6+ hours	NA	2-hr ER	2–6
SteadyStateRun (SSR)	7	20–60 min	30 min– 2 hours	5–8:1	2-hr ER with 2 × 30 min SSR, 5-min recovery between intervals	2–4
TempoRun (TR)	8 or 9	8–20 min	30–60 min total	2:1	2-hr ER with 3 × 12 min TR, 6-min recovery between intervals	2–3
RunningIntervals (RI)	10	1–3 min	12–24 min total	1:1	90-min ER with 6 × 3 min RI, 3-min recovery between intervals	2–3

time-at-intensity for a single RunningInterval workout should be 12 to 24 minutes and the work-to-recovery ratio is 1 to 1, so a 2-minute RunningInterval should be followed by 2 minutes at RecoveryRun pace or hiking. A typical workout might be six 3-minute RunningIntervals with 3 minutes of recovery between efforts. The important consideration with VO_2max intervals like this is scheduling adequate recovery afterward. Although back-to-back days of VO_2max intervals may be effective and appropriate for some runners or at certain times, the rule of thumb is to schedule only two (maybe three) VO_2max workouts in a week during a focused block of this type of work. Leave a full day of recovery between workouts, so if you do RunningIntervals on Tuesday, your next RunningInterval workout should be no sooner than Thursday.

Table 7.2 presents a summary of the five key running workouts.

When I started working with Dakota Jones, structure wasn't one of his strong suits. He knew how to dig deep but wasn't familiar with doing it on cue or on a

///// *DAKOTA JONES* INTERVALS

Before I had a coach, I had the general idea that training involved long runs, speed work, hill work, crosstraining, stretching, and . . . other stuff. I was right—training does involve all those things. But the difficult part was putting them together in a meaningful way. All these different aspects of training felt so vague and undefined. I ran a lot, sometimes fast, and competed enough that I improved quickly. But after about two years of winging it, I realized that to continue to improve, I would need help. My ability was being limited by my lack of knowledge of the science of training.

Working with Jason gave a structure and logic to my training that I had never enjoyed before. But you know what he makes me do? Intervals. Lots and lots of intervals. We started out the year with 5 × 3-min intervals, and depending on the race for which I am training, those have fluctuated up to 4 × 12 min, 4 × 20 min, and even a few 2 × 30 min intervals. Each type of interval works different energy systems for different purposes, but they all share one thing in common: They rock my world. No longer is "training" just a bunch of long runs in the mountains. Nowadays, more often than not I find myself sprinting at absolute maximum capacity up dirt or paved roads, pacing myself by time and effort. Sometimes I'm inspired, sometimes I'm destroyed, but at the end of every set I am always proud of myself. The structure of training allows me to work really hard at the times that matter and to relax the rest of the time, knowing that I really am doing all that I need to be a better athlete.

Although sometimes I might prefer to just run in the mountains, I know that doing intervals will make me faster. My goal is to be the strongest, fastest, best mountain runner in the sport. And I know that doing intervals will give me the aerobic ability to compete on the stratospheric level at which ultramarathons are regularly run these days. Plus, I do still get to go on long runs. But interspersing my long mountain runs with focused intervals several times a week undoubtedly makes me faster, and that's a sacrifice I'm willing to make for the overall goal.

>

And you know what? I like the intervals, too. I don't just suffer through them in order to be faster on race day; they are some of the most rewarding runs I do. Few other workouts provide the empirical structure that allows me to gauge my ability like intervals do, and rarely elsewhere do I get the amazing sense of accomplishment that intervals provide. By doing intervals, I know that I am making myself better within the confines of the sport I have chosen. Everything else in my life seems so ambiguous, but the intervals give my life at least one area of satisfying objectivity.

What's it like? Nose running, spit flying, my vision almost eclipsing, I can feel my heartbeat in my throat. I pump my legs as hard as possible. They feel heavy, thick, swollen. Only the balls of my feet touch the road, and as the incline steepens, my steps seem to make no progress at all. I can feel the parts of my body that aren't getting enough blood, like my hands, growing colder, and I can feel the invigoration of oxygen in each breath. Everything in my body depending upon everything else, and I'm dying, man. This is it, I cannot keep this up, but I have two more minutes and how can I go on?

I don't know. Just don't stop. I usually imagine another competitor catching up from behind me, and that makes me push a little bit harder. When the interval finally ends, I maintain a jogging pace that is little more than moving up and down on my toes. Eventually I recover enough to jog slowly downhill. And after just a few minutes I turn around and do it all again. And it hurts just as bad.

But I'm young and strong and getting better with each step. The competition drives me to be the best that I can be. Hopefully that inspiration will carry me through my training and well into the next race. And even if I sometimes have to forsake the sanctity of the mountains for the crush of the road, I'll do it to improve, to grow, to be my best in an arena that makes me feel like I can do anything.

Source: Used with permission from iRunFar.

/////

schedule. He took to structured intervals like a duck to water and later wrote about his affinity for hard work on irunfar.com. A word of caution: Dakota's description of his intervals (see sidebar) is based on his goal of winning the sport's biggest races. Your intervals will be strenuous as well, but you won't necessarily have to—or be able to—dig as deep as he does.

THE RIGHT STRUCTURE FOR INTERVAL WORKOUTS

Many run training programs define precise warm-up and cooldown periods to bookend specific interval work. Typically, and somewhat arbitrarily, the warm-up and cooldown periods are exactly 15 minutes each. The 15-minute number is not magical. The background for this structure is rooted in track and field, where the warm-up and cooldown can be done on roads near the track (and can thus be exactly 15 minutes in duration) and the intervals on the track itself. In trail running, I find this approach impractical. I am far more interested in the specificity of the intervals, which should include both the intensity and appropriate environment (either surface or grade characteristics) for the desired adaptation. Many times this will require the athlete to run for 17 or 19 or 22 minutes to get to the section of trail that is ideal for the task. Therefore, when I prescribe a workout that includes intervals, I use the EnduranceRun duration to define the total time of the workout and intend the intervals to be completed within that time. For instance, a 2-hour EnduranceRun with 3 × 10-minute TempoRuns and 5 minutes of recovery between intervals means "Run a total of 2 hours, and within those hours complete three 10-minute TempoRun efforts separated by 5 minutes at RecoveryRun pace." This gives the athlete a flexible amount of time for the warm-up and cooldown periods. My only parameters are that the warm-up be between 10 and 30 minutes and the cooldown be at least 10 minutes. Often I will also prescribe 4–8 RunningStrides of 20 seconds each after the warm-up and before any intervals.

THE TIME-CRUNCHED ULTRAMARATHONER

How much time do you really need to train? Most of us are limited by time, with our training somehow crammed into busy lives. Taking an hour at lunch or waking up an hour earlier to get a run in is more often than not the way most normal people with lives, jobs, and a family fit in their training. It is extremely easy, particularly if you are an aspiring ultrarunner, to conclude that you don't have enough time to train. But I find most athletes overestimate the amount of time truly required to train for an ultramarathon. They linearly expand their marathon training to accommodate longer distances: "If I trained 8 hours per week for a marathon, I need to train 16 for a 50-miler." On the surface that type of thinking is entirely logical, so I don't blame athletes for approaching the idea of training for an ultramarathon with trepidation. The fact is, though, there is not a linear relationship between the training required for a marathon and the training required for an ultra. A 50-miler does not require twice the amount of training as a marathon, nor does a 100-miler take twice as much training as a 50-miler. The reality is, most people are limited by available time. Therefore, reality dictates that most people train with a similar amount of volume irrespective of the distance they are training for. This limitation underscores the need for high-quality structure in your training. After all, if you ain't got much, you better make the most of what you do have.

There is, undoubtedly, a minimum amount of training time required to be successful at an ultramarathon, although it's not the same for everybody or for every distance. I always present this concept in terms of the minimum amount of time you need to be able to devote during your period of highest training volume. This "minimum maximum" sets a reference point for what you can expect to achieve on race day and helps you determine if the distance you have chosen is reasonable. While you do not need to always have this "minimum maximum" amount of training time available, you do need to have it for key weeks during the season:

- 50K and 50 miles: minimum maximum of 6 hours per week for 3 weeks, starting 6 weeks before your goal event

- 100K and 100 miles: minimum maximum of 9 hours per week for 6 weeks, starting 9 weeks before your goal event

In other words, you need at least 6 hours per week of training, for at least 3 weeks, to be successful at the 50K and 50-mile distances. For the 100K and 100-mile distances, you need at least 9 hours of training per week for 6 weeks. Outside of this 3- or 6-week period, you can have a lower volume and be perfectly successful, as long as you also do higher-quality training. Although this formula does not guarantee success or maximum performance, not being able to achieve these critical minimum maximums can lead to failure and underperformance.

When setting goals for a season, you need to carefully consider this minimum maximum concept. You need to be well informed that, according to your goals, you will need to meet these minimum time requirements in key training weeks in order to achieve success. If you can't commit the time, you are less likely to meet your goals; it's that simple. However, if you do have the required time, 6 hours per week for 3 weeks, or 9 hours per week for 6 weeks, you have every reason to believe that you can be successful. How successful you are with that time has entirely to do with how effective your training is!

CHAPTER 8

ORGANIZING YOUR TRAINING: THE LONG-RANGE PLAN

Ultramarathon (\ˈəl-trə-ˈma-rə-thän\ n.): a footrace longer than a marathon

Ask any runner what an ultramarathon is, and this is the definition you're likely to hear. While it may technically be correct, from a training perspective, an ultramarathon cannot be thought of as merely longer than a marathon. The stressors and success factors in an ultramarathon are not solely greater or more numerous than those in a marathon. And preparation for an ultramarathon should not be merely longer than preparation for a marathon. Successful preparation for an ultramarathon incorporates correct mileage, volume, intensity, nutrition, vertical specificity, terrain specificity, environmental adaptation, and the like. Yes, you have to physically go out and run in order to train properly. You have to deliberately practice what you will do on race day, not simply "get your butt over the bar." However, organizing your season does not start with the demands of the event, a specific type of interval, or any other physiological phenomenon. It is actually quite the opposite. First and foremost, organizing your training has to do with putting the pieces in place that will maximize the physical work you will do down the road.

CHOOSING YOUR EVENT

Every winter, thousands of ultrarunners eagerly await the results of the coming summer's race lottery processes. Some athletes take a "throw your hat in all the rings" approach, entering every lottery out there and letting the lottery gods sort it out. Others hedge their bets on one lottery, trying to stack the odds in their favor for a singular desired outcome. Whatever your approach, organizing your training should always start with one question: "What events am I the most passionate about?" The answer to that question revolves around many facets. You can't control the random outcome of the major ultra lottery processes, but you can control which events you focus on. Nowadays, there are more ultras than you can shake a stick at. Some have elaborate race management and support systems; others are more low-key. Some are "fast"; others are "slow." Some are in high alpine environments; others are in the desert. Whatever your preferences regarding an event's management style, terrain, and environment, chances are you can find a race that suits your desires. Organizing your training starts with choosing the events that you are the most passionate about, those that enhance your emotional engagement with what you are doing. The event might attract you because of its difficulty. Maybe you have a history in the region or an attraction to its flora and fauna. Whatever the case, *pick what you are passionate about.*

After you have determined what events are going to rile you up, it's time to bring the people you live and run with into the loop. Rarely does one run an ultra without support from other people. Your family, friends, colleagues, and running groups can all enhance the outcome of the events you have chosen. You may even depend on these people to crew and pace you come race day. So get some firepower in your corner. Tell your family, friends, and fellow runners what you are training for and what your goals are. After all, it will make sense when you walk into the office still wearing your headlamp if your colleagues know what the heck you are doing with your free time. Your chosen peer group can help you out, even if they don't run a step with you in training.

CREATING A LONG-RANGE PLAN

Open any book on endurance coaching and training and you are sure to see three words: "foundation," "preparation," and "specialization." The history behind these words goes back many decades, to some of the founding fathers of periodization. These labels are used to compartmentalize training into discrete sections. These books describe the foundation phase being reserved for building an aerobic base, similar to laying the foundation for a house. The preparation phase "develops your cardiovascular fitness, readying you for higher-level work." Finally, the specialization phase is reserved for higher intensities that are "specialized" to the event.

I dislike these generalizations and get enormously frustrated with the labels, which don't accurately describe the process. Isn't an athlete always preparing? I would rather name each training phase based on what it is—specifically, by referring to the particular aspect of physiology that the athlete is focusing on the most: endurance (EnduranceRuns and SteadyStateRuns), lactate threshold (TempoRuns), or VO$_2$max (RunningIntervals). Make no mistake, you are always training all aspects of your physiology. But, for the purpose of organizing a season, I prefer to define the segments of the year by the workouts you are doing and thus the primary physiological adaptation you're after during each period of time.

STARTING AT THE END

When I design training plans for athletes, it is always a "pick and choose" exercise rooted in determining what is going to benefit the athlete the most. I have an unlimited number of workouts to choose from: speed workouts, long runs, fartleks, ladders, progressive tempos, strength training, crosstraining, plyometrics, downhill intervals, uphill intervals, and more. However, after the planning process is all said and done, I end up using only a small handful of the arrows in my quiver, defined primarily by the five workouts described in the previous chapter. You always have far more total options for how to improve than you do practical ones. These five primary workouts set the framework of how to organize a season.

Once I have athletes pick their goal events and determine the time frame they have available to be the most prepared, I begin the process of designing a long-range plan (LRP). These plans offer a season-long snapshot of what I want an athlete to focus on at any point during the season. The plans are generalized in the sense that their level of detail is limited to weeks (not days), overarching training intensities (RunningIntervals, TempoRun, and SteadyStateRun), and other miscellaneous components of training (amount of vertical, type of surface, environmental adaptations). I do not outline the specific days per week or the specific combination of intervals I want the athlete to do at this stage; that is reserved for the short-range plan, explained in Chapter 9. The purpose of the LRP is to ensure that an athlete is employing proper strategies throughout the year. It keeps a check on how much and when to do peak volume, when to incorporate intensity, and how the race-and-recover cycles fit into the year. Like many aspects of training, there is no one-size-fits-all approach. Each LRP I develop is for an individual athlete based on his or her goals. Despite this individual nature, I rely on three common principles (in order of priority) in putting together the LRP for each of my athletes.

Principle 1: Develop the physiology that is most specific to the event closest to that event, and develop the least specific physiology furthest away. Figuring out the demands of an event is a very large part of what I do as a coach. I take this analysis starting from the very high-level cardiovascular physiology that is specific to the event, and extend it all the way down to the surface characteristics of the race, the distance between aid stations, the environmental conditions, and how one copes with the stress of eating and drinking. Even though the practical applications might be overly broad or extremely narrow, the principle is the same. If the aspect is highly specific to the event, work it closer to the event. A classic example of this can be seen in connection with the Hardrock 100. Hardrock is very specific in that hardly anyone actually runs the uphill portion of the race. Even the fastest "runners" hike the majority of the uphill and then run the descents. Therefore, applying Principle 1, I have my athletes do the majority of their hiking training in the weeks leading up to the race because it is so specific to the race in question. You can extend this thinking to many other areas such as cardiovascular intensity, surface, environmental conditions, and the average grades of the course. Anything that is very specific to the race in question you will want to work on as close to the race as possible. Most runners who go out and recon a course in the weeks leading up to an event are applying this principle correctly. They are training specifically for the grades, surface, and environmental conditions they will face on race day.

In contrast, I have my athletes do the least specific aspects of training the furthest away from the event as they can logistically manage. Again using Hardrock as an example, I cannot think of anything less specific in that race (inconsequential might be a better way of characterizing it) than one's velocity at VO$_2$max. In other words, a Hardrocker's pace at VO$_2$max is likely the least important factor in the whole scheme of success. But it is still important to develop (see Principle 2). Being the *least* important should not be confused with being *un*important! So, from a practical standpoint, many of my Hardrockers do flat, fast, high-intensity running very early in the year. They improve the least specific aspects furthest away from the event.

Principle 2: At some point during the season, incorporate each of these three critical workouts: SteadyStateRun, TempoRun, and RunningIntervals. It is important to visit all the various intensities because over the course of months, athletes will reach a point of diminishing returns for any one adaptation in particular. The various intensities build off of each other throughout the year, allowing the athlete to achieve better fitness. I once had a colleague ask me why it was important to train at various intensities if the event in question had a very low intensity, say, a 30-hour Leadville finish. To him it made all the sense in the world to train at that very low but specific intensity for as long as possible during the entire course of training. As I've talked about previously in this book, the flaw in this logic is that all the energy systems are connected and there are improvements to be made at the relatively easy aerobic pace that can be achieved only by raising an athlete's maximum sustainable pace (lactate threshold) and maximum aerobic capacity (VO$_2$max). To illustrate this concept, I pointed out some of the lab data that we have collected from elite and amateur ultrarunners throughout the years. One of the common themes we find in ultrarunners whom we test just as we start coaching them is that their sustainable intensity is very, very close to their maximum intensity. In other words, their lactate threshold intensity is nearly their VO_2max intensity. Sometimes, this difference is as little as 3 percent.

Practically speaking, this means that only a handful of seconds per mile separate the pace they can maintain for long periods of time (hours) from the pace they can handle for only a few minutes. Normally, as a coach, I would do a backflip if I got this result from my athletes; I'd love it if their sustainable intensity were as close to their maximum intensity as possible. That is a much-coveted outcome of the training process. However, where do you go from there? Certainly, your sustainable pace cannot exceed your maximum pace. That would not be possible. When we see this situation in the lab, the training protocol becomes quite simple. The athlete needs to *first* raise VO_2max, *then* work on lactate threshold. This will give the athlete a little room between VO_2max and lactate threshold before he or she goes back and works on sustainable pace. You have to do it in that order. But you also have to return to SteadyStateRun intensities during the year because you can't withstand the stress of VO_2max and lactate threshold intervals forever, nor would you make continual progress even if you could. Targeting different intensities throughout the year allows you to make measurable gains in each area, and each time you get stronger in one area you also gain the tools to make further improvements in the other areas.

Principle 3: Work strengths closer to the race and weaknesses further away. Most runners are aware of their natural strengths and weaknesses. We come to these realizations during group runs and races; anytime you run with a companion serves as a barometer. If you are passing people on the climbs and getting dropped on the technical descents, then your strength is climbing and your weakness is technical running. Therefore, according to Principle 1, you should try to improve your technical running as far away from your key event as possible and your climbing as close to the event as possible.

A CLOSER LOOK AT THE LONG-RANGE PLAN

The template for the LRP is a simple color-coded spreadsheet that delineates the specific types of workouts (RunningIntervals, TempoRun, and SSR), higher-volume and lower-volume periods, critical events throughout the season, and other variables of training (vertical, trail versus road, etc.). I have supplied an example of this from Dylan Bowman's 2014 season later in this chapter (Table 8.1, page 164, and Table 8.2, page 165) and also provided a blank LRP template in the Appendix. There is also a case study based on Dylan's 2014 season in the following section.

The LRP offers me a season-long picture of what the athlete needs to work on at any given point. It also gives a heads-up to the athlete on when to expect higher volume and higher intensity, and when to focus on other aspects of the event such as nutritional planning. However, only so much can go into the plan at this point. You will always need to adapt as the season goes along. Nevertheless, starting out with a solid plan from the get-go will ensure that you're keeping your priorities straight during the year, so when push comes to shove, you know what to push and what to shove!

///// DYLAN BOWMAN MY 2014 SEASON

August 2013 served up a moment of desperation for my ultrarunning career. I'd just sustained a serious ankle injury while in Chamonix preparing for the Ultra-Trail du Mont-Blanc, which forced me to reexamine my training methods and goals in the sport. As someone who came into ultrarunning without any formal training background, I was ignorant about how to recover from my injury or develop athletically. For the first couple years, I'd been able to steadily improve simply by gaining experience and general fitness. By the time I'd arrived in France, however, that trajectory had clearly slowed, and my improvement curve had begun to plateau. When the ankle injury occurred, it was an opportunity to either walk away from the sport or evolve as an athlete. I wanted to progress, but it was clear that I needed outside assistance.   >

I contacted Coach Koop and asked for his help. After an initial interview, he agreed to take me on.

Ironically, the first task under his guidance was to not run at all. I needed time to recover fully from my ankle injury. We started with uphill cycling intervals to reinvigorate my cardiovascular system and prevent further detraining as a result of my injury. Once my ankle regained sufficient strength, we set about planning for the 2014 racing season.

Koop asked me to consider what races would provide deep motivation. For me, it was the 2014 Western States 100-Mile Endurance Run. At that point, I'd completed the race twice. While I'd finished in the top 10 on both occasions, I was not satisfied with either performance. This feeling of unrealized potential is what gave me the deep motivation Koop sent me searching for. My goal in 2014 was to finish on the podium. Given my history at the race and my general progression as an athlete, this felt ambitious but accomplishable.

Once the goal was set, it was a matter of working backward, constructing the season from the end point and final goal. We chose B races that would provide me opportunities to gain race fitness and experience and to practice nutrition and hydration strategies. Koop then designed training blocks to plug in at appropriate times around these races to give me the best chance at success. That progression was diametrically opposed to what you'd generally see with traditional run training. Typically coaches have their athletes start the year doing low-intensity, aerobic running (generally referred to as "building a base"). I started the year doing VO_2max intervals. This usually meant hammering uphill for 3 minutes as hard as I could go for 6 to 8 repetitions, usually 3 times per week. The improvement was immediate. When we discussed the purpose of this unorthodox strategy, Koop explained his reasoning: *Train the physiological system most important to the goal race in the training block chronologically closest to the race itself and train the physiological system least important to the goal race chronologically furthest away from the race itself.*

My goal race was 100 miles long and almost seven months away. Because I would never hit VO_2max intensity in a race of that distance, it made sense to develop VO_2max first so that the adaptation could bolster my capacity to hold intensities more specific to the goal race at a later time.

Although we focused on only one system at a time, Koop also had me do a mix of longer endurance runs, short recovery runs, and days off to prepare me for my first race of the year—the Sean O'Brien 50-miler in California. I was thrilled to win the race by a fairly comfortable margin in a competitive field.

Not long after that, I received an invitation to race the Transgrancanaria 125K in the Canary Islands, only four weeks removed from Sean O'Brien. It didn't fit in the plan Koop and I had drafted at the beginning of the year, and I didn't have a lot of enthusiasm for the race itself. When Koop and I discussed it, he was careful not to try to sway me on the matter, but he reminded me to guide my decision based on motivation. Although the race didn't motivate me at the time, I couldn't bring myself to turn down the opportunity. I ended up making the trip with very little specific training, a body still fatigued from the Sean O'Brien race, and a last-minute travel itinerary to the other side of the world. In retrospect, I was clearly setting myself up for failure. I suffered a lot and finished a disappointing ninth place. I went from the confidence of winning a big American race to struggling to finish on the international stage, but I learned a valuable lesson. It was time to go back to the drawing board.

Luckily my mistake didn't totally compromise the ultimate goal; it just forced some readjustments. Koop shuffled things around to accommodate my need to recover while still having time to gain the requisite fitness for the Western States 100. It was now early spring and time to switch the intensity.

After early rounds of VO_2max work in January and February, we focused on developing the lactate threshold system. This phase was to run from March through April and into May, when I would race my next B race, the North Face 50 in Bear Mountain, New York. Koop described the goal intensity as being about 80 percent of maximum effort. Rather than heart rate or pace, we based   >

it simply on perceived exertion. While the VO_2max intervals were designed to make me fail (or at least slow down dramatically), lactate threshold is based on repeatability. The intervals are less intense, but they're also longer (usually between 10 and 20 minutes), and the total training volume is higher. I usually did these intervals going uphill to simulate race situations and improve as a climber. This intensity is much more specific to 50-mile racing than VO_2max. May rolled around quickly, and I managed to win the North Face 50. My confidence had returned.

The final training block began as soon as I had recovered, and it was again time to switch the intensity. Because this was the last training block for the Western States 100, it was time to train the system most specific to the race. Again the intensity decreased (70 percent of maximum effort), but the interval length increased (between 30 and 60 minutes). This is what Koop refers to as SteadyStateRun intensity. Because there is less fluctuation in effort output and more of a focus on consistency, these workouts are very helpful in preparing specifically for 100-mile races where steadiness is key.

We also lengthened my long runs and added more volume to help build the deep strength needed to complete 100-mile races. It was a very difficult training block both physically and mentally, but I arrived in Squaw Valley motivated and well prepared. I ran a smart race and was diligent with nutrition and hydration, which helped me run what was by far my best 100-miler to date. I finished third overall and accomplished my goal of being on the podium.

/////

DYLAN BOWMAN'S 2014 SEASON:
APPLYING THE 3 PRINCIPLES OF LONG-RANGE PLANNING
PRINCIPLE 1

Develop the physiology that is most specific to the event closest to the event, and develop the least specific physiology furthest away. The demands of the Western States 100 are well known. The race is hot, it contains about 400 feet of elevation change per mile, and Dylan needed to be capable of running under 16 hours to finish among the top three. To better handle heat, I had Dylan employ a sauna protocol aimed at improving his thermoregulatory capabilities. For the six weeks leading up to the race, he followed a passive sauna exposure protocol developed by Dr. Stacy Sims. The protocol allows for heat acclimatization *without interfering with his day-to-day training*, so Dylan could improve his fitness at the same time. Remember those prioritized adaptations from Chapter 2? Fitness is first; environmental adaptation is not first. So, finding a way for Dylan to cope with the searing Western States 100 heat and *not* compromise his fitness was key.

To match the event's specific biomechanical demands, I had Dylan target training grounds that were similar to the racecourse. Figure 8.1 shows his training statistics, where he averaged very close to the 410 feet per mile that he would experience during the Western States 100. Finally, the most specific intensities to that race performance are SteadyStateRun and EnduranceRun. These two workouts were the bread and butter of his final training.

The least specific intensity to the Western States 100 is VO_2max. This extremely high, unsustainable intensity was "least important" (not unimportant). Naturally, VO_2max gets developed first. Dylan's early-season preparation included weeks of RunningIntervals, mainly uphill to maximize the aerobic stress.

Application of Principle 1. Develop SteadyStateRun and EnduranceRun closest to the race. Focus on heat acclimatization closest to the race. Develop VO_2max (RunningIntervals)as early as possible.

PRINCIPLE 2

At some point during the season, incorporate each of the three critical workouts (SSR, Tempo-Run, RunningIntervals). Dylan had two different things to work on close to the race: lactate threshold (one of his strengths) as a by-product of Principle 3 and SteadyStateRun (most specific to the race) as a by-product of Principle 1. It is common during planning that the different principles come into conflict, and the

MAY 2014

MONDAY	TUESDAY	WEDNESDAY	THURSDAY	FRIDAY	SATURDAY	SUNDAY	WEEKLY SUMMARY
12	13th	14	15	16	17	18	SUMMARY
Rest Day	1:00 RecoveryRun	2:00 EnduranceRun with 1 × 45 min SSR	1:30 EnduranceRun	1:00 RecoveryRun	3:00 EnduranceRun with 2 × 30 min SSR, 5 min recovery between intervals	5:00 EnduranceRun. Work on your nutrition plan for WS.	Total miles: 89 Total elevation change: 36,756 ft Elevation change/ mi: 413 ft
19	20	21	22	23rd	24	25	SUMMARY
Rest Day	2:00 EnduranceRun with 1 × 45 min SSR	2:00 EnduranceRun with 1 × 30 SSR	1:30 EnduranceRun	1:00 RecoveryRun	3:00 EnduranceRun with 2 × 30 min SSR, 5 min recovery between intervals	4:00 EnduranceRun. Work on your nutrition plan for WS.	Total miles: 79 Total elevation change: 33,254 ft Elevation change/ mi: 421 ft
26	27	28	29	30	31		
Rest Day	1:00 RecoveryRun	3:00 EnduranceRun with 2 × 30 min SSR, 5 min recovery between intervals	1:30 EnduranceRun	1:00 RecoveryRun	3:00 EnduranceRun with 2 × 30 min SSR, 5 min recovery between intervals		

JUNE 2014

MONDAY	TUESDAY	WEDNESDAY	THURSDAY	FRIDAY	SATURDAY	SUNDAY	WEEKLY SUMMARY
						1	SUMMARY
						6:00 EnduranceRun. Work on your nutrition plan for WS.	Total miles: 107 Total elevation change: 45,098 ft Elevation change/ mi: 421 ft
2	3rd	4	5	6	7	8	SUMMARY
Rest Day. Start your sauna protocol this week.	2:00 EnduranceRun with 1 × 45 min SSR	2:00 EnduranceRun with 1 × 30 SSR	1:30 EnduranceRun	1:00 RecoveryRun	3:00 EnduranceRun with 2 × 30 min SSR, 5 min recovery between intervals	4:00 EnduranceRun. Work on your nutrition plan for WS.	Total miles: 91 Total elevation change: 34,580 ft Elevation change/ mi: 380 ft
9	10	11	12	13	14	15	SUMMARY
Rest Day	1:30 EnduranceRun	1:00 RecoveryRun	2:00 EnduranceRun with 1 × 45 min SSR	2:00 EnduranceRun with 1 × 30 SSR	1:30 EnduranceRun	3:00 EnduranceRun with 1 × 30 SSR	Total miles: 80 Total elevation change: 28,372 ft Elevation change/ mi: 354 ft

FIGURE 8.1 *Dylan Bowman's final training phase leading up to the 2014 Western States 100. Note that the elevation change per week is similar to that of the Western States course (410 feet of elevation change/mile).*

decision about what to do first and what to do second is not black and white. As a coach, my default is to err on the side of the demands of the event before either of the remaining principles. However, this is a judgment call and part of the art

RACE INTENSITY

The phenomenon of the most specific race intensity being SSR/EnduranceRun and the least specific being VO_2max is common in ultrarunning. Even in shorter ultramarathons, race times routinely exceed 4 to 6 hours, plenty long enough that EnduranceRun and SSR are the most specific. Exceptions are rare and consist of Skyrunning races as well as 50K and 50-mile events for elite runners. Elites in those race distances run for a shorter duration (because they are faster) and can run at higher intensities for longer periods. In these races, the elites can actually run within 10 to 15 percent of their threshold for much of the race.

of coaching. When presented with a similar conundrum with a different athlete, I might choose differently.

With Dylan, I chose to develop lactate threshold first, then SteadyStateRun and his endurance closer to the race. The decision was a function of the race demands of the Western States 100. I also wanted Dylan to be very confident going into that race. Thus, when he got his butt kicked at Transgrancanaria (knocking his confidence down) and had the opportunity to race the North Face 50 Bear Mountain, I viewed that race as a chance to simultaneously develop his lactate threshold system and build back his confidence. Therefore, I doubled down on developing lactate threshold before doing any SteadyStateRun work because lactate threshold intensity is more important for Dylan's success at the 50-mile distance. Additionally, Dylan rearranged other races in the middle of the season. When we were doing initial planning early in the season, the Transvulcania 80K and Lake Sonoma 50 were on the table. These were replaced by the North Face Bear Mountain 50-mile race, and we changed the duration of the lactate threshold work to coincide with that race. This change gave Dylan the opportunity to develop that physiology to a greater extent and race in an area of his strength when he was the most fit.

TABLE 8.1 Dylan Bowman's Initial 2014 Long-Range Plan

	WEEKS					
MONTH	January	February	March	April	May	June
RACE NAME	Sean O'Brien	Transgrancanaria		Lake Sonoma 50	Transvulcania	Western States 100
RACE PRIORITY	C	B		B	B	A
PHASE GOAL	VO₂max. Improve maximum aerobic capacity.		Lactate threshold—build to 4 × 15 T. Build long run.		Maximize long runs. Back-to-back long runs. 60-min SSR.	
Recovery						
EnduranceRun/SSR						
TempoRun						
RunningIntervals						
Taper						
Other		Maybe one round of heat work			Race nutritional planning, heat acclimatization.	
Notes	Lowest volume, highest intensity		This is typically the hardest phase, great time for 50 mile/100K.		Highest volume, lowest intensity	

(Note: PHASE GOAL "VO₂max. Improve maximum aerobic capacity." = VO_2max)

(See Table 8.1 for Dylan's LRP and Table 8.2 for how Dylan's LRP changed as the season progressed.)

Application of Principle 2. The bookends of Dylan's strengths and weaknesses (see Principle 3) and event demands dictated that, by default, he would hit all three critical intensities during the season. Thus, accomplishing all three principles was an easy task. This is not always the case. Sometimes, the time frame dictates that you have to pick and choose among the three principles, leaving out one of them. More often, you skimp on one to develop another. These are judgment calls, and thus there are few right and wrong approaches. In general, though, I tend to favor training for the demands of the event as an ever-so-slightly higher priority than the other two.

| TABLE **8.2** | Dylan Bowman's 2014 Long-Range Plan Adapted After Transgrancanaria |

MONTH	January	February	March	April	May	June
RACE NAME		Sean O'Brien	Transgrancanaria		TNF Bear Mountain	Western States 100
RACE PRIORITY		C	B		B	A
PHASE GOAL	VO₂max. Improve maximum aerobic capacity.		Lactate threshold—build to 4 x 15 T. Build long run.		Maximize long runs. Back-to-back long runs. 60-min SSR.	
Recovery						
EnduranceRun/SSR						
TempoRun						
RunningIntervals						
Taper						
Other		Maybe one round of heat work			Race nutritional planning, heat acclimatization	
Notes	Lowest volume, highest intensity		This is typically the hardest phase, great time for 50 mile/100K.		Highest volume, lowest intensity	

Note: The races have changed, and the TempoRun phase has been extended to coincide with the North Face 50 Bear Mountain.

PRINCIPLE 3

Work strengths closer to the race and weaknesses further away. I knew from the onset that one of Dylan's strengths was his physiology at lactate threshold. I could tell this from his performances at 50-mile and 50K races, which generally trended better than his other performances. In contrast, athletes with great endurance but less ability to maintain a strong pace at lactate threshold often perform better at 100-mile distances but lack the speed for great performances at the 50-mile and 50K distances. He also knows the Western States 100 course well, which was another strength come race day. Looking back at his previous training, and after his initial interview, I concluded that two of his weaknesses were technical running and his cardiovascular VO_2max.

Application of Principle 3. Prioritize the demands of the event and develop Dylan's SSR closest to Western States 100 and TempoRun closest to any 50-mile or 100K races. Develop lactate threshold closer (but not closest) to the event and VO_2max furthest away. Table technical running, which is not critical to the Western States 100 for Dylan.

TRAINING PHASES

Generally speaking, each training phase should last approximately 8 weeks, and Dylan's ultimate LRP conveniently fits into this time frame. This is merely a coincidence, however; Dylan's example of nice, neat 8-week time frames would not be applicable to every athlete. In reality, my athletes are switching intensities anywhere from 4 to 12 weeks, with the number of weeks based on three distinct facets: **intensity**, **significance**, and **rate of adaptation**.

INTENSITY OF THE PHASE

Typically, higher-intensity phases can be shorter than lower-intensity phases. I commonly have athletes go through a VO_2max phase that is as short as 3 weeks. An endurance phase that includes SteadyStateRuns and EnduranceRuns and lasts 12 weeks is equally common, with rest at appropriate times. This is because your physiology at high intensities adapts over a shorter time course and vice versa. Stephen Seiler (2006) has developed a useful theoretical curve to visually explain this phenomenon and its impact on performance (Figure 8.2). It neatly describes how an athlete's VO_2max and lactate threshold can improve and plateau over time.

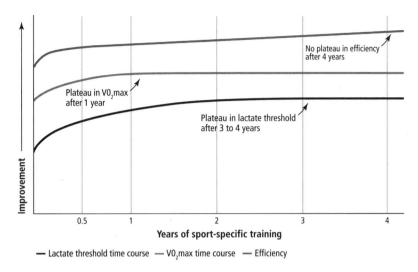

FIGURE **8.2** *Time course for training adaptation*

Source: Adapted from Seiler 2006.

SIGNIFICANCE OF THE PHASE IN THE OVERALL PLAN

Significance is quite easy to determine and correlates to Principle 1 described in the LRP planning process. Quite simply, if the training aspect is more critical to success, I will have an athlete develop it for a longer period (typically 8 weeks or more). This also happens closer to the race according to Principle 1. If the aspect is less important, I have the athlete work for a shorter period (8 weeks or less) and typically further away from the event.

POINT OF DIMINISHING RETURNS

The concept of diminishing returns can be illustrated by the example of eating cookies. The first cookie is delicious, melting in your mouth with a warm, buttery, sugary goodness. By the time you eat the fourth or fifth cookie, meh, it's OK but not nearly as satisfying as the first. The enjoyment you get from the treat diminishes as each subsequent cookie is devoured. Physiologically speaking, the concept of diminishing returns is also a reality. From a training standpoint, the returns on your hard work diminish as time and training move forward. Additionally, as you become more fit, it takes a longer amount of time to improve less (again, see Figure 8.2). This is generally a good thing, as it means you are becoming stronger and faster. Depending on the type of stress, this point of diminishing returns can come after weeks, months, or even years. Figure 8.2 also points out that even though these physiological phenomena can reach their points of diminishing returns, the athlete's efficiency (and therefore performance) can still improve.

While the figure specifically describes physiological changes at lactate threshold and VO$_2$max, put very simplistically, higher intensities produce changes in an endurance athlete more quickly but to a lesser extent, and they reach the point of diminishing returns sooner as compared with lower intensities. By knowing this simple physiological phenomenon, you can better gauge when this point of diminishing returns is reached, which is the third facet in determining how long to focus on what stress.

TAKEAWAYS ON THE LONG-RANGE PLAN

- Start at the end, do the most specific things last, and do the least specific things first.
- Get in all three critical intensities during training.
- Develop weaknesses furthest from the event and strengths closest to it.
- Start with 8-week training blocks, working one intensity at a time.
  - Shorten a block if
    - The intensity is high
    - The intensity is less important
  - Lengthen a block if
    - The intensity is low
    - The intensity is more important
- If you are designing your own training, err on the side of shorter training blocks, switching the stimulus more frequently.

BALANCING SIGNIFICANCE AND DIMINISHING RETURNS

While the general intensity of the phase can set the premise for how long or short a phase should be, the aspects of significance and diminishing returns need to be balanced while actually constructing the details of the phase. During the planning process, significance takes priority. *How important is the phase to the end result?* This dominates the phase duration philosophy because the reality of training has yet to take place. You as an athlete, and I as a coach, have yet to see how the training and adaptation actually unfold. So, we make an educated guess about when our neat little blocks are going to begin and end when we formulate the LRP. Sometimes those nice, neat blocks run true to form, but sometimes they change.

Once reality takes hold, we can prioritize training based on what we observe about the aspect of diminishing returns. As a coach, I evaluate training on a daily basis, looking at how fresh and fatigued an athlete is. Even more important, I use that information to determine whether an athlete is better after a rest phase, and I either keep the original LRP or alter it accordingly. It's a tricky balance because I want to see the athlete fatigue during the course of training and then improve just after coming out of a recovery phase. Athletes need to literally get worse before they rest and thus get better; they need that amount of stress in order to adapt. Needing an athlete to get worse before getting better can be taken only so far before the stress is too much. When I see an athlete fail to improve shortly after a recovery phase, it's one indication that he or she is ready for a different stimulus. For athletes who are designing their own training programs, I encourage you to switch in and out of training phases more quickly, rather than forcibly wringing out every last ounce of improvement. This errs on the side of caution, keeping the training stimulus novel and helping to prevent burnout. For the athletes I coach, I look at a range of variables to indicate that a change is needed and appropriate, including interval metrics, cumulative training load, acute training load, training stress scores, qualitative feedback, and workout comments from the athletes' training logs. I have outlined some of these variables in Chapter 6, "The Technology of Ultrarunning."

CHAPTER 9

ACTIVATING YOUR TRAINING: THE SHORT-RANGE PLAN

The short-range plan is where the rubber meets the road. It is what most people refer to as their daily schedule. Some will refer to it as a single "block" of training. This schedule lays out the specific workouts and rest periods for the days and weeks to come. Your short-range plan contains the precise volume, intensity, intervals, recovery, and terrain specificity on a day-by-day basis.

It is in vogue for coaches and athletes to arrange their short-range plans in tidy 4-week periods of 3 weeks "on" and 1 week "off." Generic 12-week plans available in magazines or online are often arranged in this fashion. While this offers a convenient way to lay out a typical 4-week month, I've always found this approach to be lazy. The fact of the matter is that various stressors affect the body differently. It takes a different amount of time to recover from high volume than from high intensity. Similarly, your body adapts along a different time course for various intensities. You cannot pigeonhole the process into rigid 4-week time frames.

The 3-to-1 work-rest paradigm is a good reference point to start from, but to get the most from your hard-earned training, this time frame needs to be adjusted to suit the adaptation you are seeking. The question is: How do you know what to adjust and in what ways? I use three primary concepts to design short-range plans, and when you apply these concepts to your training and your goals, you'll find that your training better suits your individual needs, is more precise, and most likely breaks the 3-to-1 paradigm.

CONCEPTS FOR THE SHORT-RANGE PLAN

Do the biggest training load when you are the most rested. You run the best when you are fresh. This is why we taper before races (though tapering tends to make ultrarunners crazy). When we are fresh and rested, we can run faster for longer periods of time. If we extend this concept to training, you are the most ready to handle the biggest training load right after a recovery phase. Following that strategy, your short-range plan should *start with the workout (or workouts) that contains the biggest training load*. Regardless of the phase you are in, you should aim to do the hardest workout you will do for the phase right off the bat. For example, for athletes who can handle a maximum of 60 minutes of SteadyStateRun, I will have them do that workout at the beginning of the phase, when they are the most rested. They might not be able to ever do a workout of that caliber for the remaining weeks of the phase, but that is fine. Many times, the hardest workout is actually a "B" race. You race hard, and the subsequent training stimulus of the race is far bigger than the stimulus you can achieve on any of the remaining training days. In any case, the fatigue induced from the initial few workouts will eventually lead to the desired adaptation. In this way, you must accept the fact that during the training process, you will get worse before you get better. If you do the right things in training, this will be intentionally so (Figure 9.1).

Higher intensity means a shorter adaptation process, longer recovery, and less frequent specific work. Most ultrarunners are intensity-averse, which means they do anything they can to avoid running very, very hard. If you are among the ultrarunning crowd that fears high-intensity work, the type of work that makes your lungs sear and your legs burn, the next paragraph will be a relief.

One of the saving graces of high-intensity work is that it takes very little of it to produce an adaptation. Hooray! The time you work at that intensity during any

MONDAY	TUESDAY	WEDNESDAY	THURSDAY	FRIDAY	SATURDAY	SUNDAY
5	6	7	8	9	10	11
Rest Day	1:30 EnduranceRun with 5 × 3 min RunningIntervals, 3 min recovery between intervals	1:00 RecoveryRun	1:30 EnduranceRun with 5 × 3 min RunningIntervals, min recovery between intervals	1:00 RecoveryRun	1:30 EnduranceRun with 5 × 3 min RunningIntervals, min recovery between intervals	2:00 EnduranceRun
12	13	14	15	16	17	18
Rest Day	1:30 EnduranceRun with 5 × 3 min RunningIntervals, 3 min recovery between intervals	1:00 RecoveryRun	1:00 RecoveryRun	1:30 EnduranceRun with 4 × 3 min RunningIntervals, 3 min recovery between intervals	1:00 RecoveryRun	2:00 EnduranceRun
19	20	21	22	23	24	25
Rest Day	1:00 RecoveryRun	1:30 EnduranceRun with 4 × 3 min RunningIntervals, 3 min recovery between intervals	0:45 RecoveryRun	0:45 RecoveryRun	1:00 RecoveryRun	1:00 RecoveryRun

FIGURE **9.1** *A RunningIntervals phase where the hardest workouts are the first four*

particular workout and the total number of consecutive weeks necessary to produce an adaptation are relatively small compared with the amount of moderate and lower-intensity work. Because of this, I never hesitate to work with "time-crunched" ultrarunners because I can take their most time-crunched periods and still get excellent adaptations at high intensities. You can see that concept reflected in Figure 9.1 and in Figure 8.2 (page 167), which shows the time course for training adaptation.

But wait, there's more! It takes longer to recover from high-intensity work, which means that, workout for workout, you need more rest and recovery between sessions to get your body ready for the next hard session. Hooray (again)! From a practical standpoint, most high-intensity phases, particularly VO_2max, need to be only 2 or 3 weeks long to elicit an appropriate adaptation. So, the total number of "hard" workouts is markedly smaller because the length of the phase is shorter and the density of the hard workouts is lower. See Figure 9.2A (SteadyStateRun) and Figure 9.2B (RunningIntervals) for a comparison between a higher-intensity phase and a lower-intensity phase. SteadyStateRun is at a lower intensity, and therefore that phase can be longer than a RunningInterval phase.

(a)

MONDAY	TUESDAY	WEDNESDAY	THURSDAY	FRIDAY	SATURDAY	SUNDAY
16	17	18	19	20	21	22
Rest Day	1:45 EnduranceRun with 2 × 30 min SteadyStateRun, 5 min recovery between intervals	1:00 RecoveryRun	1:45 EnduranceRun with 2 × 20 min SteadyStateRun, 5 min recovery between intervals	1:00 RecoveryRun	2:00 EnduranceRun with 2 × 30 min SteadyStateRun, 5 min recovery between intervals	3:00 EnduranceRun
23	24	25	26	27	28	29
Rest Day	1:45 EnduranceRun with 2 × 30 min SteadyStateRun, 5 min recovery between intervals	1:00 RecoveryRun	1:45 EnduranceRun with 2 × 20 min SteadyStateRun	1:00 RecoveryRun	2:00 EnduranceRun with 2 × 20 min SteadyStateRun	3:30 EnduranceRun
30	1	2	3	4	5	6
Rest Day	1:45 EnduranceRun with 2 × 20 min SteadyStateRun, 5 min recovery between intervals	1:00 RecoveryRun	1:45 EnduranceRun with 1 × 30 min SteadyStateRun	1:00 RecoveryRun	1:30 EnduranceRun with 1 × 30 min SteadyStateRun	4:00 EnduranceRun
7	8	9	10	11	12	13
Rest Day	1:00 RecoveryRun	1:00 RecoveryRun	1:00 RecoveryRun	1:00 RecoveryRun	2:00 EnduranceRun with 2 × 30 min SteadyStateRun, 5 min recovery between intervals	3:00 EnduranceRun

(b)

MONDAY	TUESDAY	WEDNESDAY	THURSDAY	FRIDAY	SATURDAY	SUNDAY
16	17	18	19	20	21	22
Rest Day	1:30 EnduranceRun with 5 × 3 min RunningIntervals, 3 min recovery between intervals	1:00 RecoveryRun	1:30 EnduranceRun with 5 × 3 min RunningIntervals, 3 min recovery between intervals	1:00 RecoveryRun	1:30 EnduranceRun with 5 × 3 min RunningIntervals, 3 min recovery between intervals	2:00 EnduranceRun
23	24	25	26	27	28	29
Rest Day	1:30 EnduranceRun with 5 × 3 min RunningIntervals, 3 min recovery between intervals	1:00 RecoveryRun	1:00 RecoveryRun	1:30 EnduranceRun with 4 × 3 min RunningIntervals, 3 min recovery between intervals	1:00 RecoveryRun	2:00 EnduranceRun
30	1	2	3	4	5	6
Rest Day	1:00 RecoveryRun	1:30 EnduranceRun with 4 × 3 min RunningIntervals, 3 min recovery between intervals	:45 RecoveryRun	:45 RecoveryRun	1:00 RecoveryRun	1:00 RecoveryRun

FIGURE **9.2**   *(a) A typical SteadyStateRun phase; (b) a typical RunningInterval phase. Note that the SteadyState phase is longer and there is less recovery between the workouts than in the RunningInterval phase.*

The lower the intensity, the longer the adaptation process, the shorter the recovery, and the more frequent the work can be. Workouts like EnduranceRuns, SSR, and to a lesser extent TempoRuns are typically at low enough intensities that it takes many weeks to accumulate enough training stress to produce an adaptation. Most ultra athletes intuitively realize this, as their day-to-day training is mainly a compilation of EnduranceRuns ad nauseam. It is important to realize that even at the slightly higher intensities of SSR and TempoRun, this can still be the case. Given the right construct, you should be able to handle back-to-back SSR and TempoRun days for at least some of the phase and be able to stay in these phases for more than 3 weeks. At the TempoRun intensity, I have my athletes do these workouts three times per week, often scheduling two of these workouts on consecutive days. For SSR, that limit gets pushed to four times per week in certain weeks.

During the long-range planning process, I always alert my athletes to what the hardest phase will be. The purpose is to better prepare them for what is to come. During that phase, it is important to focus on recovery, get proper sleep, try to reschedule big work projects, and avoid other life stressors. If they are trying to lose weight, it is best to do it at some other point in the season. During this hardest phase, all of their spare energy will be needed for hard training and purposeful recovery. Ninety percent of the time this is the TempoRun, or lactate threshold, phase. Although this phase is not the most intense and does not have the biggest volume, it hits the right balance of volume and intensity. That balance tends to grind an athlete down over the course of time more so than higher intensities (with less volume) or lower intensities (with higher volume).

THE CASE FOR BACK-TO-BACK HARD DAYS

Should you run on tired legs? Yes, but not for the reason you might think. Many ultrarunners have adopted a strategy with their long runs in which they intentionally run long and far on consecutive days. The theory is that this type of training teaches your body to "run when it is tired," mimicking the demands of

MONDAY	TUESDAY	WEDNESDAY	THURSDAY	FRIDAY	SATURDAY	SUNDAY
	5	6	7	8	9	10
	...anceRun) min, 5 min between intervals	1:30 EnduranceRun with 3 × 8 min TempoRun, 4 min recovery between intervals	1:00 RecoveryRun	1:00 RecoveryRun	1:30 EnduranceRun with 3 × 10 min TempoRun, 5 min recovery between intervals	1:30 EnduranceRun with 3 × 8 min TempoRun, 4 min recovery between intervals
11	12	13	14	15	16	17
Rest Day	1:00 RecoveryRun	1:30 EnduranceRun with 3 × 10 min TempoRun, 5 min recovery between intervals	1:30 EnduranceRun with 3 × 8 min TempoRun, 4 min recovery between intervals	1:00 RecoveryRun	1:30 EnduranceRun with 3 × 8 min TempoRun, 4 min recovery between intervals	2:00 EnduranceRun
18	19	20	21	22	23	24
Rest Day	1:00 RecoveryRun	1:30 EnduranceRun with 3 × 8 min TempoRun, 4 min recovery between intervals	1:30 EnduranceRun with 3 × 8 min TempoRun, 4 min recovery between intervals	1:00 RecoveryRun	1:00 RecoveryRun	1:30 EnduranceRun with 3 × 8 min TempoRun, 4 min recovery between intervals
25	26	27	28	29	30	31
Rest Day	1:00 RecoveryRun	1:00 RecoveryRun	1:00 RecoveryRun	1:30 EnduranceRun with 3 × 12 min TempoRun, 6 min recovery between intervals	1:30 EnduranceRun with 3 × 10 min TempoRun, 5 min recovery between intervals	2:00 EnduranceRun
RECOVERY PHASE						

▨ Hard workout

FIGURE **9.3** *A back-to-back-style training plan. There is one additional hard workout, as compared to Figure 9.4. Even in this example, the hardest workouts are still early in the phase.*

MONDAY	TUESDAY	WEDNESDAY	THURSDAY	FRIDAY	SATURDAY	SUNDAY
4	5	6	7	8	9	10
Rest Day	1:30 EnduranceRun with 3X10 min TempoRun, 5 min recovery between intervals	1:00 RecoveryRun	1:30 EnduranceRun with 3X8 min TempoRun, 4 min recovery between intervals	1:00 RecoveryRun	1:30 EnduranceRun with 3X10 min TempoRun, 5 min recovery between intervals	2:00 EnduranceRun
11	12	13	14	15	16	17
Rest Day	1:30 EnduranceRun with 3X10 min TempoRun, 5 min recovery between intervals	1:00 RecoveryRun	1:30 EnduranceRun with 3X8 min TempoRun, 4 min recovery between intervals	1:00 RecoveryRun	1:30 EnduranceRun with 3X8 min TempoRun, 4 min recovery between intervals	2:00 EnduranceRun
18	19	20	21	22	23	24
Rest Day	1:30 EnduranceRun with 3X8 min TempoRun, 4 min recovery between intervals	1:00 RecoveryRun	1:30 EnduranceRun with 3X8 min TempoRun, 4 min recovery between intervals	1:00 RecoveryRun	1:30 EnduranceRun with 3X8 min TempoRun, 4 min recovery between intervals	2:00 EnduranceRun
25	26	27	28	29	30	31
Rest Day	1:00 RecoveryRun	1:00 RecoveryRun	1:00 RecoveryRun	1:30 EnduranceRun with 3X12 min TempoRun, 6 min recovery between intervals	1:00 RecoveryRun	1:30 EnduranceRun with 3X10 min TempoRun, 5 min recovery between intervals
RECOVERY PHASE						

▨ Hard workout

FIGURE **9.4** *A non-back-to-back-style training example. There are only 9 hard workouts, as compared to the 10 in the back-to-back style.*

an ultramarathon. I adopt the back-to-back training strategy with my athletes in nearly every phase, so needless to say, I'm a fan. However, I take it a step further. Although I have my athletes do back-to-back long runs, I also have them do back-to-back days with SSR, TempoRuns, and, in certain circumstances, RunningIntervals. While using this strategy, you will certainly be more tired on the second day than the first. Your legs will feel like bricks, and if you have done the first workout correctly, you can't perform quite up to the level that you did on day 1.

But I do not have my athletes do back-to-back days to teach them to "run on tired legs." I do it because the effect on the aerobic engine is greater because you are concentrating your training load, and typically you can get in one or two more quality sessions per phase (compare the examples in Figures 9.3 and 9.4). This is important because athletes tend to look at training from the standpoint of weekly volume, but you also need to consider your total workload for an entire phase of training. When you can schedule in an extra workout or two within a period, while still maintaining appropriate amounts of rest, you can wring greater gains out of that period of time. Much of the practice of this strategy is adopted from other sports such as cross-country skiing and cycling (Rønnestad, Hansen, and Ellefsen 2014; Rønnestad et al. 2015). Even though running is a different sport and should be treated as such, many of the same principles apply across all aerobic sports. Taking all this into account, I've adopted this block-style, load-concentration training for the athletes I work with. Without a doubt, it's tricky to get right, and it requires careful monitoring of fatigue and performance. If you are designing your own training, I encourage you to first try back-to-back workouts at the SSR intensity to see how you react. Do it once in a phase, preferably at the beginning. If you react well, you can try it across the course of the entire phase and then try it at different intensities.

TAPERING FOR YOUR EVENT

Iñigo Mujika, a highly regarded sports physiologist known for his work on tapering and detraining, has defined tapering as "a progressive nonlinear reduction of the training load during a variable period of time, in an attempt to reduce the

///// ERIK GLOVER   BACK-TO-BACK WORKOUTS

Like many ultrarunners, I often field "How? What? Why?" questions about ultra-running from incredulous friends, family, and random people on airplanes. When I try to answer "Why?," I often confound the person asking the question. Apparently, "because it sounds painful" is not a widely accepted rationale for how someone should spend their spare time. However, when I address "How?" and "What?" questions, I believe there is a fairly sensible answer. I enjoy training. I have found that preparing for an ultra is an exercise in patience and commitment over many months, by me and my family. Further, as a time-crunched athlete, I view the months of training as a balancing act of mind, body, and logistics. To make it all work, I must enjoy putting in the hours and get genuine gratification from the week-to-week training regimen.

Based on my schedule and location, I enjoy the challenge of a period-ized, high-intensity training program that emphasizes high-quality workouts and increases my fitness level rather than sheer volume of activity. The high-intensity training includes several essential workouts that challenge me week in and week out. Out of all these workouts, I love TempoRuns the most, par-ticularly on consecutive days. Depending on the phase of my program, I will complete 2 or 3 TempoRun workouts per week that include 3 to 4 intervals of between 10 and 14 minutes just below lactate threshold effort. TempoRun workouts require focus and strategy to put together a set of consistent inter-vals just on the inside edge of where the wheels come off. TempoRuns are painful and often give me "pre-race butterflies" during warm-up, but I find them intensely gratifying because they test mental and physical toughness. Back-to-back TempoRuns force me to think about consistency over two days' effort. I want to push the first day hard, but I need to keep enough in the tank so the second day's effort does not fall off.

/////

physiological and psychological stress of daily training and optimize sports performance" (Mujika and Padilla 2000a, 80; Mujika and Padilla 2003, 1183).

Contrary to what most popular literature with clickbait headlines will tell you, tapering will not make or break your race. On average, you stand to gain 3 percent from a properly constructed taper (Mujika and Padilla 2003). That's 43 minutes in a 24-hour event. However, the difference is minimized when you consider that 3 percent increase is from the baseline of implementing no taper at all. With simple, reasonable rest before your event, you might gain 2 percent. If you designed the most scientific and effective taper ever, you would gain 3 percent. That's a difference of 1 percent, which is not much for most athletes. Yes, you should still implement a taper before your event. But you should also be realistic about what you expect to gain from it, be reasonable about the duration of your taper, and don't worry too much if things don't go perfectly to plan. Remember, Mujika talks about reduction of psychological stress as a goal of a taper, so stressing about achieving the perfect taper is counterproductive.

BEFORE YOU TAPER

Train. One of the primary pitfalls of tapering occurs when athletes go into their goal event lacking confidence in their fitness. Remember Figure 8.3 and the time course for adaptation? Another point that chart illustrates is that if you are training properly, after a period of time, each subsequent workout results in fewer positive adaptations than the last. So, put in the work early. During the final 2 months of training, it's all about fine-tuning the fitness you have built.

THE BASICS OF TAPERING

The purpose of a taper is to simultaneously reduce the negative aspects of training (fatigue) and enhance the positive ones (fitness). This combination will leave you more fit and psychologically prepared for race day. The great thing is, by reducing the negative aspects of training, you naturally enhance the positive ones. From a strategic standpoint, this is crucial. Tapering fundamentally revolves around *first* reducing certain training variables; *then*, as a consequence of that reduction, adaptation takes place. In this way, *tapering is not "maintenance,"* which is a word that is carelessly thrown around (as in, "I am going to maintain my fitness"). No athlete has ever come to me in my coaching career with "maintenance" as a goal. It should not be yours during the tapering process. Tapering is not maintenance. Tapering improves your physiology, leaving you more fit and ready for performance.

Training is a combination of volume, intensity, frequency, environment, and running cadence. These five variables can be used to describe nearly every workout for an ultrarunner. When talking tapering, it's best to break it down into how the five variables should be manipulated. Before breaking tapering down by these variables, though, we need to talk about perspective. I love science. It provides a platform from which we have the opportunity to work and explore. The fundamentals provide the base, and we get to build on top of it. Every so often, though, science gets too caught up in the minutiae. Tapering is one of those areas.

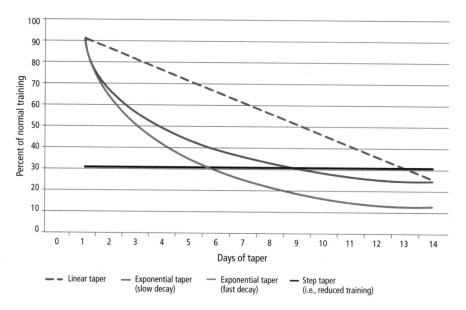

FIGURE **9.5** *Schematic representation of the different types of tapers*

Source: Mujika and Padilla 2003.

If you review the best literature on tapering, the research will recommend a "nonlinear, fast-decay reduction" of training load. This reduction takes the shape of the orange line shown in Figure 9.5, which illustrates two types of nonlinear reduction, fast and slow decay, as well as a step reduction (reducing training load by a set percentage all at once) and a linear reduction (reducing training load at a fixed percentage day after day). While I love the ingenuity of this graph and the countless hours spent on its development, this level of minutiae is impractical. For example, if you follow a "fast-decay" tapering process, on day 5 your daily training volume is supposed to be at 32.5 percent. If you were normally doing a 2-hour run, this means that your run for day 5 should be 39 minutes. Not 40 or 38, but exactly 39. There's nothing magical about 39 minutes of running on day 5 of a taper or any other day. Athletes are human beings, not machines or lab rats. In my experience, it's best to understand the science and then find ways to use it in more practical ways. The text box below shows how I encourage you to plan your taper as you approach an event.

Now, with a bit of perspective in hand, let's look at the best overarching strategies for tapering, based on the current literature. For the purposes of calibration, in this discussion of the components of training, I am assuming a 3-week tapering process for a runner who is training 10 hours per week.

KEY STRATEGIES FOR SMART TAPERING

- Start tapering two to three weeks out from an event.
- Reduce your overall training load (volume and volume of intensity) quickly at first, then gradually toward the end.
- Reduce overall volume.
- Reduce the volume of intensity (but not the intensity itself).
- Slightly reduce the frequency (days per week) or do not reduce the frequency at all.
- Maintain specificity (environment and running cadence).

Volume: Reduce

Adjusting volume is your first step in the tapering process. Using a fast-decay tapering model, volume should decrease very quickly at first, and then level off toward the end. Thus, if you start with an overall volume of 10 hours per week, you should reduce that to 4 to 5 hours (40 to 50 percent of training volume) per week the first week, 2 to 3 hours (20 to 30 percent of normal training volume) the second week, and 2 hours maximum (<20 percent of normal training volume) in the last week.

Intensity: Reduce the Amount, Not the Type

Intensity is where things get a little tricky. The overarching strategy is to reduce the volume of intensity you do during the week but not the type of intensity. The amount that you reduce the intensity should follow the "fast-decay" strategy. Thus, similar to how you would reduce volume, you would reduce the volume of intensity quickly at first, then more slowly toward the end. For example, if in a normal training week you are doing 4×10 min TempoRuns for a workout, during Taper Week 1 you would do 3×5 min TempoRuns (37.5 percent of the normal TempoRun volume). In Week 2 you would do 2×5 min TempoRuns (25 percent of the TempoRun volume), and in the last week 1×5 (12.5 percent of the TempoRun volume).

Maintenance of training intensity is a critical part of the tapering process. This is because the small amount of intensity that is done prevents a decline in the hard-earned benefits you have worked for in training (Hickson et al. 1985; Sheply et al. 1992).

Frequency: Maintain or Slightly Reduce

Frequency should be maintained or slightly reduced. This means that if you are running 5 days per week, continue running 5 days per week. If you are doing 2 specific workouts per week (TempoRun, SSR, etc.), continue doing those 2 specific workouts per week using the guidelines above for reducing the volume of intensity in those workouts.

Specificity: Maintain

Whatever terrain and vertical specificity you have been doing in training leading up to a race, maintain that during the taper. This means if you have been running on trails, continue to run on trails. If you have been running on road, run on road. One of the mistakes I see over and over again is athletes who are training for mountainous trail events and who train on specific trails for those events, but then change that specificity for their taper. They run around the track in Chamonix in preparation for the Ultra-Trail du Mont-Blanc. That strategy violates the final tapering strategy of specificity.

THE TAPER TANTRUMS

The previously mentioned strategies are primarily (but not exclusively) aimed at improving your physiological state before an event. Your psychological state is just as important. And although the tapering strategies presented here have been demonstrated to also improve psychological qualities (Morgan et al. 1987; Raglin et al. 1996; Hooper, Mackinnon, and Howard 1999), many athletes still struggle with this aspect of race preparation. They feel as if they are losing fitness or missing out on training. The two to three weeks spent reducing training seem to go on forever, and they doubt the process. They become antsy for the event, feel sluggish during their day-to-day life and runs, and become irritable and difficult to live with. This is normal, and it is important to understand that the "taper tantrums" are part of the process.

Angst and unease are normal psychological reactions to a taper. During the taper, you have more time and energy available than during your earlier training. That excess time and energy has to go somewhere, and many athletes utilize it simply to fret. To release their energy, they pack and repack their luggage, obsessively analyze splits, and second-guess their choice of socks. Any rational person observing these actions from the outside would probably get a chuckle.

To better handle your taper, trust your training. If you have done the right things in training, the taper becomes easier to handle. Have confidence that the miles, vertical, and intensity you have put in over the previous months are going to pay off. Even if your training has not gone perfectly, if you have been conscientious and dedicated to the process, you should trust that you have done enough.

I routinely ask my athletes to review their training just in advance of their taper. Specifically, I have them look at the sheer quantity of time they have dedicated to the process. The enormity of what they have done over the last several months puts the last few workouts in perspective. Those last workouts are a very, very small part of the entire process.

Avoid the taper tantrums by trusting your training and the tapering process. If you trust that you are going to come out on the other side of a taper refreshed and ready for the event, the times you spend not running suddenly have purpose.

This is an excellent time to put your excess energy into rest. Yes, this takes just as much focus and energy as training, maybe even more so for ultrarunners. Take the time you had previously set aside for training and *deliberately, intentionally* set it aside for a purposeful rest.

CHAPTER 10

FUELING AND HYDRATING FOR THE LONG HAUL

Ultrarunning is an eating contest on the go, an assertion supported by the fact that gastrointestinal distress is the leading reason athletes fail to reach the finish line in 100-mile footraces. I've already shown you that your ability to physically complete the distance is not a limiting factor for success, and that with structured training and smart planning you can overcome the challenges inherent in any ultramarathon course. But all that comes undone when your nutrition and hydration strategies fail. To optimize your performance and have the tools to work through adversity, you need a clear understanding of the fueling challenges specific to ultraendurance sports, as well as nutrition and hydration strategies that work specifically for you.

ESSENTIAL ELEMENTS OF SPORTS NUTRITION

Before we can talk about the nutrition challenges that are specific to ultraendurance athletes, we need to be on the same page in terms of the principles of sports nutrition. There are entire textbooks—and an entire profession—devoted to this topic, but in this book I'm going to cover only the essentials so we can move on to information that's more specific to ultrarunning.

MACRONUTRIENTS AND ENERGY PRODUCTION

Food contains three macronutrients: carbohydrate, protein, and fat. All the energy you expend comes from burning calories from these three sources, and you derive energy from all three sources at all times and at all levels of activity. The percentage of energy derived from each macronutrient depends on how quickly you need to produce energy and how much of a supply of each nutrient you have. Sitting and reading this book, you're deriving the vast majority of your energy from fat, although your brain (which is very engaged in learning, right?) is using primarily carbohydrate. Not to be left out, protein is quietly working in the background repairing muscle damage from your last run, bolstering your immune system, growing skin and blood cells, and so forth.

When you go for a run or increase your demand for energy through any activity, your body responds by ramping up the rate at which macronutrients are broken down into usable energy. This happens primarily in mitochondria, organelles in muscle cells that take in carbohydrate and fat and produce carbon dioxide, water, and adenosine triphosphate (ATP), the molecule that produces energy when broken down to adenosine diphosphate (ADP). Mitochondria are massively important for endurance performance; having more and bigger mitochondria gives you the ability to process more fuel per minute.

As you ramp up energy production in response to increased demand, the composition of your fuel mixture changes. The percentage of calories from carbohydrate increases, and this increase grows exponentially as your exercise intensity rises from an endurance pace to lactate threshold and above. We'll get into the reason for this a bit later. For now, what's important to remember is that while the percentage of calories from carbohydrate increases dramatically, the absolute amounts of fat and protein being used for energy also increase.

There has long been a misconception that low-intensity exercise is fueled by fat and high-intensity exercise is fueled by carbohydrate, and that there's a magical switch that gets thrown when you cross a certain pace. There's no switch. Fat utilization does not decrease as you go from an easy pace to an endurance pace. It doesn't even decrease when you reach lactate threshold. Only at extremely high intensities does fat utilization decline. At the speeds and intensities that occur during ultrarunning training and competition, the absolute amount of fat you break down for energy each minute increases as your pace increases.

The reason people misunderstand fat utilization is because they confuse a decrease in the *percentage* of energy derived from fat with a decrease in the *amount* of energy derived from fat. Fat is a great energy source, but compared with carbohydrate, it takes longer for your body to break down. As exercise intensity increases and your demand for energy rises, your body can't produce energy from fat quickly enough. This, by the way, is the fatal flaw of extremely low-carbohydrate nutritional strategies for athletes. When you severely limit the amount of carbohydrate available to working muscles, you may have stored energy from fat to continue exercising, but you are limited by the rate at which your muscles can process it. As a result, you can keep moving forward, but you will be doing so slowly.

At rest and at low exercise intensities, you don't use much carbohydrate for energy. In fact, as you sit there reading this book, 80 to 90 percent of your energy is coming from fat. At very low exercise intensities (20 to 25 percent of VO_2max), you still rely on fat for about 70 percent of your energy because your body naturally conserves carbohydrate whenever it can. This conservation strategy is necessary because you can store only about 1,600 to 2,000 calories of carbohydrate in your muscles, liver, and blood. In contrast, even a lean athlete (70 kg and 10 percent body fat) has more than 53,000 calories of stored fat. As you reach 40 to 60 percent of VO_2max, fuel utilization reaches about a 50-50 balance between fat and carbohydrate. Athletes with greater aerobic fitness will reach and maintain this 50-50 balance at a higher relative workload than will athletes who are less fit. As exercise intensity increases from 60 percent of VO_2max, the relative contribution from carbohydrate increases dramatically; but remember, even when you're burning a lot of carbohydrate at higher exercise intensities, you are still processing fat and carbohydrate using aerobic metabolism. Once you exceed your lactate threshold intensity (70 to 90 percent of VO_2max, depending on your fitness level), more than 80 percent of your energy is being derived from carbohydrate.

The great thing about carbohydrate is that once you reach the point at which you are demanding energy faster than you can produce it from fat, you can still increase the energy coming from carbohydrate to fill the gap.

Carbohydrate can be broken down into usable energy faster than fat because carbohydrate metabolism is not a single-stream process. Normally carbohydrate and fat are broken down using aerobic metabolism in mitochondria, as described earlier. This yields the greatest amount of energy per unit of fuel processed. But when energy demand increases, some carbohydrate can be partially broken down to release a portion of its potential energy more quickly. This is called *glycolysis*, and though it yields less energy per molecule of carbohydrate, it gets energy flowing to working muscles faster. Glycolysis is the reason the percentage of energy derived from carbohydrate starts increasing dramatically as exercise intensity exceeds 60 to 70 percent of VO_2max.

What happens to the leftovers from glycolysis? Well, the component that matters most in this discussion is lactate. This is the stuff that's unfairly gotten a bad rap for years. It has been blamed for the burning sensation in your muscles when you surge above your sustainable pace. It has been blamed for delayed-onset muscle soreness. People have tried to massage it away, flush it out, and buffer it. But the best way to get rid of lactate is to reintegrate it into normal aerobic metabolism to complete the process of breaking it down into energy, water, and carbon dioxide. This is one of the primary goals of endurance training: to increase the amount of lactate you can process per minute so you can exercise at a higher-intensity level before lactate accumulates significantly in your blood. This training adaptation also enables you to recover from hard efforts more quickly because deriving energy from glycolysis is like buying energy on credit. You have to pay the bill by slowing down, but when you can process lactate faster, you don't have to slow down as much or for as long.

Glycolysis is the reason carbohydrate is known as an athlete's high-octane fuel. When you need energy quickly, glycolysis allows you to burn carbohydrate faster. The downside to burning carbohydrate quickly is that you can run out of it. At most endurance intensities, you burn 5 calories per

HOW TO DETERMINE YOUR CALORIC BURN RATE

One calorie per kilogram per kilometer on flat, level terrain is a standard way to calculate the energy cost of running. That provides a good starting point, but what about runs that include a lot of climbing? To account for significant climbing, use a 1:10 ratio between vertical gain and horizontal distance. In other words, 1 meter of vertical gain equates to the energy cost of 10 meters of horizontal travel, or 1,000 meters of vertical gain equates to the energy cost of traveling 10 kilometers on flat ground. Based on a 70-kg runner on a 20-km run with 1,000 m of vertical gain, you would calculate 70 calories/km (70 × 20 km = 1,400 calories); to account for the climbing, you would add the energy cost of an additional 10 km (70 × 10 = 700 calories) and get a total of 2,100 calories. Hikers have used this 1-to-10 ratio for many years, and although it is not 100 percent accurate, it is adequate for making broad estimations on longer runs.

liter of oxygen consumed. (Note: To avoid confusion, I will use the more common spelling of food calories, using a lowercase *c*, even though the scientifically accurate terminology would either be "kilocalories" or "Calories" with a capital *C*.) A 70-kg midpack runner may have a VO_2max of 3.5 L/min, and an elite ultrarunner of the same weight may have a VO_2max of 4.75 L/min. At that intensity, most (but not all) of your caloric burn comes from carbohydrate. This means a 70-kg athlete's caloric burn rate may reach 17 to 24 calories/min, or around 4.5 to 5.5 g of carbohydrate per minute at VO_2max intensity. That might not sound like much, but if you could maintain that intensity for an hour (which you can't), you would burn close to 270 to 330 g of carbohydrate! More realistically, a midpack 70-kg runner maintaining a pace of 9:00 min/mi on flat ground will burn 12 to 13 calories/min. About 50 percent of that (6 calories/min) comes from carbohydrate, which is about 1.5 g of carbohydrate/min or 90 g/hour.

FORGET FAT ADAPTATION

The notion of optimizing your fat-burning capabilities to improve performance has been a hot topic for endurance athletes over the past few years. Ultrarunners, in particular, seem to gravitate toward this nutritional theory, perhaps because they associate lower-intensity exercise with fat-burning. This has led many ultrarunners to eat and train with the goal of becoming more "fat-adapted," meaning they intend to increase the amount of fat they burn at a particular intensity level, compared with their pre-fat-adapted state. The pro–fat adaptation argument is that you have a virtually unlimited source of energy in your stores of body fat. Proponents of this theory claim that if you train and eat properly, you can change the way your body burns energy, shifting the focus from your body's limited carbohydrate stores to the more plentiful, almost unlimited fat stores. Sounds like a great deal! If it were that simple, I'd take it.

The truth is that to produce these fat-burning adaptations, you have to make a fundamental compromise. You sacrifice developing the aerobic energy system to its maximum in order to produce the coveted fat adaptation qualities. From a practical standpoint, you have to train at a lower intensity, reduce your total workload at medium or high intensities, or reduce the frequency of any hard training (from, say, three days per week to two days per week of hard workouts), or some combination of all these. When you make such compromises, you are not developing the aerobic engine to its fullest capabilities. Most people realize this intuitively through their race efforts. When you race, you want to run as fast as possible to get to the finish line. To do so, you supplement with gels, drinks, and foods all aimed at delivering exogenous carbohydrates so you can run faster. When push comes to shove, you know you will run faster in your 50K if you get in a few gels along the way. In this sense, going through the fat adaptation process by restricting carbohydrates during training (one, but not the only, strategy for becoming fat-adapted) always produces a workload that is suboptimal. Faster running = greater workload.

To maximize improvement of the cardiovascular system, I have an athlete train at specific intensity levels for as much time and as frequently as possible. It is a very clear choice between the two strategies. You can become more fat-adapted and burn more fat, but you will arrive at the race with less fitness due to reduced training workload. Or you can eat a high-carbohydrate diet, burn less fat, complete higher workloads in training, and arrive at the race with greater fitness. For me the choice is easy, but that's because part of my philosophy is rooted in maximizing the cardiovascular system. Fat adaptation may cause a shift in how you produce energy, but it doesn't help you deliver energy more quickly to working muscles. As a result, it doesn't make you faster, and unless you are starving and running an ultramarathon simultaneously, it won't help you go farther, either. Whenever it comes to choosing a training or nutritional scenario, I always pick the one that will build a bigger cardiovascular engine.

Mile for mile and effort for effort, ultrarunners stand to gain more from improving their cardiovascular engine than from anything else. Have you ever heard anyone say, "Dude, I totally kicked your butt up that climb today because I was burning more fat than you"? Of course not. Listen to interviews with the elite ultrarunners describing how their races play out. They say things like "I could tell that so-and-so was going too hard" or "The pace on the first climb was very easy." These anecdotes correlate to how well tuned their cardiovascular engines are. The better the tune and the bigger the engine, the easier they can run at a given pace, the faster they can run at a sustainable pace, and the farther they can run at any pace.

So, where is protein in all this? Some people push protein as the preferred fuel, perhaps because high school biology taught us that muscle is made of protein, and therefore we need to eat protein in order to use our muscles. Protein is indeed necessary for building and maintaining muscle tissue, but it's not a very good fuel for exercise. For the most part, it has to be transported to the liver and be converted into carbohydrate (a process called *gluconeogenesis*, literally "creating new glucose") so it can be transported back to muscles and burned as fuel. Protein plays important roles in sports nutrition (muscle maintenance, immune function, production of enzymes, etc.), but those roles don't include being a primary fuel source. Some protein does get broken down for energy, but regardless of exercise intensity, protein contributes only 10 to 15 percent of your total caloric expenditure. As total expenditure increases, the absolute amount of protein you process—and therefore the amount you need to consume—goes up, but protein is not a major source of energy for exercise.

MICRONUTRIENTS

Vitamins and minerals are micronutrients. Although you don't derive energy directly from them or need to consume them in quantities anywhere near as large as macronutrients (hence the name), they are essential for your health and performance because of their roles in producing energy, binding oxygen to red blood cells, maintaining bone density, producing muscle contractions, and more. Because my focus here is sports nutrition for training and competition, in this section I focus on the vitamins and minerals that impact performance most directly.

Micronutrients like calcium, magnesium, zinc, and iron are important. So are vitamins A through K. But during training sessions and competitions you neither lose very much of these micronutrients through sweat nor use very much to keep going. You are, however, eating quite a bit of food to replenish the calories you are expending. Micronutrient consumption, then, is not much of an issue for ultrarunners because you are consuming plenty in the foods you are eating, and you are not losing or using much (relatively speaking) in the course of a training session or even an ultramarathon. In terms of performance, a normally healthy person—someone who does not have a condition causing a micronutrient deficiency—won't really improve performance by focusing on micronutrient intake or supplementation. It's an area that doesn't have a lot of room for optimization; your body is already doing everything that needs to be done.

THE ESSENTIAL ROLES OF FLUIDS

When it comes to sports nutrition for ultraendurance events, fluids are even more important than calories. During exercise, macronutrients have one essential job: to provide energy to working muscles. Water, in contrast, plays a wide variety of roles, and each of them is mission-critical.

CORE TEMPERATURE REGULATION

Regulating your core temperature is water's most obvious role during exercise. As you exercise, some of the energy you burn produces the work that moves you forward, but unfortunately even more energy is wasted as heat. This is the price we pay for our overall lack of efficiency. The problem is that the human body operates properly only within a narrow temperature range, from 95 to 104°F. A lot of the heat generated from exercise has to be dissipated in order to maintain core temperature within the optimal range.

Sweat is the body's primary cooling mechanism, with evaporative cooling carrying heat away from the body. As your core temperature rises, sweat glands all over your body start producing more sweat by drawing in fluid from the space around them and secreting sweat onto the surface of the skin. That fluid gets replaced by fluid from your blood plasma, making your blood volume a major reservoir of potential sweat.

As we'll cover in more detail later in this chapter, the amount of fluid an athlete needs to consume depends largely on sweat rate, which can vary greatly depending on exercise intensity, air temperature, wind conditions, and humidity.

GUT MOTILITY AND DIGESTION

Without enough fluid, you cannot digest food, which means your nutrition strategy is entirely dependent on your hydration status. After food gets broken down in the stomach and travels to the small intestine, the nutrients, fluid, and everything else you want from that food have to be transported through the selective semipermeable membrane that makes up the wall of your intestine. To get carbohydrate from the intestine into the blood, you need to have enough water in the intestine to facilitate the transport. If you don't, the food sits there until enough water becomes available, either because you drink more or because it is pulled from your body into your intestine. This latter mechanism isn't ideal in any circumstance, but it is not a big problem when you are at rest and well hydrated. When you are exercising and pumping sweat onto your skin to cool off, however, your body prioritizes thermoregulation over digestion, and digestion slows dramatically. This is often the tipping point for gastrointestinal distress because once gut motility drops, it can take a long time for it to return to normal, and food that sits in the gut generates gas and is jostled around, leading to pressure, bloating, and a cascade of gastrointestinal issues you want to avoid.

BLOOD VOLUME

You have about 4.5 to 5.5 L of blood in your body, and it never stops moving. Athletes and coaches focus on the blood's role in delivering oxygen to working muscles, but blood also delivers the nutrients your cells need and takes away the waste they produce. It carries heat away from the core to the extremities and skin in order to maintain a healthy body temperature. And blood plasma provides the fluid that ends up being excreted as sweat. One of the key responses to training and acclimatization to heat and/or altitude is an increase in blood plasma volume. It's your body's way of filling the reservoir to be prepared for the anticipated activity and environment.

When you run low on fluids and plasma volume drops, your body starts prioritizing how to use what's left. In cold temperatures or in a cold summer rainstorm at high elevation, athletes with a better hydration status stay warmer longer.

Dehydration hastens the onset of hypothermia. When it's hot outside and your plasma volume gets a little low, your resting and exercise heart rates increase. Your heart has to pump faster to deliver the same amount of oxygen using less fluid. When plasma volume gets even lower, your body prioritizes sweating over digestion, and if the situation gets dire, it prioritizes oxygen delivery over sweating, and you end up with heatstroke.

WASTE REMOVAL

Removal of metabolic waste products is another crucial role for fluids. This is of particular importance to ultrarunners because of the amount of muscle damage sustained during 50- and 100-mile events. The kidneys filter waste products out of your blood and excrete them in urine. With mild dehydration, your urine production diminishes, and the color of your urine starts to darken. More severe dehydration can damage your kidneys and alter the pH of your blood.

DAY-TO-DAY HYDRATION STATUS

Fluid and electrolyte replenishment during exercise is heavily dependent on sweat rate and temperature. Fluid loss can range from 500 ml/hour to more than 2 L/hour, and electrolyte loss is greatly influenced by the composition of your sweat. Recommendations for fluid and sodium intake become far more complex during training and ultradistance competitions. I will cover those issues in more depth later in this chapter, but to start, let's examine recommendations that will help you stay well hydrated on a day-to-day basis.

Dehydration is often evaluated based on body weight. But many athletes don't realize they start their day or their workout already dehydrated, so a 2 percent loss of body weight during your workout may not be truly 2 percent dehydration, but perhaps 4 percent dehydration if you started the day already low on body fluid.

Researchers Cheuvront and Sawka (2005) devised a simple Venn diagram that is useful for evaluating day-to-day hydration status (Figure 10.1). To use the diagram, you need to evaluate three things immediately after waking up: your weight (W), urine color (U), and thirst (T). If only one observation suggests dehydra-

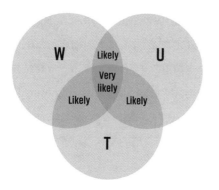

FIGURE **10.1** *The WUT diagram helps you monitor your daily hydration status and the likelihood of dehydration*

Source: Cheuvront and Sawka 2005

tion but the other two are normal, dehydration is less likely. If two observations indicate dehydration, the condition is more likely. And if all three indicate dehydration, you're very likely to be dehydrated.

First, how thirsty are you? When you are low on body fluid, your body responds with the sensation of thirst. Although there is wide variability from person to person, research suggests dehydration of about 2 percent of body weight is associated with the sensation of thirst (Kenefick et al. 2012). Next comes urine color. The color of your urine is a common ballpark measure of urine concentration. Clear to straw-colored urine is not suggestive of dehydration, but be careful not to automatically equate clear urine with ideal hydration. Urine will often be clear if you are hyperhydrated or hyponatremic, too. If your urine is the color of apple juice or darker, it is suggestive of dehydration. This color observation should also be from your urine stream or collection cup rather than from diluted urine in a toilet bowl. After urinating, weigh yourself without clothing. From day to day, your weight should remain virtually unchanged. Even if you are gradually gaining or losing weight due to changes in fat or muscle mass, those changes will be very small within a 24-hour period. A loss of 1 to 2 percent of body weight between one day and the next is more indicative of a change in total body fluid.

If two of the three or all three of these indices for evaluating body fluid indicate dehydration, then you have not done an adequate job of replenishing fluid losses over the preceding 24 hours. This doesn't necessarily mean you didn't drink enough during the previous day's workout. It also doesn't mean drinking a ton of fluid in the evening is the solution (that will increase first-morning urine volume and likely lighten its color, but much of that fluid is likely to pass right through you). It more likely means your overall daily fluid intake was inadequate to replenish losses from exercise, thermoregulation during normal activities (sitting outside on a warm day, working in a warm office, etc.), respiration, and water loss due to normal bodily function.

It's typically not a big issue if the WUT diagram indicates minor dehydration one day here and there, nor does one day of minor dehydration necessitate major changes in your habits. It is best to use the WUT diagram over a rolling three-day period. If you are consistently seeing indications of diminished hydration status over two or three days, you should make adjustments to your overall daily hydration habits. This often happens when athletes increase their training load, travel to a warmer climate or elevation, or experience a change in weather or seasons. The typical solution is to increase water consumption throughout the day rather than simply guzzling a large volume of water to counter the indications of dehydration. It is also important to use the recommendations later in this chapter to make sure you're consuming adequate fluids during training sessions.

If you can prevent two of the three indices or all three from indicating dehydration, you are starting your day in a better position to maintain ideal body fluid for the rest of the day. You are also more likely to start your workout with adequate body fluid so that a 2 percent weight loss during a run is an actual 2 percent body weight loss due to dehydration, not a net 4 percent body weight loss because you started the day and the workout already 2 percent down from day-to-day dehydration.

SPORTS NUTRITION GUIDELINES FOR RUNNING

The three primary substances you can ingest before, during, and after running to support your activity level are calories, fluid, and electrolytes. More specifically, within these categories, it is most important to ingest carbohydrate, water, and sodium, which, when you distill sports nutrition to its essence, are the three consumables that make or break athletic performance. The key is to figure out how much you need of each, when you need them, and how to get them.

The vast majority of your training runs will be shorter than 4 hours. Certainly your long runs will be longer than this if you are training for a 50-miler or 100-miler, but even preparing for these distances, your weekday interval runs are going to be in this 1- to 4-hour range. To have a high-quality training session, you have to start out properly fueled and well hydrated. The sports nutrition recommendations for training sessions of this duration are similar to those for the entire duration of your ultramarathon; if you can master your nutrition and hydration strategies for training runs, you are well on your way to mastering them for ultramarathons.

POSTWORKOUT NUTRITION

I like to start the discussion of nutrition with postworkout recommendations because they are a lot more important than the recommendations for what to do immediately before a training session.

In terms of carbohydrate, you want to start workouts and competitions with full glycogen stores. You can store about 1,600 to 2,000 calories of glycogen in your muscles and liver, with a bit more circulating in your blood. This carbohydrate energy will be burned alongside fat and a bit of protein in muscle cells as you exercise, but of the three, it is the only one you can realistically deplete during a single bout of exercise, and it will certainly be depleted during an ultramarathon.

Fortunately, it is relatively easy to ensure your glycogen stores are topped off before your next workout. Your body is primed to replenish muscle glycogen stores most rapidly within the first 30 to 60 minutes following exercise, and the sooner the better. During this period, known as the *glycogen window*, there literally are more gates or "windows" open to allow sugar to enter muscle cells. Consuming sodium after a workout helps replenish sodium lost in sweat, but it also plays an important role in transporting carbohydrate out of the gut and into the bloodstream. And of course, fluid is important for replacing the water that evaporated off your skin to keep you from overheating. This is why many athletes start postworkout replenishment with a carbohydrate-rich recovery drink. These specially formulated mixtures contain the three components you need most: carbohydrate, sodium, and fluid. Perhaps most important, these drinks are easy to consume so that you start getting nutrients into the system faster.

In terms of total amounts, your goal *within the first two hours* after exercising should be to consume 500 to 700 mg of sodium and enough water to equal 1.5 times the water weight you lost during the exercise session. In other words, if you lost 2 pounds (32 ounces) during your workout, you should drink 48 ounces of fluid in the 2 hours after you get back. *Within four hours after training*, you should consume 1.5 g of carbohydrate per kilogram (g/kg) of body weight. For a 70-kg (154-pound) athlete, 1.5 g/kg means 105 g of carbohydrate. That can be quite a challenge, especially when you add in the protein and fat calories that come with that carbohydrate, and obviously it becomes even more challenging for heavier athletes. That's why this recommendation applies to a 4-hour period. Ideally you should consume the first 50 to 60 g of that carbohydrate within the first 30 to 60 minutes so you can take advantage of the glycogen window, but the rate of glycogen replenishment doesn't magically go to zero after 60 minutes.

MEASUREMENTS: IMPERIAL VERSUS METRIC

At times in this book I use imperial units (feet of elevation, miles of distance), and at other times I use metric units (VO_2 expressed as milliliters per kilogram per minute or energy expenditure expressed as 1 calorie per kilogram per kilometer). In this chapter I will be using grams per kilogram to describe the amounts of a nutrient to consume based on your body weight. Why not stick with either imperial or metric throughout? I'm walking the fine line between using common terms for a US audience and correctly representing data used in the sports science and sports nutrition professions. It wouldn't make sense to translate grams per kilogram into ounces per pound or to create an imperial version of VO_2max values. As you read this chapter, there will be some sample conversions from kilograms to pounds. To determine your weight in kilograms, divide your weight in pounds by 2.2.

The glycogen window is important, but it is also important to keep replenishment in perspective. We used to think immediate postworkout consumption of carbohydrate was absolutely crucial for maximizing glycogen replenishment. While it is a good idea to get started with replenishment in the first hour because muscle cells are very receptive to taking in carbohydrate, glycogen replenishment will reach 100 percent within 24 hours after exercise regardless. During a period when you are training once a day for 1 to 4 hours, you won't need to take dramatic or inconvenient steps to fully replenish glycogen stores before your next workout. I mention this because many athletes gorge themselves on huge postworkout meals because they look back over the hours they've just spent running and overestimate both the calories they need and the urgency to replenish them immediately.

As you move through the rest of your day, aim to consume about 60 to 65 percent of your total calories from carbohydrate, 13 to 15 percent from protein, and 20 to 25 percent from fat. For a 70-kg athlete consuming about 2,500 calories/day, this comes out to a total of about 6.0 g/kg of carbohydrate (420 g), about 1.2 g/kg of protein (84 g), and about 1 g/kg of fat (70 g).

DURING-WORKOUT NUTRITION

The goal of sports nutrition during a workout or event is to supply your body with the energy, fluid, and electrolytes necessary for optimal performance. Consuming too little of any of them leads to underperformance, and consuming too much will generally lead to gastric distress, which in turns hinders performance.

The recommendations from the American College of Sports Medicine (ACSM) provide a good starting point. They specify consuming 60 to 90 g of carbohydrate and 500 to 700 mg of sodium per hour, and enough fluid to avoid weight loss greater than 2 percent of your body weight. While these recommendations provide a good starting point, they need to be adapted for ultrarunners. In particular, for training and events in hotter temperatures where fluid intake is high, 500 to 700 mg of sodium per hour might be inadequate. Later in this chapter, I describe an exercise we commonly do at our running camps to further individualize these recommendations.

Carbohydrate

The recommendation to consume 60 to 90 g/hour of carbohydrate is based on the fact you are able to absorb and utilize about 1 g of exogenous carbohydrate per minute during exercise; with training and a combination of carbohydrate sources (different types of sugar), you may be able to increase this to about 1.4 g/min, or about 84 g/hour. Consuming more carbohydrate than you can effectively utilize can lead to gastric distress because too much carbohydrate remains in the gut, and with the reduced gut motility commonly experienced from reduced blood flow to the intestines during exercise, bacteria in the intestine act on that excess carbohydrate and create gas, which leads to bloating and nausea.

However, this recommended carbohydrate intake fails to take into account either your weight or your energy expenditure. Lighter athletes who are exercising at relatively low intensities may not need even 60 g/hour, and even heavier athletes who are working at light intensity levels may not need 90 g/hour. A better way to determine your hourly carbohydrate needs is to consume 30 to 40 percent of your hourly energy expenditure. Using our previous example of a 70-kg midpack runner maintaining a pace of 9:00 min/mi and burning approximately 12 to 13 calories/min, hourly expenditure would be 720 to 780 calories/hour. (To determine your individual burn rate, see "How to Determine Your Caloric Burn Rate," page 189.) Thirty to 40 percent replenishment at this intensity would equal 216 to 312 calories, or 54 to 78 g/hr. It is also important to note that exogenous carbohydrate replenishment is only necessary during workouts lasting more than 60 to 75 minutes. For shorter training sessions, you have enough stored carbohydrate to fuel even the highest-intensity VO_2max workout.

Fluid Consumption

In addition to making sure you're consuming enough calories to support your workouts, you also have to make sure your fluid intake is adequate. The easiest way to determine whether your fluid consumption is keeping up with your fluid losses is to weigh yourself without clothing before and after your workouts (excluding long runs). Any weight you lose during this time is due to fluid loss. Although

CALORIES IN YOUR POCKET, HYDRATION IN YOUR BOTTLES

What should be in your bottles during workouts: water or a high-carbohydrate/ electrolyte sports drink? For the vast majority, a high-carbohydrate drink is not necessary. While high-carbohydrate drinks have a place in sports nutrition, separating calories from hydration is a better and more versatile strategy. What's in your bottle or hydration pack should serve the purpose of hydration, and the food in your pocket should serve the purpose of fueling. As workload and temperature change, your fluid and calorie needs change independently. When it is hot, you need more fluid per hour, sometimes twice as much as during a cool run. This often happens during the course of an ultramarathon where you start in the cool morning and run through the heat of the day. If your fluids contain 35 g or more of carbohydrate per 20-ounce serving, you'll consume 35 g if you drink one bottle and 70 g per hour if you drink two bottles. That's at the top end of the recommended range of 60 to 90 g of carbohydrate. Any further calories can lead to gastric distress. Even worse, after the first bottle and 35 g of carbohydrate, you may not feel like drinking because you intuit that you don't need or want more carbohydrate. So you delay drinking and start digging a dehydration hole that can take hours to recover from. Remember, you can come back from a caloric deficit easily and within minutes by eating. Returning to normal hydration status takes much longer, and being dehydrated during that time can have more deleterious effects on your performance.

Separating calories from hydration allows you to ratchet up fluid intake in response to high temperatures and dial it back in cooler conditions without greatly affecting your calorie supply. It also allows you to vary carbohydrate sources more easily because they are not tied to what you are drinking. This is important because your food choices can supply a large amount of the sodium you need to replenish. In many cases you can consume the recommended amount of sodium entirely through food sources while drinking plain water.

there is some evidence that athletes can lose 2 percent or more of their body weight due to dehydration with no decline in performance, and in some cases with an increase in competitive performance due to reduced body weight, in training there is no benefit to exceeding 2 percent weight loss during workouts.

A good starting point for fluid intake is to consume a full handheld bottle (20 ounces) per hour. If you are exercising in the heat, you will need to increase this, potentially to two or more bottles per hour, at which point a hydration pack is a far more convenient option.

Over the years, the notion of a 2 percent loss of body weight negatively impacting performance has become almost ubiquitous. I even included a table in Chapter 4 that referenced this range (Table 4.3, page 71). It is definitely a good rule of thumb, but the duration of ultrarunning events and the extreme temperature swings experienced during 15–30-hour events mean that losing more than 2 percent of body weight may be inevitable and not as detrimental as it would be in shorter, higher-intensity events. Skin temperature is moderated mainly by air temperature, whereas core temperature is moderated more by workload. When skin temperature is low and/or core temperature is not elevated, dehydration of up to 4 percent of body weight may not hinder endurance performance. That's not to say it's going to improve performance or that this level of dehydration should be a goal. But it does provide perspective for ultrarunners, who are very likely to lose at least 2 to 4 percent of body weight during an ultramarathon, who may run a significant portion of their event in cool nighttime temperatures, and who maintain a relatively low intensity level throughout. If everything else is normal—you're eating, clearheaded, not suffering from nausea—a 3 to 5 percent loss of body weight may not be ideal, but in the last third of your event it may be inevitable and in itself not necessarily a cause for great concern.

FROM MOUTH TO BLOODSTREAM

It is easy to get too caught up in trying to determine the ideal formula of a sports drink or the perfect ratio of carbohydrate to electrolyte. What many people overlook is that whatever you ingest gets combined in the stomach, and how it combines determines how quickly it gets into the small intestine, which determines how quickly it gets into your bloodstream. This is particularly important for ultrarunners because long runs require frequent fueling from varied sources over many hours. The properties of an individual drink or food are less relevant than having a broader understanding of how carbohydrate, fluid, and electrolytes get from your mouth to your bloodstream.

From Stomach to Intestine

One of the primary roles of the stomach is to prepare food and fluid for entry into the small intestine. Your stomach doesn't just break food down from a mashed solid to a liquidy slurry; it will hold on to that slurry until the mixture has the right chemical balance before opening the gates to the intestine. The rate at which this happens is called *gastric emptying*, and as an athlete you want that process to be rapid.

A few things slow gastric emptying, including highly concentrated foods or solutions (think energy gel or highly concentrated sports drink). These concentrated carbohydrates sit in your stomach until enough fluid is available to dilute the mixture, which is why it is imperative to consume 8 ounces of water with an energy gel.

Taking in too much food and/or fluid can also slow gastric emptying. To a point, increased volume in the stomach accelerates gastric emptying, and you can train your system to go faster. However, even with training there is a limit, which is why consuming smaller volumes of fluid a few times per hour is preferable to guzzling the entire amount needed once an hour. When you overload your system, gastric emptying can't keep up, and you get a sloshing belly.

Absorption from the Intestine

Once the things you've eaten get to the small intestine, it's time to get them into the bloodstream! As with other systems in the body, there are several processes going on at the same time.

The wall of your intestine is a selective, semipermeable membrane, and water and other materials can pass through it in a number of ways. Some things move from the inside of the intestine into the cells of the intestinal wall and then out the other side to the interstitial space between the intestinal wall and the capillaries carrying blood. Other things squeeze between the cells of your intestinal wall into this same interstitial space. When you consume plain water, you are likely to have a low-concentration solution in your intestine, meaning there's a bunch of fluid and not that much stuff dissolved in it. In contrast, the fluid in the interstitial space on the other side of the intestinal wall has a lot of stuff in it. The overall amount of stuff dissolved in a fluid is referred to as its osmolality; in this scenario, the fluid in the interstitial space has a higher osmolality than the fluid in the intestine. Water travels through a semipermeable membrane from an area of low osmolality to an area of high osmolality (it seeks to dilute the high-concentration area). Practically, this means water moves from the intestine to the interstitial space through the spaces between the cells of your intestinal wall, which is what you want (see Figure 10.2).

Whereas water moves passively through the intestinal wall, carbohydrate has to be actively transported. You have distinct channels for different types of sugar: glucose uses door 1, sucrose goes through door 2, and so forth. This is important for endurance athletes because it means you can take in energy faster when you consume multiple sources of sugar. Think of it as being like trying to get into a football stadium: Fewer doors mean longer lines and more waiting; more doors

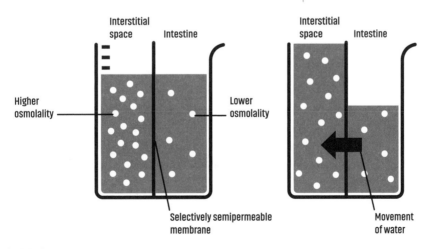

FIGURE 10.2 *How water moves through a semipermeable membrane from an area of lower osmolality to higher osmolality*

Source: Illustrated by Charlie Layton

mean less waiting. Another benefit to the active transport of sugar is that sugar drags water with it, creating a second method for water to move from the intestine into the interstitial space.

There are also passive and active methods for getting sodium from the intestine to the interstitial space. Like water, sodium can be moved passively through the small spaces between the cells of your intestinal wall. But there are also two active transport methods for sodium. The first is a cotransport with carbohydrate. The cells in your small intestine have "gates" that enable cotransport of sugar and sodium together (one glucose molecule and two sodium ions) from the intestine into the cell of the intestinal wall. As a result, sodium and carbohydrate move into the bloodstream more quickly when they are present together, which is why even low-calorie electrolyte-rich sports drinks contain some sugar.

Once in the cell, glucose and sodium go their separate ways. Both end up in the interstitial space, but sodium uses a second active transport method: the sodium-potassium pump, which utilizes energy to pump three molecules of sodium out of the cell and bring two molecules of potassium in from the outside. The sodium-potassium pump is crucial because you are actively moving sodium from an area of low sodium concentration (inside the cell) to an area of higher concentration (the interstitial space), which is the opposite of what would happen normally. This movement of sodium further increases the osmolality of the interstitial fluid, which in turn draws more water from the intestine.

Getting into the Bloodstream

With all these passive and active methods moving fluid, carbohydrate, and sodium from the intestine into the interstitial space, the pressure in that space increases. At this point the pressure gradient becomes the active driver. The water in the space could go two ways: back to the interior of the intestine or forward into the bloodstream. The capillary membrane on the bloodstream side of the space is more permeable than the tighter membrane on the intestinal side. Because water moves from an area of higher pressure to lower pressure, it moves through the capillary membrane into the bloodstream, taking the sodium and carbohydrate with it.

WHAT THE HECK IS IN MY SPORTS DRINK?

A sports drink is essentially water with stuff dissolved in it. Some drinks have lots of different kinds of stuff dissolved in them, most of which just waste space. There is only so much room to dissolve solutes in a drink, and drinks with fewer ingredients can use more of that room for important things such as carbohydrate and sodium. The simplest drinks are the best because they are easiest on the gut and facilitate the transport of sugar and electrolyte across the semipermeable membrane of the intestinal wall better and faster.

The concentration of sports drinks is important. When you change the osmolality of the fluid (the total molecular concentration of everything in the drink—carbohydrate, electrolyte, flavoring, additives—per unit volume), it changes how the drink influences the overall mixture in your stomach, and hence how that mixture makes it into the intestine. Sports drinks are formulated to optimize the absorption of carbohydrate, fluid, and electrolyte. If the osmolality of the sports drink is too high because of a bunch of additives, it may contribute to slower gastric emptying. When the osmolality of sports drinks is lower, it is more likely to contribute to faster gastric emptying (depending on what else you're eating and drinking), and if it's being consumed on an empty stomach, it is formulated to get into the intestine quickly.

If you are designing a sports drink to have a relatively low osmolality but you want it to deliver moderate to high amounts of sodium and/or carbohydrate, you have to eliminate other stuff to make room. That's a big part of the reason we've seen drink manufacturers shift to drinks with shorter ingredient lists.

The ingredients, primarily sugar, sodium, potassium, and flavoring, are in the drink for good reason. Putting electrolytes and flavoring into a fluid makes you want to drink more frequently and consume more fluid each time you drink. There's actually a lot more to the way your sports drink tastes than marketing mumbo jumbo. A lightly flavored drink is preferable to a stronger one   >

because when you consume half a bottle in one long slug, the stronger-tasting drink becomes overwhelming and you stop drinking. A drink that tastes almost watered down when you are at rest will taste just about right when you are running. This is why athletes have long diluted commercial sports drinks like original Gatorade, which these days are often flavored to appeal to convenience store customers instead of athletes.

Even taste components and mouth feel are important. A slightly tart drink will encourage you to drink more than an overly sweet one, and citrus flavors also increase the drive to drink. It should be no surprise, then, that almost every drink company has some version of lemon-lime and/or orange in its product line. In addition to the flavor, a sports drink needs to clear the mouth well. When a drink leaves a film in your mouth, as is often the case with overly sweet drinks, it's not only unpleasant, but you're not likely to drink again soon.

Rather than dilute sports drinks, it is better to find a drink with a lighter taste so you can comfortably consume it at full strength. The reason you don't want to dilute heavily flavored commercial sports drinks isn't really because doing so lowers the concentration of sugar in the drink but because it reduces the sodium concentration. Again, this is relative to all the other foods and fluids you are consuming, but if you are consuming a sports drink with the primary goal of staying hydrated—that is, maintaining proper fluid and electrolyte levels—then consuming a watered-down drink provides a lot of fluid and reduced sodium, which over time could contribute to inadequate sodium replenishment in relation to fluid intake.

As we discuss the ingredients of sports drinks (see the sidebar "What the Heck Is in My Sports Drink?"), recommended foods for race day, and the balance of hydration status and sodium levels (later in this chapter), understanding these mouth-to-bloodstream pathways helps you make decisions about the drinks and foods you're consuming.

Making Sure You're Getting It Right

There's a simple way you can make sure your carbohydrate, fluid, and electrolyte intake is on target during workouts. An exercise I use at ultrarunning camps is to have athletes hold on to the wrappers from everything they consume during a 4-hour endurance run. After the run, we lay them all out and record the following for each item: carbohydrate calories, milligrams of electrolytes, and milliliters of fluid.

After tallying up everything you have consumed, do some simple math. You are aiming for consumption of 600 to 800 mg of sodium per liter of fluid consumed and a total of about 30 to 40 percent replenishment of total caloric expenditure in carbohydrate calories. Why 600 to 800 mg of sodium per liter of fluid consumed? While the ACSM recommends 500 to 700 mg of sodium *per hour,* it did not have ultramarathoners specifically in mind when determining this recommendation. Calibrating your sodium intake in conjunction with your fluid intake allows you to drink more or less depending on the conditions and maintain the proper ratio of sodium to fluid needed to replace what is lost during the activity. Quite simply, if it's hotter, you need more fluid *and* sodium.

An example of this, detailed in Table 10.1, is a 70-kg runner returning from a 34-km (approximately 4-hour) run, having consumed 2.1 liters of fluid as well as two gels, two bars, and three sleeves of Bonk Breaker drink mix. Looking at all the empty wrappers, we see that this intake adds up to 734 calories from carbohydrate and 1,320 mg of sodium. Using the formula of 1 calorie/kg/km, you can calculate

TABLE 10.1 Tallying Up Carbohydrate, Sodium, and Fluid

FOOD/FLUID	CARBOHYDRATE CALORIES	SODIUM (MG)	FLUID (ML)
2 × Carb Boom gel	220	100	0
2 × Bonk Breaker bar (whole bar)	304	320	0
3 × Bonk Breaker RealHydration mix, single-serve sleeve	210	900	1,800
Water bottle	0	0	300
Totals	734	1,320	2,100

Total calories burned on run: 2,400
Percent of expenditure replaced: 734/2,400 = 31%
1,320 mg Na/2.1L = 629 mg Na/L

that the run cost approximately 2,400 calories. Consuming 734 carbohydrate calories during the run means replenishing 734/2,400, or 31 percent of energy expenditure. Consuming 1,320 mg of sodium and 2.1 L of fluid leads to 629 mg of sodium per liter of fluid. All of these are in the recommended ranges.

PREWORKOUT NUTRITION

The most important aspect of the last full meal you eat before a training session is to ensure that it's out of your stomach and digested before you start training. This is especially important for interval workouts because higher-intensity efforts tend to be downright unpleasant on a full stomach. A relatively light meal that's rich in carbohydrate (preferably about 70 percent of total calories) is a good choice because meals that contain a lot of fat or protein stay in the stomach longer and are digested more slowly. That's a good thing if you're trying to feel full longer, but it's not good if you're about to go out for a hard workout. Examples of good meal choices are pasta, a turkey sandwich, or oatmeal with fruit.

When it comes to your preworkout or pre-race meal, a good rule of thumb is that meal size should get smaller the closer to the workout or race you get. For instance, you can consume 1.5 g of carbohydrate per kilogram of body weight when your final preworkout meal is three hours before your run (Table 10.2), but keep it closer to 1 g/kg if you're going to train two hours after your last significant

TABLE **10.2**	Recommended Grams of Carbohydrate per Kilogram of Body Weight in Last Significant Preworkout Meal			
BODY WEIGHT (KG)	**3–4 HOURS PRIOR**	**2–3 HOURS PRIOR**	**1–2 HOURS PRIOR**	**0–60 MINUTES PRIOR**
	(1.5–2.0 g/kg)	(1.0–1.5 g/kg)	(0.5–1.0 g/kg)	(0.25–0.5 g/kg)
55 (121 lb.)	83–110	55–83	28–55	14–28
60 (132 lb.)	90–120	60–90	30–60	15–30
65 (143 lb.)	98–130	65–98	33–65	16–33
70 (154 lb.)	105–140	70–105	35–70	18–35
75 (165 lb.)	113–150	75–113	38–75	19–38
80 (176 lb.)	120–160	80–120	40–80	20–40
85 (187 lb.)	128–170	85–128	43–85	21–43

JASON KOOP'S SECRET RICE BALLS

One of the greatest truths about sports nutrition is that even the best foods are useless if they stay in your pocket. You have to put those calories, electrolytes, and fluids into your body for them to do you any good. That means you have to like how they taste, how they smell, how they feel in your mouth, and how easy they are to unwrap and get down your throat. When I was a novice endurance athlete, I loved Krispy Kreme doughnuts, and one of my early experiments in sports nutrition was to cram three or four into a sandwich bag and squeeze them out a torn corner, as you would a carbohydrate gel. My tastes and my cooking skills have improved since then, and I developed two variations of a rice ball that meet the during-workout and during-competition nutrition guidelines in this chapter and have the taste, texture, and convenience characteristics that make them a go-to favorite for several of my athletes.

Bacon and Egg Rice Balls

MAKES ABOUT 12 RICE BALLS

2 eggs

2 strips bacon

1½ cups uncooked basmati rice

2 oz. grated Parmesan cheese

Salt to taste

1. Cook the rice.
2. Scramble and cook the eggs.
3. Cook the bacon. Drain excess fat and chop.
4. Combine rice, eggs, bacon, cheese, and salt in a large mixing bowl.
5. Scoop small portions into sandwich bags and tie the ends off.

Per ball: Calories: 133 / Carbohydrate: 18 g / Protein: 4 g / Fat: 5 g / Sodium: 354 mg

Sweet and Salty Rice Balls (vegetarian)

MAKES ABOUT 12 RICE BALLS

2 eggs

1½ cups uncooked basmati rice

2 Tbsp. honey

1 Tbsp. soy sauce

1. Cook the rice.
2. Scramble and cook the eggs.
3. Combine rice, eggs, honey, and soy sauce in a large mixing bowl.
4. Scoop small portions into sandwich bags and tie the ends off.

Per ball: Calories: 115 / Carbohydrate: 20 g / Protein: 2 g / Fat: 3 g / Sodium: 327 mg

meal. And you shouldn't try to fill your daily fiber requirement at this time. The American Heart Association recommends 25 to 30 g of fiber a day to reduce LDL cholesterol (the bad kind) and lower the risk of heart disease, but fiber slows digestion, so it's better saved for other meals.

Preworkout Snack

Preworkout snacks don't supply the bulk of the energy or hydration you'll utilize during your workout; rather, that comes from the nutrition choices you made during the 18 to 24 hours between your last run and today's training session. But your preworkout snack can have a big impact on how you feel. Eat the right things, and you'll feel strong, invigorated, and energized. Eat the wrong things, and you'll feel bloated, sluggish, and nauseated; it's hard to have a great workout when you feel like you're carrying a bowling ball in your gut.

The key is to choose foods that will get out of your gut and into your blood quickly. There are many choices available, and it's important to experiment with various combinations until you find a solution that doesn't come back up halfway through your workout. As you can see in the following list, many snack combinations provide 50 to 75 g of carbohydrate and would work in the hour leading up to training. You can easily bring this down to 40 to 60 g by using smaller portions. Regardless of the option you choose, it's imperative that you also consume 16 to 24 ounces of fluid, be it water or a sports drink, in the hour before training.

- 1 cup vanilla yogurt + ½ cup Grape-Nuts + 2 tablespoons raisins
- 1 cup vanilla yogurt + 1 cup fresh fruit
- 1 cup juice + 1 banana
- 1 slice banana nut bread + 1 cup skim milk
- 1 energy bar + 8 ounces sports drink
- Smoothie: 2 cups skim or soy milk + 1½ cups mango or berries + 2 tablespoons soy protein
- 1½ cups multigrain cereal + 1½ cups skim milk
- 1 bagel + 1 banana + 1 tablespoon nut butter
- 1 cup cottage cheese + 8 whole wheat crackers + 1 apple

Commercial sports nutrition products like bars, gels, and sports drinks are also good options for a preworkout snack, especially in terms of convenience. Because they are designed for rapid absorption, you are likely to fully digest the carbohydrates in a gel, bar, or sports drink and have all that energy available for your muscles. To aid in the digestion and absorption process, make sure you consume at least 8 ounces of fluid any time you eat a gel or bar. In terms of carbohydrate content, a bottle of sports drink, for example, may have 22 g of carbohydrate, a Carb Boom energy gel has 25 g, half a Bonk Breaker bar has 19 g, and a serving of Bonk Breaker energy chews has 24 g. For a 70-kg runner, a bottle of sports drink and half a Bonk Breaker bar provide about 41 g of carbohydrate, or 0.58 g/kg, which falls in the correct range if our runner is one to two hours away from a workout.

ADAPTING SPORTS NUTRITION GUIDELINES FOR ULTRARUNNING EVENTS

Using the recommendations and strategies discussed here, most ultrarunners can consistently fuel their workouts and maintain a good hydration status in training. It is during events that nutrition and hydration strategies frequently go off the rails. Gastrointestinal distress is the number one reason athletes fail to finish, and even athletes with in-depth knowledge and experience with the nutrition challenges of ultramarathons get knocked out of events by dehydration and upset stomachs.

ULTRA-SPECIFIC CHALLENGES OF ULTRA DISTANCE EVENTS

One of my colleagues at CTS boiled the ultramarathoner's nutrition strategy down to this: Develop the ability to simultaneously run and eat as much as you can without barfing. While that is a drastic oversimplification of the goals and challenges of fueling yourself through an ultramarathon, it is nonetheless true. It is especially true at the 100-mile distance, where caloric expenditure far exceeds the body's stored carbohydrate levels. You have to consume a lot of calories and a lot of fluid over the course of many hours in order to finish an ultramarathon, and you have to overcome several challenges that competitors in shorter events do not face.

Prolonged Exposure to the Elements

Challenge. The simple fact of being outdoors, awake, and on your feet for many, many hours creates a nutritional challenge. Athletes in shorter events can eat a pre-race meal, consume calories and fluid to support their energy expenditure and thermoregulation needs, and then finish their event before needing another meal. They can deplete their energy stores faster and dig deeper into their reserves because post-race replenishment is only a few hours away. They can even race themselves into significant dehydration and gastrointestinal distress and reach the finish line before experiencing a significant decline in performance. Ultradistance competitors cannot be so cavalier or take as many risks because the duration and distance of the event will force them to deal with the consequences well before they reach the finish line.

Adaptation. Ultramarathon runners must develop the ability to consume and digest a steady stream of calories over the course of many hours. Some of those calories need to be from solid foods with more bulk, more fat, and more protein than carbohydrate-only foods like gels and sports drinks. While the nutritional focus needs to be primarily on fueling with carbohydrate calories, it is important to realize your race foods are also taking the place of meals during longer events. Fat and protein are satiating, meaning they stave off feelings of hunger better than carbohydrate does. If you respond to feelings of hunger by overconsuming carbohydrate, you increase the likelihood of gastric distress. By incorporating solid foods containing fat and protein, you can continue to base your carbohydrate intake on your caloric expenditure rather than on a growling stomach.

Long Distances/Times Between Aid Stations

Challenge. Major urban marathons have aid stations nearly every mile. That's 20 or more aid stations in 26 miles, with food and fluids available at the finish line. At the Western States 100-Mile Endurance Run, there are 21 aid stations in 100 miles, with distances between stations ranging from 5 to 7 miles in the first third of the race and from 3 to 4 miles in the final third. Depending on your pace and the terrain, that can mean well over an hour between aid stations. If you have trouble between aid stations that causes you to stop, that time can increase dramatically.

Adaptation. With long distances between aid stations, you will require gear that allows you to fuel along the way. Train with the gear you plan to use on race day. If you rarely run with a hydration pack in training and then have to run with one during a 100-miler, it may become uncomfortable and a constant source of annoyance. The same goes for hydration bottles or that fuel belt you just picked up online. Some races mandate required gear that you must carry at all times. Make sure you can fit it into your pack, that the pack is still comfortable, and that you can run effectively when fully loaded. If you will have pacers or support crews in aid stations, make sure they know how to quickly and efficiently refill your pack so you don't have to stop and wait.

Dramatic Changes in Environmental Conditions

Challenge. If your event starts in the dark and proceeds through an entire day and into the night, and perhaps into the following morning, you are going to experience dramatic shifts in environmental conditions. Ultramarathon runners can face temperature swings of 40 or more degrees and high-altitude rain or snowstorms (even in summer). These changes greatly impact your sweat rate and your perceptions of hunger and thirst.

Adaptation. Use your equipment to minimize changes in your core temperature due to changes in environmental conditions. If it's going to get hotter, you want to take steps to stay cool: Wear lighter clothing, remove layers, soak your clothing, drink cool beverages, and so forth. If it is going to get colder, use your equipment to stay warm, such as by wearing more layers and swapping wet clothing for dry clothing. In both situations, you need to stay hydrated. As weather changes, be aware of changes in your sweat rate because that directly impacts your hydration strategy. As temperatures climb and sweat rate increases, you need to anticipate this and start consuming more fluid. The longer you wait, the more behind you get in hydration status. In cold weather, your sweat rate will decline; it's important to recognize that and reduce fluid intake to avoid overhydration. If you are behind in hydration already, you can also take advantage of cooler temperatures to gradually get back on track in terms of hydration status. If you anticipate dramatic changes in temperature during your event, know your sweat rate for a variety of temperature ranges. Dramatic environmental changes also disrupt your routine and strategy. You may forget to eat as you struggle through a thunderstorm or focus on staying warm through the predawn hours. This is where practice and a knowledgeable support crew can be invaluable.

General Fatigue and Diminished Decision-Making Ability

Challenge. When you are very tired, you make decisions you would never make in a less fatigued state. You might leave an aid station without refilling a hydration pack. You might zone out and not consume anything for miles. You might scrap your nutrition plan entirely and scarf down enough cookies to make you sick. I've seen all these things and many more, all caused by extreme fatigue.

Adaptation. Habits and routines pay huge dividends for an ultradistance competitor. Develop habits that are consistent from everyday training sessions to your longest races, so they become ingrained to the point you stick to them even when you are unbelievably fatigued. Develop a routine you use every time you pick up your hydration pack: Check for water, standard food choices, and standard equipment (like a rain shell). Make sure you at least have your bull's-eye foods (more on that in a later section) with you whenever you leave an aid station. Keep these routines simple and minimal; you don't have to have everything all the time, but you always need to have something to eat, something to drink, and something to protect yourself from the elements. Dakota Jones's story (see sidebar, page 218) illustrates the concept well. When you are fatigued and in the heat of battle, have a routine. If you don't . . .

Food Fatigue

Consuming small amounts of food and fluids over and over again during the course of many hours is exhausting. Many athletes reach a point where they don't want to expend the effort required to eat or they no longer have a taste for the food options available. This is rarely a problem in shorter events because less food is needed to complete the race. As a result, athletes competing in shorter events can utilize a narrower range of food options, whereas ultradistance athletes typically need to find a wider range of foods they are willing to eat and that work for them without causing stomach upset. I have spent so much time working through the challenge of food fatigue with athletes that I have developed a specific strategy to deal with it.

The bull's-eye nutrition strategy. During training, particularly during the longer runs, I have athletes experiment with different—and sometimes counterintuitive—foods to help them reach their target calorie ranges. Foods that work are easy to open

///// DAKOTA JONES THE TIME I ATE A LOT OF SALT

There is hot debate in the world of sports science about whether or not salt has anything to do with cramping during endurance events. But I do my best to avoid science. So when I was running a race in California a few years ago and started cramping, I followed the conventional wisdom and turned to salt for my cure. The problem was—I had no salt!

Cramping, no salt, and 30 miles into a fast 50-mile race. What was I to do? Well, there ain't much in the woods out there, so I couldn't do much except keep going. But eventually I came to the next aid station, and the first thing I looked for was salt.

But let me back up a little. I'd like to note with no small amount of pride that I was winning the race. Or rather, I was running neck-and-neck with Mike Wolfe, both of us in the front position. And it was hard to complain about my cramping because he was at that very moment bleeding freely from the forehead. He hadn't gotten quite low enough when ducking beneath a fallen tree early in the race and had opened up a major head wound. But hey—cramping hurts too! It was happening all up and down my inner thighs and starting to make me run like I had just gotten off a big horse.

Since we were in front of the race, we were in a hurry. You might even have called us frantic. Well, me at least. I ran up to the table at the aid station and shouted, "Salt! I need salt! Do you have any salt pills?"

The volunteers looked at me in surprise. "Well, we don't have salt pills," one ventured, "but we do have salt." She pointed at a bowl of table salt situated next to some boiled potatoes. I looked at the salt in dismay, but, having no other option, I decided to just go for it. The cramping was getting worse.

I picked up the bowl of salt and put my whole face in it, licking the salt off the top. At that very moment I thought, "Oh, no! What an asshole! Other people might want to use this bowl of salt!" So I put the bowl down and looked up at the volunteers, who were gaping at me. "I'm so sorry!" I stammered.

"I shouldn't have done that." But it was too late; Mike was already leaving the aid station, and I needed to go. So I put my fingers into the salt and pulled out a huge pinch that I just stuffed into my mouth. It must have been at least a tablespoon.

The second I swallowed, the world ended. The salt catalyzed some sort of horrible reaction in my belly that caused a hurricane of nausea to boil up into my throat and cheeks. I could feel the back of my mouth start salivating heavily, and the cramping migrated from my legs to the spaces between my ribs and in doing so magnified in intensity tenfold. The pain in my ribs prevented me from breathing, and I was suddenly stumbling along taking quick gasps of air with my head hanging down, drooling. Mike was just ahead of me, and as we plunged back into the forest, he started pulling ahead.

I didn't stop. But I couldn't run normally either. I just kept charging along as well as possible without being able to breathe. Every step was a jarring nightmare in my chest, and barely a minute after leaving the aid station, I threw up everything I'd recently eaten with a horrible retching sound. Thin green fluid—the remnants of many gels in the past four hours—spattered the ground and my shoes. Mike was far enough ahead that he didn't even notice, but I suddenly felt a lot better. My cheeks weren't salivating anything like they had been.

The problem that remained was my ribs. The pain kept me from taking full breaths. I ran along the trail hunched over like an old witch without her staff. Even standing up straight was a strain. Mike pulled a significant lead on me, and I was never able to catch him, even as the pain gradually cleared up. In the end I managed to hang on to second, but I sure as hell didn't take any more salt.

Perhaps the scientists will one day figure out why we cramp during races, but even if they tell me it's salt, I'm not sure I'll be willing to listen.

/////

and eat on the run. They taste good, don't get stuck in your teeth, and make you run as well as or better than you were running before eating them. Foods that don't work are difficult to open, messy, crumbly, and hard to hold in one hand. They get stuck in your mouth, are too dry, or are tough to swallow without choking. Most of all, they sit in your gut like a calorie bomb, make you feel bloated or full, and slow you down. Your goal is to find three to five foods you can count on to work in any situation. These are your bull's-eye foods.

All the food options you try can be categorized by where they fall on a target. Your bull's-eye foods are your tried-and-true favorites. If these core foods begin to fail, because you're tired of eating them, craving more sweetness or saltiness, or craving a different texture, then you can choose foods from the next ring of the target. These are foods you may not eat all the time, but you have tried them in training and know they work for you.

Beyond this ring are foods that you haven't tried but that are similar to foods you have tried. For instance, you may know that chocolate chip cookies work for you, but there are only oatmeal cookies in the aid station. Or you like regular potato chips, but only BBQ-flavored chips are available.

Anything beyond this ring is off target altogether. These are the foods you know don't work for you and foods similar to foods that don't work for you. It is important to list these foods out as well so that you and your crew are reminded of the things you have tried that have not worked in training.

Developing your bull's-eye foods. Variety is important in your short list of bull's-eye foods. The end goal is to find a combination of three to five foods that, together, meet all the following criteria:

- At least one real food—something you make or assemble or that is not made specifically for running (rice ball, peanut butter and jelly sandwich, or pretzels)
- At least one engineered food (gel, chewable, or sports drink)
- Something sweet
- Something savory
- Something salty

If you construct this combination correctly, these bull's-eye foods can be rotated and substituted during any race as needed according to your target calorie range as identified earlier in the chapter (30–40 percent of calorie expenditure). After these core foods have been fully vetted, experiment with backup (outer-ring) foods. These backup foodstuffs are what you can confidently fall back on if you lose your taste or craving for your bull's-eye foods. The typical fallback plan revolves around the aid station fare of cookies, soup, fruit, and sandwiches. Third-ring foods are variations of second-ring foods.

The bull's-eye strategy is easy to visualize and easy to explain to your support crew. Figure 10.3 is an actual example of one runner's bull's-eye strategy. At any point during a race, either the athlete or his or her support crew can quickly consult the target and make a good decision.

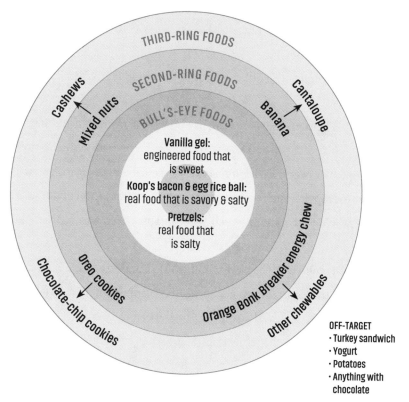

FIGURE **10.3** *A sample bull's-eye nutrition strategy*

ING HYDRATION AND SODIUM: THE ULTIMATE CHALLENGE FOR ULTRARUNNING

al body water and your sodium concentration will affect performance in

ways. Further complicating the matter is the fact that at any point in time,

your hydration and sodium balance can be normal or you could have too much or too little of either one.

Hydration state can be measured relative to your body weight, and your natremic state is measured by the concentration of sodium in your blood (measured in millimoles per liter). To understand how hydration status and sodium concentration change, it's important to first understand some terminology.

- **Euhydrated:** Normal body weight, typically less than 3 percent weight change
- **Hypohydrated/dehydrated:** Greater than 3 percent decrease in body weight
- **Hyperhydrated/overhydrated:** Increase in body weight
- **Normonatremic:** Normal blood sodium concentration (135 to <145 mmol/L)
- **Hypernatremic:** Too much sodium in the blood (>145 mmol/L)
- **Hyponatremic:** Too little sodium in the blood (125 to 135 mmol/L)

Table 10.3 helps us to better visualize how these hydration and natremic states converge. It resembles a tic-tac-toe board, with the various natremic states on the horizontal rows and hydration states in the vertical columns. As with regular tic-tac-toe, occupying the center square puts you in a position of power. This is the desired physiological state in which you can run faster, run farther, and tolerate heat better.

Assuming you start your event euhydrated and normonatremic, during the course of an ultramarathon you are going to consume a lot of fluid, a lot of calories, and a lot of sodium. You will also be exposed to varying temperatures and weather conditions, and you will spend times at a variety of intensities. All these things, along with the sheer length of time you will be out on the course, will shift your hydration and natremic statuses. No scenario is more advantageous than being euhydrated and normonatremic, but some of the other scenarios are worse than

TABLE **10.3**	How Hydration and Natremic States Converge		

		NATREMIC STATES		
		LOW	**NORMAL**	**HIGH**
		HYPONATREMIC	NORMONATREMIC	HYPERNATREMIC
HYDRATION STATE	**LOW** DEHYDRATED	Dehydrated and hyponatremic	Dehydrated and normonatremic	Dehydrated and hypernatremic
	NORMAL EUHYDRATED	Euhydrated and hyponatremic	Euhydrated and normonatremic	Euhydrated and hypernatremic
	HIGH OVERHYDRATED	Overhydrated and hyponatremic	Overhydrated and normonatremic	Overhydrated and hypernatremic

others. The one that gets the most media attention is the scenario in which an athlete is overhydrated and hyponatremic, specifically a slow marathoner who drinks way too much plain water and gains weight during the event. Hyponatremia happens in ultrarunning, too, but it can also manifest as euhydration and hyponatremia. This means the athlete is at normal body weight (less than 3 percent body weight loss) but has not replenished enough sodium to offset losses from prolonged hours of sweating. It's dilution of the blood by removal of sodium, rather than dilution of the blood by the addition of too much water.

During an ultramarathon your sodium-hydration balance is one of the most important aspects of biofeedback to pay attention to. As you eat, drink, run, and spend more time in the elements, this balance is constantly shifting. Your goal is to stay in or get back to that center square!

The following sections represent the various combinations of hydration and natremic states you could end up in during the course of an ultramarathon. Some are more dangerous and affect your performance more than others. Similarly, some are easier to get into and easier to correct than others. To better explain them, each state is described by the level of hydration, level of sodium, the prevalence of the occurrence, how you got there, what the symptoms are, and how you can get back to the center square (euhydrated and normonatremic).

Occurrence rate for hydration and natremic states (adapted from Hoffman, Hew-Butler, and Stuempfle 2013):

- **Extremely rare:** <1 percent
- **Rare:** 3–6 percent
- **Somewhat common:** 10–15 percent
- **Common:** 30 percent or greater

Dehydrated and Hyponatremic

Hydration: Low
Sodium: Low
Occurrence: Rare (3–6 percent of 100-mile finishers)

How you got here. You can get to this state if you have lost a lot of electrolytes through sweating and you have gradually fallen behind in both sodium and fluid replenishment. Rising temperatures during an ultramarathon can lead to this problem as well because you have been losing sodium throughout the race, and then sweat rate increases dramatically and accelerates both fluid and sodium loss.

Symptoms. Dry skin and mouth, thirst, craving for salty foods, dizziness on standing, weight loss, and low/no urine volume. At risk for heat stress in warm conditions.

How to get back to the center square. Consume sports drink, salty broth, and/or a combination of water and salty foods. Don't consume only water. In warm/hot conditions slow down, wet your clothing, and douse with water to alleviate heat stress.

Euhydrated and Hyponatremic

Hydration: Normal
Sodium: Low
Occurrence: Rare (3–6 percent of 100-mile finishers)

How you got here. This is a relatively easy state to reach in an ultramarathon, especially if you experience food fatigue and gradually start taking in less food or fewer sodium-containing drinks. Athletes who are salty sweaters can also end up in this state because they have higher sweat losses over time. This condition does not put you at elevated risk of heat stress, since you have plenty of body fluid for sweat; however, it can become much more serious if sodium balance is not corrected.

Symptoms. Normal weight and thirst, moist mouth, craving for salty foods but nausea upon eating, normal urine output.

How to get back to the center square. Consume sports drink, salty broth, and/or a combination of water and salty foods. Try ginger or another remedy to alleviate nausea.

Overhydrated and Hyponatremic
Hydration: High
Sodium: Low
Occurrence: Rare (3–6 percent of 100-mile finishers)

How you got here. This dangerous condition requires immediate action. Athletes who consume too much plain water and not enough sodium are at risk. Even those who know better can end up in this situation when food fatigue and overall fatigue cause poor decision-making. Some stop eating due to nausea but continue consuming a lot of plain water in hopes of calming the nausea by getting the gut to start moving again. Hot conditions combined with frequent aid stations can make this worse, as sips of low-sodium fluids (cola, ginger ale, water) at aid stations add up.

Symptoms. Increased weight, puffy hands, high output of clear urine, cognitive impairment, disorientation, sloshing stomach, nausea, possible vomiting. Low risk of heat stress because there is plenty of fluid available for sweat.

How to get back to the center square. If symptoms are mild and the condition is caught early, you may be able to return to a more euhydrated and normonatremic state by consuming salty foods and restricting fluid intake. Even if symptoms are mild, it is recommended that you stay in an aid station where medical professionals are present. The support crew needs to monitor the runner's condition closely because it can deteriorate quickly. A runner who is exhibiting frequent vomiting, seizures, or significant neurological impairment needs immediate attention from medical staff. When in doubt, seek medical help.

Dehydrated and Normonatremic

Hydration: Low
Sodium: Normal
Occurrence: Somewhat common (10–15 percent of 100-mile finishers)

How you got here. In this case, you are consuming plenty of sodium from a variety of foods but either are not consuming enough fluid or are underestimating your sweat rate. At high altitudes the air is dry and sweat evaporates quickly, so skin may seem pretty dry even though you are sweating profusely. You also lose more body fluid through respiration in dry air. This can lead runners to underestimate sweat rate and fail to replenish fluids adequately. In warm environments some athletes run low on fluids based on the amount they are carrying. Rationing fluid is better than running completely dry, but eventually it will lead to dehydration.

Symptoms. Weight loss, dry mouth, strong thirst, normal appetite for food, possible dizziness upon standing, fatigue, loss of focus, low urine output, urine may be the color of apple juice or darker. Elevated risk of heat stress in warm environment.

How to get back to the center square. Consume water. Sports drink and/or salty broth can be consumed but are not necessary. In warm/hot conditions slow down, wet your clothing, and douse with water to alleviate heat stress.

Overhydrated and Normonatremic

Hydration: High
Sodium: Normal
Occurrence: Common (>30 percent of 100-mile finishers)

How you got here. This scenario sometimes happens in cooler weather when sweat rates are relatively low and you are eating plenty of sodium-rich foods but also consuming more fluid than necessary. Sometimes athletes who follow a regimented fluid-con schedule end up here because they don't reduce fluid intake when cool weather, rainstorms, and wet clothing reduce their sweat rate. However, even when the temperature rises, athletes can be susceptible to this issue. Simple paranoia about dehydration can lead them to overdrink. Research performed by Martin Hoffman during the Western States 100 and the Rio Del Lago Endurance Run has found that this scenario is the most common (aside from euhydration and normonatremia) for athletes (Hoffman, Hew-Butler, and Stuempfle 2013).

Symptoms. Nausea, sloshing stomach, bloating, low thirst, slight weight gain or absence of expected minor weight loss, puffy hands, normal taste for salty foods but diminished hunger due to feeling full.

How to get back to the center square. Restrict fluid intake to just moisten mouth. Consider just swishing fluid in the mouth and spitting it out. This is not a scenario that increases the risk of heat stress because there is plenty of fluid available for sweat.

Dehydrated and Hypernatremic
Hydration: Low
Sodium: High
Occurrence: Extremely rare (<1 percent of 100-mile finishers)

How you got here. The difference between this scenario and being dehydrated and normonatremic may be the absence of urination. With high sodium concentration in the blood, your body holds on to the water it has instead of making fluid available for urine. Athletes sometimes end up in this condition due to overconsumption of sodium through salt tablets or losing track of sodium intake from multiple sources (chips plus salt tablet plus electrolyte drink, etc.). The challenge with this scenario is that the high sodium consumption may lead to nausea, which reduces the appeal of drinking.

Symptoms. Weight loss, dry mouth, dry skin, cessation of urination, strong thirst, salty foods may taste bad. Athlete is at elevated risk of heat stress in warm environments.

How to get back to the center square. Consume plain water and restrict sodium intake. If you need calories, seek low-sodium carbohydrate sources. Sip small amounts of water to mitigate nausea. In warm/hot conditions slow down, wet your clothing, and douse with water to alleviate heat stress.

Euhydrated and Hypernatremic
Hydration: Normal
Sodium: High
Occurrence: Extremely rare (<1 percent of 100-mile finishers)

How you got here. This state is caused by consuming too much sodium in too short a period of time. Athletes who use salt tablets when they don't need them can end up here easily, which is one of the reasons I recommend food and fluid sources of sodium rather than salt tablets.

Symptoms. Normal weight, strong thirst, no dry mouth, salty foods may taste bad but appetite is generally normal, normal urination frequency but urine is the color of apple juice or darker. Risk of heat stress is not elevated.

How to get back to the center square. Restrict sodium intake and continue with normal consumption of water. If you need calories, seek low-sodium carbohydrate sources. The condition will improve as you lose sodium through sweat and urination, but be careful not to restrict sodium long enough to swing all the way to euhydrated and hyponatremic.

Overhydrated and Hypernatremic
Hydration: High
Sodium: High
Occurrence: Extremely rare (<1 percent of 100-mile finishers)

How you got here. This is a scenario that's relatively hard to achieve. To get here you have to overconsume both fluid and sodium. It can happen, however, if an athlete is moving slowly in cool weather (low sweat rate) and consuming large amounts of salty food and/or large volumes of salty broth or high-sodium sports drinks. When you are moving slowly, it is easier to consume large volumes of food and fluids because the intensity is low and there is less jostling to upset the stomach.

Symptoms. High thirst, slight weight gain, salty foods taste bad, high urine output, puffy hands, possible confusion or poor decision-making. This scenario shares some characteristics with the more dangerous overhydration and hyponatremia, including puffy hands, possible confusion, weight gain, and high urine output. The key differences are that with this scenario you will be thirsty, salty foods will taste bad, and your urine will have more color (although it is still light).

How to get back to the center square. Restrict fluid intake to just moisten mouth. Consider just swishing fluid in the mouth and spitting it out. Restrict sodium intake. If you need calories, seek low-sodium carbohydrate sources. This is not a scenario that increases risk of heat stress because there is plenty of fluid available for sweat.

Euhydrated and Normonatremic

Hydration: Normal
Sodium: Normal
Occurrence: Common (>30 percent of 100-mile finishers)

How you got here. You're doing everything right and adjusting fluid and sodium intake appropriately for changing conditions. Congratulations! The important thing is to stay here, which requires foresight.

Symptoms. Weight is stable or slightly low but within 3 percent of starting weight. Normal appetite and sweating, and normal urine output. Mouth is moist, and you have no nausea.

How to stay in the center square. Think about how the conditions are going to change in the next few hours and plan accordingly. If fluid loss is likely to accelerate based on rising temperature, higher elevation, or greater intensity, plan to carry more fluid and gradually increase sodium consumption (or at least have sources of sodium with you).

With so many variables in play, there are bound to be errors that take you away from the center square. While continuing to move forward, the preferable hydration and sodium errors are slight dehydration and slight hypernatremia. As you head in the direction of overhydration and/or hyponatremia, running becomes uncomfortable because of nausea, puffy hands, bloating, and a sloshing stomach. Heading in the direction of dehydration and/or hypernatremia will be increasingly uncomfortable as well, characterized by increased thirst, dry mouth, and dry skin. While these symptoms are unpleasant, they are more easily solved (get water, wet skin to mitigate heat stress) and less likely to stop you completely.

FINAL WORD

Your biggest takeaway from this chapter is this: Sports nutrition is dynamic. There is no singular formula that will produce optimal results for all athletes in all conditions. This is an area where as an athlete you have to become an expert in manipulating carbohydrate, fluid, and sodium based on exercise intensity, duration of activity, and environmental factors. Hopefully you now have a better understanding of how these three key ingredients interact with each other and are affected by numerous factors.

Sports nutrition is also trainable. The first step is to determine the food and drink combinations that work best for you based on the ideas presented in this chapter. Then, over time, you can train to increase the amounts of those foods and drinks you can consume without causing stomach upset.

CHAPTER 11

CREATING YOUR PERSONAL RACE STRATEGIES

Creating your personal race strategies is the final piece of the training process leading up to an event. Your personal race strategies bring your hard-earned training to life on race day. Setting race goals, deciding on nutritional strategies, and choosing your crew and pacers are the last pieces you complete in the weeks before the event. Many times, I have my athletes put the finishing touches on during the taper, as a means of providing an outlet for their pent-up energy. In any case, last is certainly not least! By being clear on your goals, nutrition, and pacing, and by choosing the right crew (or not having one at all), you maximize the impact of the work you have done and the fitness you have attained.

STEP 0: REVIEW YOUR TRAINING

Your personal race-day strategies start with a little homework: Go review your training. Regardless of whether you keep a paper training log, work up your own spreadsheet, or use technology such as Strava, TrainingPeaks, Movescount, or Garmin Connect, pore over the last several months of training. Find where you were strong, find the places where there were chinks in the armor. Look at the paces, grades, food, and fluids you utilized in training. This homework serves as the basis from which you will derive your race-day strategies. The effectiveness of your training sets a realistic framework for your goals. The nutrition you used in training is the platform you use to build your race-day nutrition strategy. The paces and workouts you have accomplished in training are analogous to how you can meter out your race-day effort. Examine what you have done, and it will tell you what you are capable of and what you need to do come race day.

WHAT IS YOUR RACE-DAY GOAL?

"What does success look like to you?" is the question I ask my athletes as the season is taking shape. The answer to this question helps me understand an athlete's goals for the season and for particular events. While I have some influence on how those goals are shaped, ultimately they are the athlete's goals. For example, the goals Dakota, Missy, Dylan, Erik, and Kaci have are theirs and theirs alone. They should run, train, and race with a purpose for the goals they have created and own.

When narrowing down your race-day goals, use a similar philosophy. The goals you have on race day are not your partner's, your children's, or your boss's. They are yours, and you must own them. This mind-set may seem selfish, but starting from this reference point allows you to focus on you first as *the* runner. Your family, friends, and peers are key parts of your support network, but in the end, your goals are yours and no one else's.

From this mind-set, the practical steps of race-day goal setting can proceed. Whereas the broad, early-season goal-setting question about what success looks like is purposefully subjective and may seem hippy-dippy, the goals you establish for race day are concrete, actionable, and focused on the task at hand. This does not mean they need to be cold and formulaic. "Run with a smile" is just as concrete, actionable, and focused on the task at hand as "Eat 200 calories an hour." Both of these are valid goals, and being creative with your goals helps personalize them. They do not have to fit into the stereotypical construct of a particular time, pace, or placing. They do, however, need to describe two things:

- Your outcome goal: This is what you ultimately want to achieve.
- Your process goals: These are the things you need to do during the race to achieve your outcome goal.

OUTCOME GOALS

I am a big fan of all sports. Although I have a particular affection for my hometown Dallas Cowboys, Dallas Mavericks, Texas Rangers, Texas A&M Aggies, and Dallas Stars, my love of sports and competition is indiscriminate. My biggest fascination with sports is the simple outcome at the end of any sporting event. While I enjoy

---

OUTCOME VERSUS PROCESS GOALS

Outcome goal: What you ultimately want to achieve.

Process goals: Intermediate checkpoints that support the outcome goal.

Example outcome goal: Finish the American River 50 in under eight hours.

Process goals:

- Eat a smart breakfast of 600 calories.
- Begin the race running 8:00 to 8:30 min/mi.
- Eat early and often, around 250 calories per hour.
- Stay positive.
- Tell the crew "thanks."

Example outcome goal: Finish the Vermont 100 having enjoyed the day.

Process goals:

- Keep the pace easy and manageable.
- Tell the crew to keep me smiling.
- Thank the volunteers at the aid station.
- Encourage other runners.
- Focus on gratitude that you get to run.

seeing how a particular play in football materializes and how all the plays through-out the game pile up for a story line in the fourth quarter, the outcome of the game is what fascinates me. Sports are inevitably an outcome-oriented affair. Wins and losses pile up at the top of the box score; the statistics are underneath. Particularly in running, where there is a starting line, a finish line, and a clock, there is always an outcome for every runner in the race. We can decide to place more or less importance on the outcome versus the process, but the outcome goal is the start-ing point for goal setting. All properly set outcome goals share a common set of characteristics that serve as a framework for formulating your particular goals:

- Outcome goals describe the outcome.
- Outcome goals are achievable.
- Outcome goals are challenging.

Outcome goals must describe the outcome. Words matter, and so does specificity. The most important property of an outcome goal is that it must accurately describe the desired outcome. Outcomes can be times, places, or actions. They can be specific (such as a time or placing) or broad (such as a time range). Examples include:

- Place in the top third of the field.
- Finish the race.
- Run under nine hours for a 50-miler.

These are acceptable outcome goals that accurately describe some phenomenon that will occur at the conclusion of the event. Sounds simple? Not so. I consistently find athletes and coaches who use the wrong language to describe outcome goals. "I just want to finish" is a common way of expressing that you want to complete the race. I would never let my athletes express their goals this way, and you shouldn't do it either. The word "just" demeans the process. And "I want" is not an outcome of the event. "Finish the race" is the right goal; it describes the outcome you want to achieve.

Risky business: balancing challenging goals and affinity for risk. Successful outcome goals strike a balance between being achievable and offering a challenge. Where you sit on the achievability teeter-totter depends on your individual tolerance for risk. As you set goals that are more challenging and closer to the limits of your capabilities, you must simultaneously accept a higher level of risk associated with those goals. The inverse is also true, but sometimes it's harder to grasp. Goals beyond your physical capabilities are not well-constructed goals. It is also important to realize that if you have a low tolerance for risk, an extremely challenging goal is just as inappropriate as a goal that is way beyond your physical capabilities.

In other words, if you are risk-averse, your goals will need to be less challenging and more within your comfort zone. To make challenging goals achievable, you have to be willing to accept greater risk. Being risk-averse is not a character flaw; nonetheless, your acceptance of or aversion to risk affects the way you need to set goals. A risk-averse athlete must put a premium on ensuring the goal is within his or her physical capabilities, even on a day when performance is below average.

Figure 11.1 illustrates the ideal balance. You have selected a goal that is challenging, and your affinity for risk is high enough that you will make the decisions and take the chances necessary to achieve your goal.

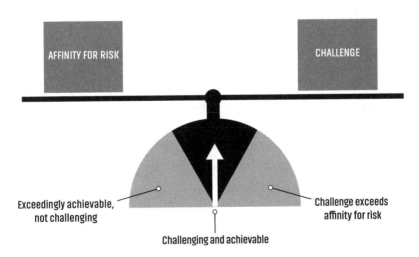

FIGURE **11.1** *A goal where the challenge is balanced with the affinity for risk*

Source: Illustrated by Charlie Layton

A goal that is more challenging requires more risk to remain in balance, as illustrated in Figure 11.2. Put another way, an athlete with greater affinity for risk can pursue goals that present greater challenges.

A goal that is less challenging needs less risk tolerance to remain highly achievable, as shown in Figure 11.3. This can be a good scenario for a beginner because affinity for risk in endurance sports typically increases with experience, which consequently helps make more challenging events increasingly achievable.

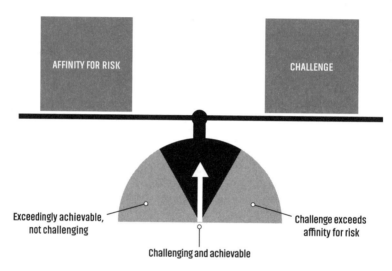

FIGURE **11.2** *A bigger challenge that is balanced with a larger affinity for risk*
Source: Illustrated by Charlie Layton

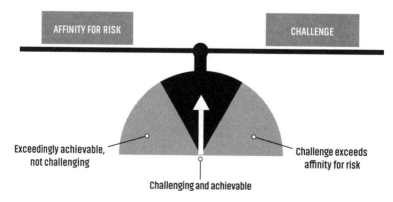

FIGURE **11.3** *An easier challenge that is balanced with a smaller affinity for risk*
Source: Illustrated by Charlie Layton

Figure 11.4 illustrates a scenario in which your goal is highly challenging but you're not tolerant enough of the risks necessary to make that goal achievable. It is highly unlikely you will achieve your outcome goal. While I encourage athletes to take on challenging goals, you can only push the challenge aspect of your goals as far as your risk tolerance will let you. You may be physically capable of achieving a more challenging goal, but you will fail over and over again unless your affinity for risk is high enough to enable you to fully apply that physical capacity to the goal.

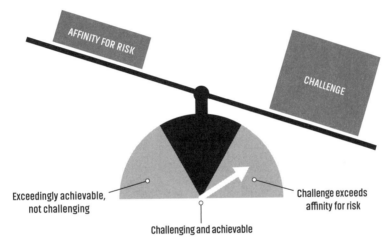

FIGURE 11.4   *A bigger challenge that is not balanced with a bigger affinity for risk*

Source: Illustrated by Charlie Layton

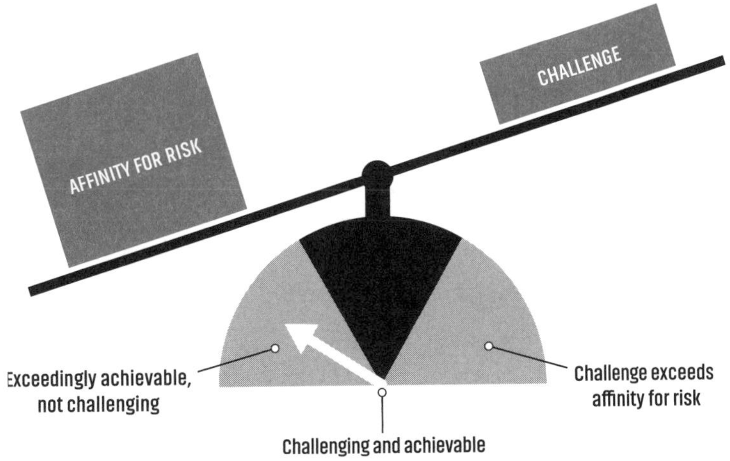

FIGURE 11.5   *An easy challenge that is thrown out of balance with a high affinity for risk*

Source: Illustrated by Charlie Layton

Finally, Figure 11.5 illustrates a scenario in which you have a high affinity for risk and your goal is highly achievable. It is virtually guaranteed that you will achieve your outcome goal. Although that may seem like a winning scenario, from a goal-setting perspective it is out of balance. The goal is simply not challenging enough. What's wrong with an easy goal? Beyond the fact that you're disrespecting your own abilities, goals that are too easy lead to complacency, lack of focus, and big mistakes. Challenging goals force you to focus because many aspects of training, nutrition, and strategy have to go right in order for you to succeed. When the goal is too easy, you don't take it seriously, you don't prepare, and you can find yourself in a surprisingly dangerous position on race day.

How many outcome goals can you have? When setting outcome goals for an event, the simpler the better. I push, prod, and facilitate the process with my athletes, but in the end it is their responsibility to craft their own outcome goals. Typically, after a few conversations, one singular outcome-based goal emerges. Any previous iterations of the outcome-based goal normally transition to process goals. When an outcome goal is a placing or a time in the particular event, most athletes will choose to set A, B, and C goals for that time/place. For example, if your outcome goal is to run 9 hours in the American River 50, you might have an A goal of 8:45, a B goal of 9:00, and a C goal of 9:15. These are all still challenging enough and within a normal range of performance. Other athletes will have an A goal of 9:00 and a B goal of finishing the race. Finally, some athletes will have *only* one goal: "I'm going to run 8:45 or bust!" When this is the case, my role as a coach is to first ensure that the goal is reasonable and balanced with the right affinity for risk. Second, I offer 100 percent support for the athlete in that goal. Once again, these are your goals. Take the time and care to craft them, and you will be on the right path.

PROCESS GOALS

Ronda Rousey is a badass. Win, lose, or draw, I admit that I am a fan and card-carrying member of the armbar nation! Aside from my fascination with Ms. Rousey, the sport of mixed martial arts (MMA) serves as one of the best examples of process goal planning. Training for MMA involves mastery of many different fighting forms. Boxers, wrestlers, Muay Thai fighters, kickboxers, and jujitsu practitioners come together and do battle in the octagon. In these matches, victory can be won in a variety of ways. You can win by forcing your opponent to "tap out," which is the grown-up, professional version of crying uncle. You can win by decision, which puts the outcome in the hands of judges sitting ringside. You can win by knockout or a referee stoppage.

As these athletes prepare for competition, their different fighting styles converge. Karate experts face wrestlers. Boxers face grappling artists. Muay Thai and jujitsu practitioners square off. As the saying in the sport goes, "Styles make fights." The athletes who choose to do battle are acutely aware of each other's strengths and weaknesses. They know their opponent has heavy hands or a penchant for a particular submission technique (like Rousey's storied armbar). Because of these different styles, fighters are forced to think about how they are going to win. They can't simply try harder and achieve victory. They must think about how they are going to use their strengths and exploit their opponent's weaknesses to achieve victory.

When you watch these athletes train, particularly as they are getting ready for a big fight, one question asked by their coaches prevails: "How do you see the fight ending?" The fighter, having already rehearsed the scenario in his or her head throughout practice, knows the answer: "I win by knockout," "I win by submission," or "I win by armbar." The "I win" part for MMA fighters is the outcome goal. The "by knockout," "by submission," or "by armbar" part peers into the *process* of achieving that goal. In training, MMA fighters rehearse how to control position, cut off angles, and wear out their opponent as different pieces of the *process* of accomplishing the outcome of winning. During the fight, pieces of the process they have rehearsed come to light as the fighters move, strike, and control the ring. These fighters know it is not good enough to simply answer their coach's question with "I win." Their answer specifies *how* they will defeat their opponent.

As in MMA, defining the outcome goal in ultrarunning is only part of the process. The remaining part relies on setting process goals that will lead to success. Planning process goals is the actionable portion of your race-day goal-setting exercise. Unlike the outcome goal, which will be influenced by variables outside of your control, you have 100 percent control of process goals come race day. They are the actions, thoughts, checkpoints, and supporting activities you do during the race to better ensure the outcome goal is achieved. In this way, process goals should dominate your thought process during the race. Thinking "I need to eat another gel to hit 200 calories an hour" at mile 30 of a 50-miler is going to do a lot more good than thinking "I need to finish in nine hours." Like outcome goal planning, process goals need to be personalized to suit you as an individual, your goals, and most important, your personality.

When I have my athletes move through the process of goal planning, highly individualized paths emerge to support their outcome goals. Many times, even athletes with very similar outcome goals have wildly different process goals. Your process is your own, but all well-set process goals meet the following criteria:

- The process goal must directly support the outcome goal.
- The runner must be able to control the process.
- The process goals must suit the runner's individual needs.

Process goals must support the outcome goal. As you move through the development of your race-day process goals, the most important question to answer is "Do the process goals support the outcome goal?" Accomplishing each process goal brings you one step closer to your outcome goal. Goals related to pace, effort level, attitude, nutritional planning, and gear selection are all valid process goals as long as they directly improve the likelihood of the outcome goal being met. Process goals that do not directly affect the outcome are frivolous and only suck valuable energy from your race. A great litmus test for a properly constructed set of process goals is to run them by your crew. If a process goal is well constructed, it should be something that your crew can easily reinforce while you are in an aid station as well as something that makes an impact down the road.

HOW YOUR CREW CAN REINFORCE YOUR PROCESS GOALS

Outcome goal: Finish the American River 50.

Process goal: Eat 200 calories an hour.

List your process goals on a cue card and give it to your crew. Have them ask questions related to the specific process goals you need to go through, such as "How many calories have you taken in? It's three hours into the race; you should have consumed 600 calories by now."

Process goals must be able to be controlled. For a process goal to be effective, you must be able to execute it during the course of race day. Process goals such as eating a certain amount of calories, running at a particular pace, and having a great attitude are all under your control. Process goals that fall outside of your control, particularly if they are dependent on another person, are not properly set process goals. "Run with Analisa for the first half" might sound like an easy goal to accomplish. But you are not in control of Analisa's running. Avoiding the weather, staying in the top 20, or beating a fellow runner are all similar; you as the runner are not in complete control.

Process goals must suit the needs of the individual. When setting process goals with my athletes, I am careful to help them tailor their goals to their individual needs, psychology, and personality. Many of the process goals you develop will include technical aspects (such as pace, calories per hour, and anything that can be quantified) and psychological facets of the event (such as "stay positive"). The emphasis on either technical or psychological aspects must be tailored to the individual, but I always encourage athletes to include at least one of each. If you run well based on tracking stats and numbers (such as calories and pace), you should have a larger proportion of those types of process goals. If you run well with more psychological cues (such as staying positive, having fun, interacting with the crew), these should constitute a larger proportion of your process goals. Similarly, when I am out at races encouraging athletes, the statistic-focused athlete will hear comments such as "You ran that section right on your target time! Great job!" from me. In contrast, an athlete who craves more psychological motivation will hear "Stay positive! This next section is your strength, and your crew is right around the corner!"

I have included an example of outcome and process goals for Erik Glover's Vermont 100K. His singular outcome goal was "Finish the race" (not "I just want to finish the race"). His process goals all supported the outcome goal, and he could control every one of them. Erik also needed a balance of technical and psychological cues. Finally, because he is a braniac it made sense for him to compartmentalize his process goals into three distinct areas: pacing, nutrition, and attitude.

Outcome goal: Finish the Vermont 100K.

Process goals:

Pacing (all three process goals supported the outcome goal by helping Erik to keep a proper intensity level)

- Hold a consistent intensity.
- Be patient and power-hike if I need to.
- Run any downhills.

Nutrition (all three process goals supported the outcome goal by keeping Erik's nutrition program on track)

- Eat every 20 minutes.
- Eat 250 calories per hour.
- Rotate between my gels and real foods.

Attitude (all four process goals supported the outcome goal by reinforcing a positive attitude)

- Smile!
- Tell my crew and aid station workers "thank you."

- Actively work out of any low points.
- Look up and take in the scenery.

GOAL SETTING IN YOUR FIRST ULTRA OR FIRST 100-MILE EVENT

The Leadville Trail 100 is notorious for having an extremely poor finish rate. Most years, it hovers around 50 percent; some years, it's even lower. While the race is certainly difficult, there are no good reasons for this level of failure in the event. Some runners will blame the altitude. Others will say the climbing is just too much. Neither of these is true. As race founder Ken Chlouber would say, "These are crybaby excuses."

The real rationale for Leadville's poor finish rate revolves around the fact that there are no prerequisites to enter the race, as there are for many other 100-mile events. An athlete needs only to survive the lottery process, plunk down an entry fee, and show up to gain a spot. As a result, many athletes who are new to the sport or using Leadville as their first 100-mile race enter the event. Many of the innocent rookies end up dropping like flies. The effort required to complete 100 mountainous miles at high altitude torments runners as they attempt to locomote through the wee hours of the night and into the next day. The athletes struggle with cutoffs, calories, and a sense of what the hell they have gotten themselves into. Sadly, many who are struggling will refuse to continue. It's a tough race for sure, but not as tough as one would expect from a 50 percent finish rate.

Far more than 50 percent of the athletes entering the Leadville Trail 100 have the necessary fitness to complete the race. For the athletes who don't finish, what they lack is not physical ability but a sense of purpose. Purpose is what will drive them in and out of the frigid Outward Bound aid station at mile 75 when a warm car ride back into town is oh so tempting. The rookie mistake is not a lack of training; it is a failure to understand what a special feeling comes from finishing one's first 100-mile race. They came to the race without that singular purpose, and it costs them.

It has taken me until this point in the book to insert a personal story about training and preparing for ultramarathons. All the earlier chapters are filled with anecdotes from my athletes, purposefully so, in order to avoid introducing my own bias. To this point, I have avoided inserting my own N of 1.

My first 100-mile event was the Leadville Trail 100 in 2008. I will always remember the year of the event. "June 13th 2009" is stamped on a band that wraps around my left ring finger. The year before, at the finish line of the Leadville Trail 100, I proposed to my wife.

An athlete's first ultra and first 100-mile race are special moments. These two accomplishments represent special achievements that are unparalleled in the runner's athletic career. Because one's *first* is such a special moment, the goal-setting process for these events must revolve around getting to the finish line, at all costs. Time, place, and performance in these circumstances are all secondary considerations.

I chose to reinforce the "finish at all costs" mentality by carrying a ring in the pocket of my shorts for the entirety of the 2008 Leadville Trail 100. For the finish line proposal, I had no backup plan. I either finished the race and got on one knee, or . . . Well, I didn't know what the hell I was going to do. For 100 miles, the ring was there, with the center stone occasionally pressing into my thigh. It was a constant reminder of how important the race was and how special the finish would be. That was my outcome goal—finish the race and have the chance to propose to my future wife, at all costs. There were no B, C, or D goals, just one goal and one focus. My process goals were similarly suited: Run conservatively, take time in the aid stations, enjoy the company of my pacers, take extra warm gear. All were aimed at finishing in any time under the 30-hour cutoff. While the race was hard, the ending of the story was a happy one. Sure, I was well prepared and fit, and I had a fantastic support team (including this book's coauthor, Jim Rutberg). But the crucial aspect of preparation was setting the all-important outcome goal and its supporting process goals. Achieving that goal meant the world to me.

THE DREADED DNF

Ultramarathons are hard. Most ultrarunners who have had long careers have at least one DNF to their credit. Sure, you will find the anomalies without a DNF, but these individuals are at the end of the bell curve. In my coaching career, I have had my fair share of athletes who have DNFed in an ultra. I have had several DNFs myself. Some could have been prevented, but others were unavoidable. While it's always heartbreaking to see an athlete underperform, I have never, not once, been upset, ashamed, mad, or embarrassed with an athlete who takes a DNF. There are three reasons for this:

- If a DNF results from some random act, such as in the 2014 Hardrock 100 when Dakota Jones rolled his foot on a rock early in the race, that's part of the game. No sense in agonizing over it. Injuries can happen on any training day and on any training mile throughout the year. It's just dumb luck if it happens on race day.

- If a DNF results from a lack of preparation, either physical or mental, that's on me. It's my job to make sure the athlete gets to the starting line prepared for the event. Similarly, my hope in writing this book is to give you enough knowledge and tools so you will be well prepared when you reach the starting line for your event.

- Some athletes choose to race at the edges of their capabilities. That is their goal. For these athletes, a DNF may be the right personal choice once their aggressive goal slips away, even when completing the race is still a possibility. It might require limping through the remaining miles or a three-hour nap at the aid station, but they could still finish. Yet they choose not to continue. These athletes have chased the goal they set and should have no shame in that DNF. If you are clear on what your goals are, then a DNF, as a potential ramification of aggressive goal setting, is just as gutsy as struggling to the end. As long as you are crystal clear on your goals, find the right balance of challenge and risk, and take the time to craft goals in a meaningful way, then you will always make the right decision if faced with the possibility of a DNF.

CREATING AN EFFORT-BASED RACE-DAY STRATEGY

Pacing for an ultra can make or break your race day. Wrist-top GPS technology can provide accurate information on pace, altitude, cadence, and heart rate to help guide the process. These data cues can be used to better prepare for race day. Reliance on this information can also ruin your plans, if you apply it incorrectly.

Pacing data from Martin Hoffman's team reveal that athletes who perform better and place higher generally have less speed variability overall and slow down less as the race progresses (Figure 11.6). The easy conclusion to make is that these athletes paced the race better, and thus slow down less and finish the race faster. However, could it be that the athletes who slowed down less were just more prepared? That question has yet to be answered.

In any case, proper pacing on race day can take three different strategies. You can choose to utilize one, or a combination that suits your needs and situation.

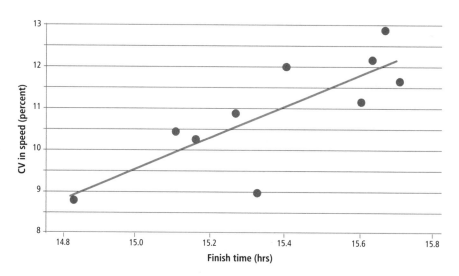

FIGURE **11.6** *Relationship between coefficient of variation (CV) in speed and finish time for the 10 fastest finishers of the WS 100. The fastest finishers had the lowest variation in speed.*

Source: Hoffman 2014.

OPTION 1: PACE

The standard race-day marathon plan invariably revolves around hitting some sort of pace for segments of the race. Even before the utilization of GPS watches, digital timing clocks lined the routes of the major marathon courses, sometimes as often as every mile. As GPS watches evolved, this proposition further evolved to monitoring between the timing clocks. For athletes looking to set a particular pace or time standard for a marathon, this is a good proposition. You have all the data you need at regular intervals to pace the race out properly. In many major marathons, you can even get customizable pacing bracelets, complete with splits for each and every mile.

Ultramarathons are not simply long marathons. Although pace can be a useful tool to execute your race-day strategy, there are limitations that you will have to account for to determine if it is a useful tool for you and your goals.

Pace is a good tool on race day in the following scenarios:

- Race terrain is flat and level without any technical elements for 50-mile and 50K distances. In this situation, you can choose to base your race-day strategy entirely on pace. If you are keenly aware of your TempoRun, SteadyStateRun, and EnduranceRun paces, your race-day paces can mirror these when appropriate. Similarly, if there is an element of flat, level terrain somewhere within a trail race, you can incorporate pace in those sections to gauge your race-day intensity.

- You are able to train on the racecourse. In this situation, if you are aware of your pace on certain segments and during certain workouts, you can use that information to calibrate your race-day pace. For example, if you consistently do SSR intervals up a climb in training and that climb is used during the race, you can check your GPS watch at various points during the climb to make sure you are at the right pace. For 50K and 50-mile races, many athletes can climb segments at their SSR or TempoRun intensities. Generally speaking, if the total number of climbing segments in the race match the training interval lengths described in Chapter 7 (see Table 7.2, page 144), you can reproduce those same intensities during the race if you have trained properly for them.

Pace is a poor tool on race day in the following scenarios:

- The terrain is different than your home training ground. The terrain will slow you down if it is more technical than your home training ground. The opposite is true if the race-day terrain is more benign. This is true at all race intensities and at all grades. Bottom line, if your race-day terrain is much more or less difficult than your home training ground, pace will be a poor tool for you come race day.

- The altitude is different than your home training ground. When you are at higher altitudes, your pace will be negatively affected. The opposite is true if you are racing at lower altitudes.

- For 100-mile and 100K events. Typically, these events are so long that you will be running much slower and easier than your day-to-day training paces and intensities.

OPTION 2: HEART RATE

As discussed in Chapter 7, heart rate is generally a poor way to determine intensity for an ultrarunner. Factors such as sleep, temperature, hydration, fatigue, and time of day may affect heart rate at any particular point in time. Furthermore, because I am an advocate of training based on rating of perceived exertion (RPE), introducing heart rate on race day would violate the tried-and-true rule of "Try nothing new on race day." Nevertheless, there is one limited scenario in which it is appropriate to use heart rate to gauge your race-day intensity.

Heart rate is a good tool on race day in the following scenario:

- When an athlete is consistently overenthusiastic at the start of the race. In this case, I recommend using a heart rate monitor as a governor for the first 25 percent of the race. The simple procedure I use is to find the athlete's normal SSR heart rate range during training (still using RPE to determine the

CALIBRATING RPE FOR RACE DAY

If you have taken the time to properly train and develop your various physiological systems, you can race as you have trained. This means that the accumulated time at the various intensities you were able to accomplish in training can, at a very minimum, be re-created in the race. For example, if you were consistently doing 4 × 10 min efforts at TempoRun intensity during training, you can accumulate 40 to 60 minutes of the same intensity during the race. The same is >

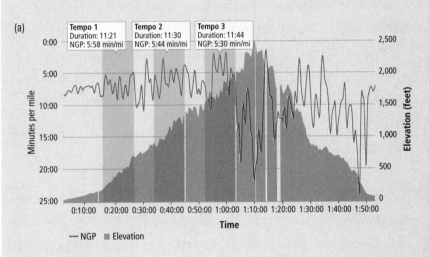

(a)

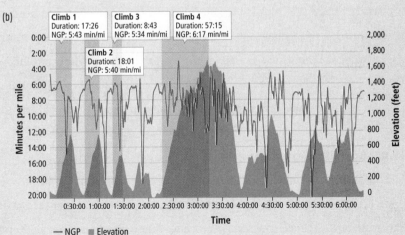

(b)

true for EnduranceRun and SSR intensities. Based on the attributes of the race you are preparing for, you can map out a plan of what RPE to target for different parts of the race. The first figure (a) is a typical TempoRun that Dylan Bowman did in preparation for the 2014 North Face Endurance Challenge, San Francisco. It shows that he can average a Normalized Graded Pace (NGP) for 3 × 11–12 min. The intervals for this workout would be at an RPE of 8 to 9. The second figure (b) is a GPS file from Dylan's 2014 North Face Endurance Challenge, San Francisco 50-mile race. The first four major climbs of the race are highlighted with the NGP Dylan was able to run. Dylan calibrated his race-day effort from his training efforts because the climb segments were similar in length to what he was able to reproduce in training. The race data validate this strategy because the NGP from the first three climbs is similar to his TempoRun NGP (5:50 min/mi), and the NGP from the fourth climb would be indicative of an SSR effort (close to 60 min in length).

intensity during the actual workouts), then have him or her use that value as a governor that is not to be exceeded during the first 25 percent of the race. For example, if during training an athlete's heart rate range is normally 160 to 165 beats per minute for SSR intervals, I will set 165 as the absolute heart rate that the athlete cannot exceed for the first 25 percent of the race. Effectively, this holds the athlete at the lower end of SSR intensity/higher end of EnduranceRun because race-day heart rates are higher at all intensities for the first 25 percent of the race due to freshness and adrenaline.

Heart rate is a poor tool on race day in the following scenarios:

- Just about everything else. Your race-day heart rate is going to be affected by a multitude of factors. Early in the race, adrenaline and the fact that you are rested will artificially elevate heart rate. As fatigue sets in, your heart rate will be depressed. All in all, heart rate is a poor choice to use come race day.

OPTION 3: RPE

Racing should be a reflection of your training. Similarly, pacing during the race should revolve around how you pace your day-to-day efforts. With my athletes, this means using rating of perceived exertion. Your internal RPE offers a calibration point that accurately identifies your intensity and is free from the errors associated with pace and heart rate. But the main reason my athletes use RPE on race day is because it is what they have used in training. Day in and day out, they are calibrating their efforts using this simple 1 to 10 scale. Race day should be no different. (For a detailed look at RPE, refer to Chapter 7.) The sidebar on page 249 illustrates how Dylan Bowman was able to take his efforts during day-to-day training and translate them into proper pacing on race day.

CREATING A RACE-DAY NUTRITION STRATEGY

If you have done everything right in training, you should not need an elaborate race-day nutrition plan because your race nutrition will be very similar to your training nutrition. Only rarely will my athletes go to a race with an elaborate workbook listing concoctions of engineered foods, sports drinks, and foodstuffs. I've seen such detailed plans and have always likened them to the biochemistry experiments I performed as a young student. In these unnecessarily complicated plans, the required food and fluid are detailed in 30-, 20-, and sometimes 10-minute increments. Puzzled and confused crew members wade through the details, asking, "Was this aid station supposed to be 8 ounces of coke with a Nutella cracker or water with half a scoop of the red powder, half a scoop of the other powder, and a peanut butter and jelly sandwich?" When watching these real-life chemistry experiments unfold, I have always wondered, "Is this how that runner trains?" To date, in all my experience as a runner and a coach, I have yet to come across an athlete who maintains such elaborate nutrition planning during training. Why, then, do they do it in a race?

Table 11.1 presents an example of such an overcomplicated nutrition plan. I adapted it from many of the flawed race plans I have seen over the years. Although the plan is well intended, it is too complicated, and the concoctions utilized are

TABLE 11.1	Overcomplicated Nutrition Strategy		
RACE SECTION	**FOOD**	**FLUID**	**SUPPLEMENTS**
Start to aid station 1	2 gels	1 drink mix in bottle 1	1 salt tab
		1 drink mix in bottle 2	1 amino acid capsule
Aid station 1 to aid station 2	2 gels	Water in bottle 1	1 salt tab
	1 energy bar	1 electrolyte tablet in bottle 2	
		Coke in aid station	
Aid station 2 to aid station 3	1 pack energy chews	½ drink mix, ½ scoop whey protein in bottle 1	2 salt tabs
	½ pack energy chews	Water in bottle 2	
		Ginger ale in aid station	
Aid station 3 to finish	2 gels	½ drink mix, ½ Coke in bottle 1	1 salt tab
	1 pack energy chews	1 electrolyte tablet in bottle 2	1 amino acid capsule

impractical to replicate in training. I once read a nutrition plan developed for an athlete that included consuming exactly 83 ounces of liquid during a 21-mile section of race. Not 82, not 84, but 83.

DEVELOP A STRATEGY, THEN A PLAN

You don't want to leave your nutrition to chance in an ultramarathon, but what you want to develop is a race-day nutrition *strategy*, after which you may or may not choose to create a race-day nutrition *plan*. A strategy encompasses the target calories, fluid, and foodstuffs you have tried and tested in training. If you develop an actual written-down-on-paper plan from that overarching strategy, it should take no more than an elementary school education to execute. If you have done a good job in training by experimenting with the right foodstuffs and drinks, the race-day strategy is simple.

Developing your nutrition strategy for race day should revolve around the following aspects:

- Eat and drink what you have tried in training.

- Target calories per hour.

- Target fluid per hour, adjusted for the temperature range of the event.

- Know when and how to incorporate things like caffeine or stomach-calming tricks like antacids and ginger.

Fluids first. As discussed in Chapter 10, your nutrition strategy is largely dependent on your hydration status. When your hydration status is in check, the foods you ingest stand a chance of being absorbed and metabolized into energy. Therefore, your race-day nutrition strategy starts with the fluid you plan to take in during various parts of the race. Consider factors such as time between aid stations, temperature, and intensity. If you plan to consume liquid with some form of calories, this also sets the beginning of your caloric range, which you need to determine next.

Find your target calorie range. As opposed to a strict "eat this at 30 minutes, eat that at 60 minutes" type of plan, I recommend first targeting a specific calorie range. Once that range is determined, the specific foodstuffs you plan to consume on race day are developed during day-to-day training. The calorie count is relatively easy: 200 to 250 calories after the first 60 minutes for most people. Some elite athletes can push that count toward 400. Kaci Lickteig breaks this formula; with her diminutive stature, she can tolerate only 160 to 180 calories per hour. In any case, finding your target calorie range (not a specific number) is the first step. This process was described in Chapter 10, "Fueling and Hydrating for the Long Haul."

Develop your bull's-eye and outer-ring foods. During training, particularly during longer runs, use your target calorie ranges and then experiment with different foodstuffs. This is how you develop the core group of bull's-eye foods that are tried and true for you. As described in Chapter 10, you also need to develop foods that fit into the outer rings of your target, those you can use for backup if your core go-to foods begin to fail. It is important to build your lists of target foods, and foods that are off target, so you can make good choices in any race, under varying circumstances, and as your preferences change during an event.

Once the core foods have been fully tested in training, experiment with your backup foods. In theory, the three to five foodstuffs developed in training will be all you need, but, in ultrarunning sometimes things don't go as planned. These backup foodstuffs are what you can fall back on when all else fails. The typical fallback plan revolves around the aid station fare of cookies, soup, fruit, sandwiches, and the like.

An example of an athlete's bull's-eye nutrition strategy is shown in Figure 10.3 (page 221). If you can stay on target and rotate through your three or four core foods during the race, then stick with them and stay in the bull's-eye. If you get tired of those foods, then move to the outer ring.

Customize intake for your race distance and effort. Your blood flow is always being balanced between digestion, cooling, and your working muscles. Different intensities will allow for different combinations and amounts of your bull's-eye foodstuffs. In general, the higher the intensity of the race, the more you will need to rely on easily digestible calories. The converse is also true. The longer the race, the more you can incorporate real food. The bull's-eye and outer-ring foods are a representation of *any* of the things you can eat, not necessarily the specific or optimal ones for a particular race. For example, you might only use gels from your bull's-eye in a 50K, gels and pretzels for a 50-mile race, and the entire rotation for a 100-mile event.

Figure 11.7 depicts a target that is customized for a more intense race. Using only three foodstuffs, this athlete would still have a real food (rice ball) and an engineered food (gel), as well as hit the sweet, salty, and savory taste profiles.

SUPPLEMENTS AND ERGOGENIC AIDS

Like bull's-eye nutrition, other supplements and ergogenic aids you anticipate using on race day should be tested in training. Yes, this means taking a caffeine pill or some crystallized ginger on a four-hour run when it is completely unnecessary! Your bull's-eye nutrition might be enough to get you to the finish line on race day. But because the distance and duration of the event are typically longer than any

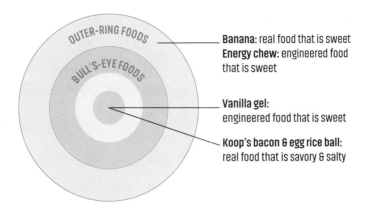

Banana: real food that is sweet
Energy chew: engineered food that is sweet

Vanilla gel: engineered food that is sweet

Koop's bacon & egg rice ball: real food that is savory & salty

FIGURE **11.7** *Target customization for a shorter, more intense ultra*

single training run, it's good to have a set of supplements and ergogenic aids that you can go to when the time comes.

CAFFEINE: THE ORIGINAL PERFORMANCE-ENHANCING DRUG

Yes, caffeine is a drug. In fact, it is the most widely consumed psychoactive drug in the world today. Yes, it can enhance your performance. I vividly remember pacing my wife during the latter stages of the Run Rabbit Run 100 and stumbling upon a ream of a dozen 200-mg caffeine pills. I wondered whether the runner who dropped the package was simply being lazy by not cutting the foil-constrained ream down into more realistic chunks of a few pills or actually intended to use all 2,400 mg of caffeine over the last 20 miles of the race. Because ultrarunners are a somewhat obsessive group, I assumed the latter. That would have been a sight! I'm glad I found the pills, and not an amped-up arrhythmic runner.

Caffeine supplementation can be used in two ways: to acutely enhance your performance or as a stimulant specifically to stay awake and alert.

Caffeine as a performance enhancer. Caffeine supplementation starts with your morning cup of coffee on race day. If you regularly drink a cup or two a day, feel free to enjoy a similar amount as you go through your pre-race routine. This supplementation then deviates, based on the race distance you are about to undertake.

For shorter races lasting less than six hours, you can supplement with occasional caffeine, up to 50 mg in any particular hour for the entire race. The supplementation should mainly come from caffeinated gels, chews, and colas. If you typically have coffee in the morning, caffeine from the coffee should be enough for the first two to three hours of the race. Therefore, I suggest waiting until after the second or third hour to start supplementing with caffeine in other forms. Furthermore, the dose response from caffeine as it relates to endurance performance is not linear, meaning that moderate doses of caffeine are likely to have the same performance effect as higher doses (Graham and Spriet 1995; Pasman et al. 1995). More isn't always better. Thus, a cautious and conservative approach will have the same performance effect as a more aggressive one.

Caffeine to stay awake and alert. Many ultrarunning events go into the night and through the following day. Runners are constantly battling the mythical-yet-real sleep monster, particularly in the wee hours of the morning, before sunrise and after 20 hours on their feet. Caffeine is one of the key pieces of ammunition against the sleep monster, and you can ingest it in many forms: pills, colas, chocolate-covered espresso beans, energy drinks, and caffeinated sports nutrition products. However, when using caffeine as a stimulant to boost your alertness, the timing, rather than the form, is critical.

For athletes competing in events lasting longer than 24 hours, caffeine is best viewed as a stimulant to stay awake and alert. In these situations, you need to focus on when the stimulation will be needed most, and then supplement at that point. This means starting the day with a normal routine, including pre-race breakfast and coffee if that is what you are accustomed to. But as the race begins, *take care to avoid caffeine.* Gels, drinks, and foods at this point should all be noncaffeinated. Sometime after midnight, when you expect a visit from the sleep monster, begin your caffeine supplementation. Doses can be as high as 100 mg/hour for three to four hours and can cease shortly after the sun rises, which helps to reset your circadian rhythms.

NAPPING

If you anticipate sleeping at any point during the event, there's a great strategy researchers have found involving caffeine and short power naps. While the findings are not specific to an ultra setting, they can be modified and applied if you anticipate needing sleep, or if an unanticipated trail nap is a must. In these situations, if you expect to take a 20- to 30-minute power nap, it is best to consume caffeine just prior to the slumber. Paradoxically, the crux of the benefit lies in the fact that the stimulant will take effect when you wake up, leaving you more refreshed and alert (Horne and Reyner 1996; Reyner and Horne 1997; Hayashi, Masuda, and Hori 2003).

STOMACH SETTLERS

As was discussed in Chapter 4, gastrointestinal distress is one of the leading problems experienced by ultrarunners, typically occurring after hours of racing, which is far past the duration of a normal training run. Even though training runs provide few opportunities to test the efficacy of any of the typical stomach settlers such as ginger, antacids, and hard candies, you may be able to rule them out by testing them during training, even when your stomach is not upset. Kaci Lickteig's 2015 Western States 100 story, described at the end of this chapter, is an excellent illustration of this. In her previous training, Kaci had not tried the ginger chews I gave her during that race. Had she done so, they probably would have had the same visceral and unpleasant effect they had during the race. The takeaway is, as with anything else related to nutrition, be sure to try stomach settlers during training, even if you don't need to.

Ginger. Ginger is available in candy form, crystallized, or in a ginger beer or brew. It has long been recommended by herbalists and doctors and used by cancer patients and pregnant women as an alternative to drugs to treat nausea. The theory is that the chemicals and soothing flavor help to calm an upset stomach. Although much of the research either shows a benefit or is inconclusive, small doses are reported to have the most benefit (Lien et al. 2003; Lohsiriwat et al. 2010; Pongrojpaw, Somprasit, and Chanthasenanont 2007; Ryan 2012). You should note, however, that most aid station ginger ale of the generic variety contains no actual ginger!

Antacids. These can be Tums or a generic alternative. When you eat, your body increases the amount of gastric acids in order to digest food. These acids can overflow up the esophagus and irritate and potentially damage the esophageal lining as well as the lining of the stomach. To combat this increase in gastric acids, antacids provide a base in the form of calcium carbonate, which neutralizes the acid. Chew one or two at a time.

Hard candies. Peppermints and butterscotch candies have long been used by runners to soothe sour stomachs. The theory is that the sucking motion of your mouth will relieve the distress. Although there is little scientific evidence to back up this claim, it's a home remedy that has been around for many years. In desperate times, it might be worth a shot. As an added bonus, you get the sugar from the candy. Butterscotch is my favorite.

This list of supplements and ergogenic aids is purposely very short. There should be no reason to incorporate anything other than real food, engineered sport-specific foods and sports drinks, and the items listed here. There are a lot of powders and packages in sports nutrition stores that promise to carry you farther and faster than ever before, but beware. Supplements are not regulated by the Food and Drug Administration. They may contain ingredients that are not listed on the label, and the ingredients listed on the label may not be in the bottle, or may be in the bottle in a different amount than listed. The combination of no regulation and inaccurate or deceptive manufacturing and labeling means that supplements from the corner store, grocery store, or specialized sports nutrition store may contain substances that are not only against the spirit of drug-free sport but also prohibited by the US Anti-Doping Agency and World Anti-Doping Agency.

NSAIDS

Don't include NSAIDs (aspirin, ibuprofen, naproxen) in your race-day plan. Ever. They increase the risk of hyponatremia (Wharam et al. 2006; Page et al. 2007) and greatly increase the demand placed on the renal system, putting you at greater risk of renal injury and rhabdomyolysis (emptying of damaged or dead muscle tissue from muscles into the bloodstream). You might ache a little less after popping a couple of ibuprofen tablets, but the downside is you could end up in the hospital with renal failure. Pretty easy choice.

MODIFIED NUTRITIONAL STRATEGY FOR RACE DAY

Table 11.1 showed a flawed, overcomplicated plan to demonstrate how not to develop a race-day nutrition plan. Now let's look at an example of what you should do. Table 11.2 shows a properly developed and streamlined race-day nutrition strategy. It is focused on target calorie and fluid ranges, not exact foodstuffs and scoops of powder. It gives the athlete the flexibility to choose to consume 100 calories of a Bonk Breaker or the equivalent amount of energy chews. The fluid is easy to manage, with target total consumption ranges from aid station to aid station. Finally, this is merely a replication of what the athlete would do in training. For a five-hour training run, the athlete would take 80 to 120 ounces of sports drink and water with 1,000 to 1,250 calories of gels, Bonk Breaker bars, rice balls, and energy chews, throughout training, similar to the five hours between aid stations 1 and 3.

RECRUITING AND INSTRUCTING YOUR SUPPORT CREW

Ultrarunning has a special community. Nearly every weekend in cities, parks, and wildlands all across the country, people are organizing and running ultra-marathons. Aid stations are stocked, and volunteers arise in the wee hours of the morning to take their places. Crews play a vital role in this community, serving as personal aid stations to weary runners as they undertake their ultramarathon

TABLE **11.2**	Streamlined Nutritional Strategy		
RACE SECTION	**FOOD**	**FLUID**	**SUPPLEMENTS**
Start to aid station 1 (2 hours)	100 calories total (1 gel)	20–30 oz. total (water)	None
Aid station 1 to aid station 2 (2 hours)	400–500 calories total (gels and Bonk Breaker bar)	30–50 oz. total (water and drink mix)	None
Aid station 2 to aid station 3 (3 hours)	600–750 calories total (rice ball, gels, energy chews)	50–70 oz. total (water and drink mix)	1 salt tab
Aid station 3 to finish (2 hours)	400–500 calories total (gels and Bonk Breaker bar)	~50 oz. total (water and drink mix)	Ginger chews or antacid if necessary

journey. With comprehensive aid station support at most ultras these days, it is certainly not necessary to have a crew for your race, but it sure is nice to see a familiar face. Choosing your crew for this adventure is not a decision to take lightly. When you choose the correct crew mates, they can push you to greater heights. They will know exactly what to say and what to give you, and may even be able to anticipate what you will need next. When you choose the wrong crew, they can drag you down. The wrong crew can drain your energy, make mistakes in execution, and worst of all cause a DNF when you are able to move forward.

The first step: Determine whether you want a crew at all. Both new and experienced runners sometimes choose to forgo crews entirely. Most races make this possible with bountiful aid stations and more than enough helpful volunteers to keep you moving. If, for whatever reason, your preferred crew (family, friends, etc.) cannot make the event, fret not. The race will most likely be able to take care of you.

If you decide you want a crew, your next move is to determine who exactly you want out there. Husbands, wives, kids, friends, and running partners can all make up a good crew. If they care for you and can get away for the weekend, chances are they would jump at the chance to help. However, just because your friends and loved ones *can* be part of your crew does not mean that they *should* be. The best crew members are the people who know you as a runner and as a person . . . and have only a small amount of sympathy. After all, it's going to be tough out there, so it's best to have someone in your corner who does not mind telling you to suck it up.

Align your crew with your goals first, and then instruct them on the tactical details. First and foremost, your crew is there to assist you in achieving your goals; handing off gels or a jacket and making soup are mere means to that end. I consistently see crews with folders, spreadsheets, and labeled baggies in the aid stations of ultramarathon events. Any kid off the street could look at a highlighted portion of a worksheet, pull the food and gear listed on it, and lay them out for the runner. You don't need a supportive, caring, and engaged crew member for that. And if that's all you empower your crew to do, you are not leveraging the people around you to enhance your performance. The mistake people make is to have crew members who are well instructed on what to do but poorly instructed on the crew's overall goals and the runner's outcome and process goals. Make no mistake, these overall goals are far more important than the number of potatoes to eat at mile 30. Beginner racers and crews tend to rely more on worksheets and minute-by-minute instructions because the structure provides confidence. Your goal, however, should be to progress to the point where, if you have properly instructed and empowered your crew on their goals and your outcome and process goals, you should need to do little more than give them an index card with those goals, a duffel bag full of your gear and nutrition, and driving directions.

DO YOU WANT A PACER?

Many ultramarathons, particularly at the 100K and 100-mile distances, allow the use of pacers to accompany the runner. In theory, the pacers can provide motivational support and offer a level of safety for their runner and other runners in the field. As an added benefit, serving as a pacer is a great way to get an introduction into the sport. Most pacers are well intended, but some end up undoing their runner's race. Personality conflicts, goal misalignments, and a lack of preparation have waylaid many an ultrarunner's best-laid plans. Using a pacer or choosing to go solo is entirely a personal preference. The decision ultimately lies with the runner.

///// *MISSY GOSNEY* SUPPORT CREWS: TO HAVE OR NOT TO HAVE

In most of the ultramarathons I have done, I chose to not utilize a crew. For me, the simplicity of having to worry about me and me alone is part of what I love about ultrarunning. Choosing to go without a crew, I am free from the constraints and necessary additional energy of worrying about other people's schedules, creating a larger footprint in the wilderness, and organizing unnecessary logistics. This leaves more time, energy, and focus that I can devote to me.

Furthermore, I have found that most aid station volunteers love helping. They are thrilled at the prospect of being pulled off of whatever routine task they are doing to find a drop bag, unpack it, and then cool down some boiling hot chicken soup. I have become an expert, dare I say guru, at coming into an aid station, finding someone who is willing to help, and instructing them on exactly what I need to get out of the aid station in the most efficient way possible. My drop bags are well-packed models of efficiency, complete with packing lists and detailed instructions for when my brain gets fuzzy. For me, no crew is the way to go.

The 2015 Hardrock was an exception to that rule. I had been unsuccessfully playing the lottery to enter for four years, and my ultimate success in gaining entry was a thrill. As I planned for the race, I decided to enlist the services of my teenaged son as my crew. Although he had little experience in the ultramarathon world, I knew he would be excellent and that the process would be a learning experience for him. As I approached the subject, I asked him one question: "Can you take care of your mom?" For me, that was his only goal. Sure, I would later go over all the finer details, such as which jacket to bring, when I wanted some soup, and when I would need coffee. But as long he could take care of his mom, that's all we needed.

/////

SUCCESS IS ALWAYS THE RUNNER'S RESPONSIBILITY

Crew or no crew, pacer or no pacer, the responsibility of finishing the race and achieving your goals is yours alone. In this way, your crew and/or pacer(s) merely catalyze the process; they are not the linchpins in the operation. Success will ultimately be up to you, your training, and the determination you put forth on race day. When you are choosing a crew or a pacer, remember that it is always your responsibility as a runner to succeed. Your crew or a pacer can help you thrive on race day, but you should not rely on them for your success.

THE ADAPT SYSTEM FOR PROBLEM-SOLVING

Everyone has a plan until they get punched in the mouth.   —Mike Tyson

If you do one single thing at a high enough intensity for long enough, every once in a while the shit will hit the fan. As much as you have trained, as patiently as you have paced, as dialed as your race-day nutrition is, and as experienced as you are, you will eventually get punched in the mouth, and it is going to hurt. Your legs will feel like lead, your effort will feel unreasonable, you will start tripping over roots and rocks, and your stomach will be in knots. If you are especially unlucky, these infirmities will all happen at once. And for many miles. Maybe not in your next race, or the one after that, but if you remain in the ultramarathon game for a long enough time, lady luck's evil doppelgänger will eventually find you.

Ultramarathons are long enough that you have the opportunity to go through (many) highs and (hopefully fewer) lows. Some of the highs will be amazing; some of the lows will be excruciating. For many, that's part of the attraction to the sport. However, having things go wrong does not necessarily mean your race is over. Fortunately, most ultramarathon cutoffs are generous enough that you can have a bad patch (or two) and still complete the event. And the more fit you are, the more bandwidth you'll have to get through a rough patch. Believe me, I would far rather my athletes never have to experience bad patches in their races. Ideally, ultramarathoners would just run and eat and run, and run and eat and run some more, and never have any issues. If you play your cards right and prepare well, this is usually the case. Nonetheless, it's wise to prepare yourself for some tough times. As the British writer and politician Benjamin Disraeli said, "I am prepared for the worst, but hope for the best."

I have developed five simple steps you can apply to get yourself out of the proverbial hole, regardless of the situation you're in. These steps form the easy-to-remember and appropriate acronym ADAPT, which also serves as a reminder of what you need to do at your lowest of lows:

Accept

Diagnose

Analyze

Plan

Take action

ACCEPT

Accept things as they are. We all live in the present. In the exact moment that things deteriorate, you have to be in the present. Sure, you can hope that Scotty will beam you up to another place and another time where your stomach is not tied up in knots, but that isn't going to happen. So, accept the fact that things suck at the moment. Accept that your primary outcome goal might go out the window. Accept that you might be stuck in the aid station for the next hour or even longer, or that you might need to curl up and take a trail nap (your water bottle or hydration pack makes for an outstanding pillow, by the way). Accept how you are in the present, however bad that might be, and get over it.

Emotion clouds judgment. It pulls an opaque veil over the situation, effectively making you incapable of rational thought and action. Acceptance of the situation allows you to move forward. When you reach the point of acceptance, you forget the past. The rock you just stubbed your toe on for the fifth time? Gone. The trail marker you missed, costing you precious time and energy on the wrong path? In the past. You can't change the fact that you've tripped and fallen three times over the last hundred yards, but you can change your outlook. Acceptance of the situation moves you from the past into the present. It lifts the fog of emotion and enables you to think and act rationally. Accept first, and then you are ready to move forward.

DIAGNOSE

Make a quick and dirty assessment of what is going on. Don't try to *solve* your problems yet, but do try to figure out what is going on. This step is easy. If you just rolled your ankle, then, duh, you have an injured ankle. If your stomach has turned, then your nutrition plan has gone awry. If you are frustrated because you have fallen, then you are simply frustrated. Don't worry about the specifics of the issue just yet or how to resolve it; just diagnose the problem. Keep this step simple and to the point. "I have an upset stomach," "I am lightheaded," or "I am frustrated" (or a combination of these) will work perfectly fine. It is also fine to identify more than one problem, but resist the urge to roll right to analysis or planning before clearly identifying the problem. When people fail at this step, they end up creating solutions to the wrong problems.

ANALYZE

Now it is time to apply some thinking to the problem and enlist whatever synapses you have that are still working. You have moved on and accepted that things suck. You have diagnosed what the issue is. It's now time to analyze the situation you are in. Where is the next aid station? How much time do you have until the next cutoff? What tools, food, supplies, and gear are available? Create a mental inventory, because these are the means you will use to get yourself out of the hole you are currently in. The outcome of the next step depends on the analysis you do!

PLAN

You have accepted the situation, diagnosed what is wrong, and analyzed your surroundings. Now it's time to actually figure out what to do and plan. This is by far the most complicated step. The plan should not require Mensa-level analysis, but it will require some brainpower. Your plan incorporates your earlier analysis of the situation and the means at your disposal. It takes the wheres and whats and weaves them into concrete steps that can lift you out of the hole you have dug. Depending on the situation, a simple plan might be to get to the next aid station and figure it out from there. If this is the case, you can share the results of your diagnosis and analysis with your crew, and they can help you formulate a new plan. One step at a time.

TAKE ACTION

When it's all said and done, you have to take action. Problems do not fix themselves. *You* as the athlete have to do something deliberate to fix them. If you believe in magic, like the Disneyland type of magic, then ultrarunning is not for you. Put your plan into action. Take action. By force if necessary.

> **Situation:** "I have just rolled my ankle on a rock."
>
> **Accept:** "My ankle is going to hurt for a bit. I am going to be slower. This is fine. I'm over it."
>
> **Diagnose:** "I have an injured ankle."
>
> **Analyze:** "I was 60 minutes away from the next aid station. Now I am about 90 minutes away if I walk. I do not have enough food or water on me for that length of time. I have crew at the next aid station."
>
> **Plan:** "I am going to walk into the next aid station. If I see another runner, I will ask them for some food and fluid. When I get to the next aid station, I am going to see if there is medical help there or some other way to tape/brace my ankle. My crew is there so they can help me with this."
>
> **Take action:** "I am going to walk down the trail now." As another runner approaches: "I am going to ask this runner for some fluid."

This example is a simple and straightforward application of the ADAPT system. Kaci Lickteig's experience at the 2015 Western States 100-Mile Endurance Run (see sidebar) is an example of how you can use the ADAPT system to work through a potentially race-ending situation and come all the way back to have a great result.

///// KACI LICKTEIG 2015 WESTERN STATES 100

My 2015 Western States 100-mile race was focused on growing from my experience the previous year. A quick recap from my 2014 Western States 100 race:

- I ran too aggressively on the descents and blew my quads and hips out by mile 40.

- The final 60.2 miles were a complete sufferfest.

- That experience brought about a new perspective and respect for the race.

- I needed to make changes for 2015 to ensure that I would have a much better race.

As I sat waiting for the 2015 start, so many thoughts were going through my mind. To say I was cool, calm, and collected would be a lie. I was scared, emotional, and a nervous wreck. I didn't know how my day was going to unfold, but I knew I was going to accept that I would make the changes necessary to start my race off on the right foot.

Standing at the starting line, I was shaking with both excitement and nervousness. Once the countdown finished, I was off on my journey. The crest at the top of Escarpment was picturesque, and I took in the breathtaking view of the sunrise. I no more than batted an eye and I made my way down the buttery singletrack trail on the other side. I stuck to my plan to stay back, remain calm, and reserve energy. I knew that I had taken these downhill descents too hard the previous year, and this year I was going to be more purposeful to take them with care.

I quickly found myself far behind the lead women. I couldn't allow myself to get caught up in the chase yet, as it was too risky. I was not happy to have to be so far behind and not get to run with the other women; however, I knew it was what I had to do for my own sake. I decided to stay in control and just cruise along, taking in all that was around me.

I continued to run my own race and within my own means. I soon found myself catching up to several of the lead women. I passed a few over the course of the next several miles. While grazing at one of the aid stations, I grabbed a grilled turkey and cheese sandwich. I hadn't eaten greasy food in ages, and this is where it all began. Somewhere up the Devil's Thumb   >

climb, issues start to flare up; I got very overheated during the ascent, and my stomach started turning sour. I figured the greasy grilled cheese was a mistake. As I left the next aid station, I took a popsicle to see if the coolness would help. My stomach revolted against the popsicle and any form of nutrition that I tried to ingest. I was in a world of discomfort. I tried to run, but every downhill jostled my stomach, making it worse. I was in a fit of panic. I thought, "Oh no, is this going to be the end of my race?" I had heard so many horror stories about "bad stomachs" and how they caused people to end their races. But this was my reality.

After my initial panic, I accepted that my stomach was upset and realized this was my reality at the present time. I couldn't let myself get overwhelmed and frustrated, as that would have just added to the stress. I diagnosed my problem: "I have a sour stomach and I am hot." I then analyzed my whereabouts and realized the next aid station was going to be at least 4 to 5 miles away. I had nothing with me to calm my stomach. Thankfully, I was running with another runner who realized I was having problems. Out of the greatness of her heart, she offered me some Tums. I gratefully accepted. I had just a few aid stations before I would arrive at Michigan Bluff, where my crew would be waiting for me. I planned to make my way there as best I could, keeping my stomach under control and trying to stay as cool as possible.

Once I made my way up to Michigan Bluff, I saw my crew and my coach, Jason Koop. I asked right away, "What do I do for a bad stomach?" He instantly said to get some ginger. I grabbed some ginger chews, but I couldn't stand the taste and I had to spit most of them out. Jason and my crew grabbed me and took me to some shade to try and cool me down and talk me through this low point. They made me realize that my legs were fine and moving; it was just my stomach that was limiting me. Coach had made me a slushy, which I took and carried with me. He told me to nurse the cool slushy and simply keep moving forward. After all, the day is long, and you never know what's going to happen. That is just what I did. I took action and started taking little sips of the refreshing slushy and pressed the bottle against my neck to cool me down. I was not moving fast, but gradually I started feeling rejuvenated and was able to start running again. My mind and body realigned, and my next plan was to run to Foresthill to pick up my pacer. At Foresthill, mile 62 of the race, I was in fifth place, nearly an hour behind the first- and second-place women.

The remaining 38 miles of the race were just that, a race. I wanted to see how fast I could run. My stomach was solid, my attitude was great, and my legs were spry. My pacer and I made our way down the river and up past Green Gate. Shortly thereafter, I realized I was in third place and on the podium. I was elated and thought to myself how much I wanted to be in the top three. Now it was time to race against myself because I didn't want to get caught. I didn't know how strong the other women behind me were, and I didn't want to find out.

We were moving smoothly, and the smile on my face kept growing. I couldn't believe how my race was shaping up. I was so thankful for every step forward. Finally, at the Highway 49 aid station, I passed another woman. "Holy smokes, I am in second place . . . SECOND PLACE!" I was on fire. As my friends say back home, "Light the fires and kick the tires." It was go time—no holding back. I felt a rush of adrenaline overtake me. We were moving quickly, making our way to No Hands Bridge aid station. I recall Coach saying, "Keep racing!!" That is exactly what we did. I couldn't believe we were running all the way up to Robie Point aid station, as it is a decent climb. Once we hit the road down to Placer High School, the finish, I was overjoyed and emotional. Coming into the stadium and crossing the finish line in second place brought me to tears. It was a dream come true. Every time I think about that day, my heart grows warm, and I think of how grateful I am to have had the day I did.

/////

Kaci's story of adapting to the race is one of my favorites. Watching her move from aid station to aid station, I knew she was very close to having her race go from bad to abysmal. She had multiple things going wrong. As an athlete, you can usually deal with one thing at a time. Your foot hurts, not a big deal. You get too hot, you can simply slow down and cool off. You have an upset tummy, you can tough it out. But if you are having more than one of these problems, the damage is worse than the sum of their parts.

By the time I saw Kaci at Michigan Bluff, this was the case. She had multiple issues (sour stomach, overheating, bad attitude). She was also far behind her 2014 splits (more than 20 minutes at Michigan Bluff and nearly 30 at Foresthill). Thankfully, though, she had already made much progress in turning her race around, even though the race splits might not have shown it. She had already accepted the fact that she had multiple problems. She diagnosed that she was hot and her stomach was sour. She then analyzed where she could get help—at the next aid station where her crew was. Her plan was to make it to that aid station and let her crew help her out. She then took action, slowly moving down the trail and trying to keep cool. When she was in the aid station, she took action on the next part of her plan by telling her crew what was going on. She successfully found something to turn her around: a cold slushy. At that point, she was still far out of the race, far off of the podium, significantly behind her previous year's times, and far from the finish. But ultramarathons are long, and even in the elite field, you have time to make mistakes and turn them around. One key is to stay in the moment and continue working on the problem right in front of you. Yes, you have to think ahead, but you have to be careful not to think about all the things that could happen hours and hours from now. Such thoughts become overwhelming and may lead you to think that a DNF is inevitable. Solve the problem in front of you and move on to the next decision, and the next. Ultimately, Kaci turned her mistakes around. She continued to take action and pulled herself out of the hole she had dug, thereby turning what could have been a disastrous race into a PR (a full 46 minutes faster than 2014) and one of the best races of her career.

WHAT IS MISSING FROM THE ADAPT SYSTEM?

Admittedly, the acronym ADAPT is a bit contrived. It represents a series of steps that are analogous to problem-solving techniques that have been used by Boy Scouts, mountaineers, adventure racers, and the military, among others. The point of using the acronym is to identify a series of concrete steps you can focus on when you are at the lowest of low points. It is also important to understand what I intentionally *left out* of the ADAPT system.

Predict. Many runners are by nature analytical people. They are experts at doing easy math and determining their pace and how long it is going to take to get to the next aid station. While under normal circumstances it is a good thing to know when and how long it will take to locomote from place to place, when one is pulling out of a low, that thinking should be kept to a minimum. You should absolutely figure out how long it is going to take you to get to the next aid station, but the math should end there. One never knows how the day is going to turn out. Kaci's story is a great example.

Radically change your race strategy. The acronym is ADAPT, not PANIC. Making small, incremental changes is always better than drastically revising your well-thought-out race strategy all at once. Many times, small changes (or adaptations) from your original plan are all that are necessary.

Guess. Simply taking a stab in the dark to fix a problem should be the last resort. If you do a thorough job of analyzing and planning, the steps out of the hole should be quite clear-cut. Fortunately for most of us, fixing problems in ultrarunning is not rocket science. There is typically a wealth of experience out on the course during race day. Your crew, aid station workers, and fellow runners can help if you get stumped. Use them if necessary!

CHAPTER 12

RACING WISELY

How many races do I need? —ALMOST EVERY ATHLETE I'VE EVER TALKED TO

Athletes frequently ask me this question as they get set to start the journey toward their goal event. Particularly if their goal is challenging, athletes often feel the need to have some logical series of races in order to prepare. The question has always puzzled me. No one really "needs" a race. Yet many people think there is some magical formula that will tell them, "If you complete x and y races, you will be prepared for your goal."

Further confounding the issue is the fact that the number of ultrarunning events grows every year. It is quite easy to find a 50K, 50-mile, or 100-mile event on any given weekend. In certain areas, the travel required to reach an ultramarathon is minimal. Given that most ultrarunners are an outdoorsy group, George Mallory's oft-quoted rationale "because it's there" becomes a reason to race and race often.

Doing a race because you feel you "need" it or simply because "it's there" is a poor way to pick and choose events. Unfortunately, many athletes fall victim to this psychology. They endlessly chase the races they feel they need because they are there. They race too much, and they race without a true purpose.

To better understand what racing means to each individual, I gathered several of my athletes on a conference call. Some of them race nearly every weekend. Others race only once in a calendar year. The conversation was fascinating. Interestingly, while the optimum quantity and types of races varied wildly from athlete to athlete, their viewpoints on why and when to race were equally dissimilar. What ultimately emerged was a different set of values each athlete placed on the racing process. That value system then set the construct for how many and what types of racing each athlete did.

Racing and what it represents to you are rooted in your personal values. The values you put on the process of racing should determine what and when you choose (not need) to race. Like many other value systems, this one is entirely individual. The same series of races that works for one athlete might be counterproductive for another, even when they are preparing for the same goal event.

In the following sections, I have summarized the racing values for the athletes who participated in the conference call. Some might fit your own value set; some might not. Your values will ultimately determine what races you pick and how many of them end up on your calendar. I encourage you to use these as a starting point for your goals. The ultimate end point is up to you to craft.

RACING AS THE END OF MEANS

I like to have a point to what I'm doing.   —Dakota Jones

For many, racing represents the simple end point of training. While from a coaching standpoint I always view training as continuous, some athletes bookend the process with the races they choose. Athletes put in miles, contrive different intervals, and sacrifice time with family and friends to make themselves better in order to race at their best. For these athletes, racing fulfills the training process. In Dakota's case, much of his specific training is spent hammering up the steep gravel roads near Durango, Colorado. Many times, this is at the expense of climbing some breathtaking peak, rock climbing, or reading (yet another) book. For him, racing validates the work and sacrifice necessary to achieve his goals. Racing is the ultimate point of what he does on a day-to-day basis. If you are an athlete who sees racing as the logical end point of a period of training or preparation, you may not feel the need to race very frequently. You are more likely to place greater value on particular races that are important to you, rather than racing for the sake of racing.

RACING AS A COMPETITIVE OUTLET

At the end of the day, I like to compete. Racing is that outlet for me. —DYLAN BOWMAN

Many of us are competitive by nature, and this innate competitive psychology drives athletes to want to race. Running against fellow athletes, or against oneself, is what racing represents. These athletes enjoy seeing how their fitness and toughness stack up. When your competitive drive is what you're satisfying, it may make sense to incorporate more high-quality racing into your annual plan.

RACING AS PART OF THE TRAINING PROCESS

I use racing to gain the things I will need to draw upon come race day. —ERIK GLOVER

Day-to-day training can only prepare you for so much. Managing aid stations, drop bags, foreign terrain, and event-day logistics are difficult to replicate in training. Racing can help to bridge the gaps that remain. Furthermore, racing can provide an opportunity for a big training stimulus. The duration and intensity of the race usually exceed what an athlete can accomplish in day-to-day training.

For me, racing is part of the training process.   —KACI LICKTEIG

Kaci Lickteig places a similar value on the racing process. Kaci races a lot, sometimes three out of four weeks a month throughout many months of the year. She races frequently because she values racing as part of the training process. I know this because I interact with her on a daily basis, and together we determine how much emphasis she should place on different races throughout the year. This assessment is crucial for any athlete who is using races as part of the training process.

There is only so much physical and emotional bandwidth available to race with. Determining each race's individual emphasis helps to manage that bandwidth.

For many athletes, races can help bridge the gaps between day-to-day training and the goal event. Sometimes they provide a great opportunity to put in a huge training day with aid station support rather than having to manage that support on your own. They provide a bigger training stimulus and provide an arena for athletes to work on the things they are going to face during their goal event.

RACING TO BE PART OF A COMMUNITY

It's the same group of idiots at every race.

—JASON KOOP

For many, racing involves community. In ultrarunning, we are lucky that the community is such a good one. The "idiots" I lovingly refer to are friends I have had the fortune of sharing the trails with on a Saturday. Many ultrarunners find that racing allows them to touch base with the community of people they identify with, much like any other social group. This is why you see many ultrarunners become aid station volunteers and attend races simply to cheer other people on. They value the community of people who make up the sport. If it's the community that draws you to races, but you struggle with balancing your purposeful training with the preparation for and recovery from frequent races, you may benefit from volunteering at events. That way, you can stay engaged with the community while still staying true to your overall long-range plan for the year.

FIND YOUR RACING VALUES

The answer to the question "How many races do I need?" comes about from first determining your racing values. The aforementioned examples are just a few. Racing can represent many things to you, and these can ebb and flow over time. When setting up your season and choosing races, first think about what those races represent to you. Is it the competition, a stepping-stone, the end point of your training, or something entirely different? Like any value system, your racing values are for you to determine. After you have done this, the distance, timing, and frequency of the races you *choose* can follow suit.

OPTIMAL RACING FOR MAXIMUM PERFORMANCE

If your race values are rooted in achieving optimal performance, there is a range of race frequency that you can utilize to ensure that you are toeing the line in the best shape possible. For purposes of simplification, the following ranges assume that you are racing only at the specified distances in a 12-month period. For example, if you want to maximize your performance at the 100-mile distance, you can do so one or two times per year, if that is the only distance you race.

- 100 mile: one or two times per 12 months
- 100K and 50 mile: two or three times per 12 months
- 50K: three or four times per 12 months

IS SUBOPTIMAL RACING OK?

Yes! You can race four 100-milers in a calendar year (or in a few short months, as in the Grand Slam of Ultrarunning). But that does not mean you can optimally prepare for each one. How suboptimal is the third, fourth, or fifth 100-mile race in a 12-month period? That's a guessing game, and the answer is rooted in your own personal physiology and psychology. The point is, if your racing values are to optimize the training process, you will be most likely to fulfill those values by limiting your racing. This does not mean that racing more is bad (suboptimal ≠ bad). It only means that when you are determining your racing values, it is important to keep in mind the practical ramifications and possible drawbacks of choosing too many races.

PREREQUISITE TRAINING DISTANCES FOR ULTRAMARATHONS

One of the persistent concepts in run training is that you must be able to complete a specific percentage of your goal distance in training in order to be prepared for your race. This idea comes from marathon training, where people are convinced they need to complete a 20-mile run as the final long run before their taper. But there is nothing magical about that 20-mile run, and there is similarly nothing magical about running 50 miles before you attempt to run 100, or 30 before you attempt to run 100 kilometers. Ironically, this is one area in which marathon training is similar to ultramarathon training: The one long run is not a prerequisite for success.

Would it be ideal if you could do it? Sure. Completing very long runs helps to reinforce your pacing, nutrition, and hydration strategies. They give you the opportunity to face adversity and work through rough patches. But the physiology necessary to successfully complete an ultramarathon is not significantly impacted by whether or not you have completed one single very long run. If you cannot incorporate such a run into your training schedule, but you can focus on developing your cardiovascular system and creating the strategies that will manage your effort level and fueling, you can still successfully complete an ultramarathon.

CHAPTER 13

COACHING GUIDE TO NORTH AMERICAN ULTRAS

Never underestimate the value of course knowledge when it comes to racing an ultramarathon. The more you know about the terrain, weather, aid stations, gradients, durations of climbs, and landmarks, the better off you'll be on race day. Ultrarunning is an intellectual pursuit as much as it is a physical challenge, and having more knowledge enables you to create a better plan of attack.

Course reconnaissance is one way athletes gain knowledge about the demands of particular races, but that's not a realistic option for a lot of runners who travel significant distances to compete in their goal events. Some runners take the long view and race an event once as a recon mission with the idea they'll return a second time to pursue a performance goal. This is effective, but it's at least a two-year process! The most accessible way athletes learn about races is by talking with other athletes who have already done the event. As with training, however, this method suffers from the N of 1 bias.

A benefit of coaching a large number of athletes over a long period is that I have been able to build a library of course-specific knowledge for major races. Together with input from athletes I work with, this coaching guide to North American ultras is designed to supplement the information you'll find on the races' websites and in their race bibles. The goal here isn't to republish every detail about these well-known races but to provide the kind of insider advice and guidance that can only come from experience.

AMERICAN RIVER 50

The American River 50, held the first weekend of April, is one of the oldest and largest ultramarathons in the United States. The point-to-point course starts at Folsom Lake, east of Sacramento, California, and roughly follows the bike path around the lake and down the American River, before doubling back on the other side and continuing into the Sierra Nevada foothills to the finish in Auburn, California.

The field of 800-plus runners enjoys a mostly flat course, especially for the first 25 miles. In fact, the race is frequently called "a road marathon followed by a trail run" thanks to its split personality. Experienced ultrarunners come to this race to notch PRs, while many newbies tackle it as their first ultra.

DID YOU KNOW? The American River 50 is known for one of the sweetest pieces of swag among ultra race finishers: a Patagonia jacket.

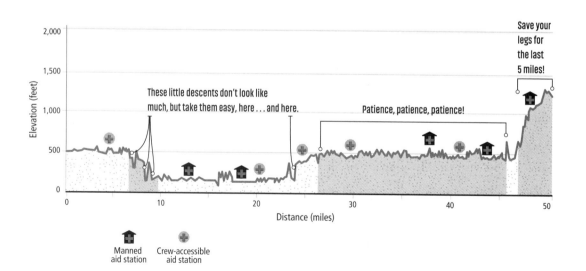

SPECS

Course record: 5:32:18 (Jim Howard, 1981); 6:09:08 (Ann Trason, 1993)

Median time: 11:07 (2015)

Cutoff time: 14 hours

Climbing:
   Total elevation gain: 3,100 feet (half of which comes in the last 5 miles)
   Total elevation loss: 2,100 feet

WEATHER. It's generally warm but not hot in the Sacramento Valley this time of year. The issue for many runners is that they aren't yet acclimated to the heat, even if that's only 75 degrees.

Rain is unlikely, but if it does rain, expect to spend the majority of the day in the wet because spring storms can take all day to move through the area.

UNIQUE WEATHER-RELATED CHALLENGE. The heat comes on in full force at the most difficult, final section of the race, which features the only long, sustained climb on the course over somewhat technical terrain (especially compared with the first half of the race).

EQUIPMENT. Despite the flat course and time spent on the bike trail, you'll want to wear trail running shoes to tackle the race's second half. You'll also need a headlamp for the first 30 minutes of the race, which you can then dump at the first aid station.

INDISPENSABLE GEAR. Carry two water bottles, as some aid stations are more than an hour apart.

CRUX OF THE RACE. The last 5-mile section is a 1,500-foot climb that few are psychologically prepared for after cruising along for the first 45 miles. The climb psychs many people out, so much so that some runners fail to finish the race even though they probably could.

CRITICAL MENTAL CHALLENGE. Runners who fail at the American River 50 tend to do so because they think it will be easier than it is. They find themselves loping along at marathon pace through the first couple of hours without even trying; they figure they're having a good day, not realizing that they're going too fast. Successful runners here have to force themselves to slow down during those first 25 miles, a challenging task when the field's size means there's always someone running faster around you.

THE PRO KNOWS. "You can run the entire race, which for many ultrarunners can be a hard concept to wrap their heads around and train for. Also, running on the bike path for so long is hard on your joints. To deal with both those situations, try incorporating longer road runs at marathon pace into your training." —*Jen Benna, first place, 2015*

TRAINING TIPS. In addition to following Benna's advice, you'll want to prepare yourself for handling technical downhill sections. They're not long, but the race's relative speed can easily overmatch your agility—and state of fatigue—if you're not ready for them.

CRITICAL TRAINING PHASE. If you are using this race as a tune-up for your primary ultras later in the summer, feel free to do VO$_2$max work leading up to the race. Although you will not tap into that energy system much, it will set the stage for those more important upcoming races. If this is your goal event, or your first ultra, you should be doing SteadyStateRun (SSR) work in the four to eight weeks before the race.

CREW TIPS. Crew access is considered very easy. The main difficulty for your crew will be dealing with other crews in a search for parking space at the aid stations. As a result, crews may underestimate travel and parking time and miss their runners. Plan out a strategy in which you only need to see your crew at certain, strategically chosen aid stations. This will be less stressful for you and them.

Pacers are allowed to join starting at mile 24.31, the Beal's Point aid station.

BADWATER 135

This legendary 135-miler, which is run from the lowest and hottest point on the planet, Badwater, California, in Death Valley National Park (280 feet below sea level), to Whitney Portal at 8,300 feet, bills itself as "The World's Toughest Foot Race" for four main reasons: It is run at the end of July when daytime highs regularly exceed 110 degrees; it is run entirely on bone-crushing tarmac; it crosses three mountain ranges; and it is 35 miles longer than the more popular 100-mile ultramarathons.

The field for Badwater is capped at 100 runners per year and racers must qualify by completing three 100-mile races, with the most recent occurring within the preceding 12 months. Applicants who complete Badwater's Salton Sea or Cape Fear races are given special consideration.

DID YOU KNOW? The original Badwater race in 1977 finished atop Mount Whitney, the highest spot in the continental United States at 14,505 feet in elevation. That was an extra 8 miles from (and 6,205 feet higher than) the current finish line at Whitney Portal.

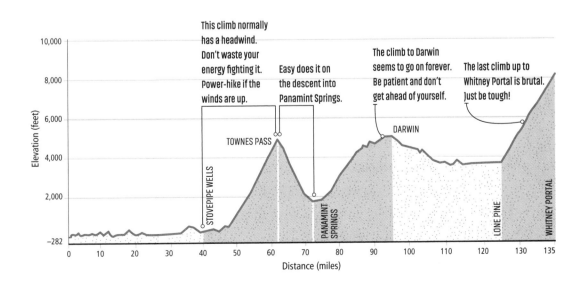

SPECS

Course record: 22:51:29 (Valmir Nunes, 2007); 26:16:12 (Jamie Donaldson, 2010)

Median time: 38:00 (2015)

Cutoff time: 48 hours

Climbing:
   Total elevation gain: 14,600 feet
   Total elevation loss: 6,100 feet

Significant climbs:
   Stovepipe Wells to Townes Pass; Panamint Springs to Father Crowley Point;
   Lone Pine to Whitney Portal

WEATHER. Think you know heat? You don't know heat until you try running in Death Valley, where the temperature can top 130 degrees, and it will stay above 100 degrees for significant portions of the race (minus a few "cool" respites of 70-degree temps on top of the mountain passes in the middle of the night). There's no rain, and you can pray for clouds, but don't expect them.

UNIQUE WEATHER-RELATED CHALLENGE. It comes down to surviving the heat and the sun. Run on the relatively cooler white stripe on the shoulder of the road because the black asphalt will be hot enough to melt your shoes and blister the bottoms of your feet. There is usually a searing headwind, with gusts of 25 to 30 miles per hour, coming out of Stovepipe Wells at mile 41.5. It will suck the moisture right out of your nose and throat and make you choke. Consider applying saline solution inside your nose to keep it moist, and pop a steady supply of lozenges to help moisten your throat.

EQUIPMENT. With the extreme exposure and heat, sunblock will not provide adequate skin protection, so you'll need to cover up in a breathable running suit made with UV-protective fabric. You will also want to wear clothes that will stay wet so you can enjoy some evaporative cooling effect. Therefore, avoid the fastest-drying and moisture-wicking fabrics. Ice sleeves are a must, as well as a hat that you can refill with ice every couple of miles.

INDISPENSABLE GEAR. Ice. Lots of ice. You'll need more than you ever thought you would, and keeping it frozen inside an armory of high-quality coolers is a huge challenge. Not helping matters: There are very few places to find ice along the route, and everyone else in the race is looking for a lot of ice, too.

CRUX OF THE RACE. The entire race is probably unlike anything you've ever put yourself through, but the last half-marathon of the course from Lone Pine to Whitney Portal is a 4,573-foot climb straight up the side of the mountain. Coming at mile 122, it hits racers at a point where they've already pushed beyond anything they've done before (run more than 100 miles).

CRITICAL MENTAL CHALLENGE. Because the ultrarunners who make up the field at Badwater are quite experienced, they are generally very good at heat acclimatization and race-day planning. The time span and the sleep deprivation, not the heat, can be the hardest challenges. Racers are out there for two nights, which is a first for many of them. Spending all that time in the race's extreme conditions can leave even well-prepared racers battling through a complete breakdown of their bodies' ability to thermoregulate. It's not the temperature itself but rather the amount of time you're exposed to it that eventually breaks you down.

THE PRO KNOWS. "Many ultrarunners can run all day and night on trails, but Badwater is a road race, not a trail race. Whereas a trail runner can do 75 percent of his or her training on dirt, training for Badwater means that more than 60 percent of your miles should be on pavement. It takes a long time to get the body used to that. I always tell people that running 200 miles anywhere else is nothing compared to finishing Badwater." —*Dean Karnazes, 10-time Badwater 135 finisher*

TRAINING TIPS. You will want to do many of your training runs during the hottest parts of the day. Regular sessions in a sauna, four to five times a week, are extremely useful to help the body acclimate to the heat. Gradually build up your tolerance, staying in the heat as long as you can.

CRITICAL TRAINING PHASE. Because the final few weeks of training should include critical heat acclimation, runners need to build their fitness and peak mileage six to eight weeks out from the race. Running your longest and hardest runs at the same time you are trying to acclimate to the heat is a recipe for disaster.

CREW TIPS. There's likely no other ultramarathon in the world where your crew is so critical to success—and so likely to suffer. In fact, more crew members than runners end up requiring medical attention for heat- and exhaustion-related emergencies. It's that brutal. Crew members need their own strict hydration and rest schedules to survive.

Successful teams need a minimum of two crew members to trade off duties, run resupply missions, and, most important, attend to their runner, who will need constant monitoring. Badwater is unique in that crews can help their runner at any time, anywhere on the course (except for certain sections of the race as specified by the race management). The only requirement is that they find a safe place to pull all four tires off the main road.

Pacers are allowed, but unlike other trail or road races, they can only run behind their runner, not in front or to the side.

Finally, read the rule book! No other ultramarathon in the United States has more elaborate rules than Badwater. To protect the integrity of the race and ensure that future races happen, crews must be keenly aware of the rules.

HARDROCK 100

One of the toughest 100-mile races in the world, the Hardrock, held in mid-July, starts and finishes in the high alpine town of Silverton, Colorado, and sends competitors on a loop around the most remote and highest mountain passes in the state, including an ascent up and over 14,048-foot Handies Peak. The route's elevation averages 11,186 feet, topping 12,000 feet 13 times.

CLOCKWISE

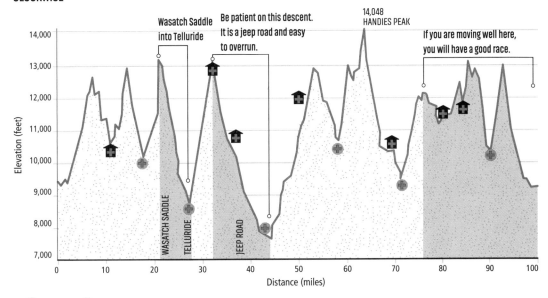

COUNTERCLOCKWISE

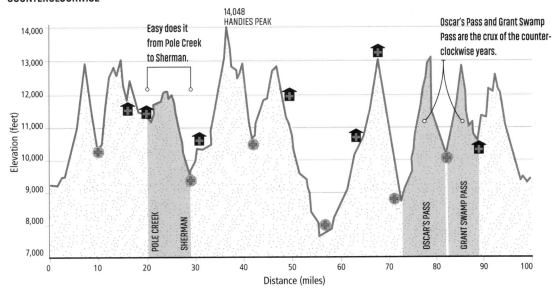

Getting into the race is almost as difficult. Runners must have completed a qualifying ultra run, and even then, there are only 47 slots available for first-time participants. In addition, there is a service requirement: eight hours volunteer work at an ultra race.

DID YOU KNOW? On even years the race goes clockwise. On odd years it runs counter-clockwise. Racers have to kiss the Hardrock, a large stone painted with a picture of a ram's head, to officially finish the race. This race also has one of the most detailed course descriptions available; read it.

SPECS

Course record: 22:41 (Kilian Jornet, 2014); 27:18 (Diana Finkel, 2009)

Median time: 39:30 (2015)

Cutoff time: 48 hours

Climbing:
Total elevation gain/loss: 33,992 feet
Critical climbs and descents: They are all hard! Hardrock is one of the most notoriously difficult 100-mile events. You are climbing or descending nearly the entire course.

WEATHER. Prepare for subfreezing nights in the high alpine sections and highs in the mid-70s in the town of Ouray. Because the race takes place in the middle of the Rocky Mountain summer monsoon season, expect late afternoon thunderstorms, some of them violent, with extreme drops in temperature and even snowfall. Fortunately, the storms move in and out quickly.

UNIQUE WEATHER-RELATED CHALLENGE. Be on the lookout for clouds developing into storms that can unleash a bone-chilling cloudburst of rain or hail. The route takes participants over multiple exposed ridgelines where lightning strikes are a very real concern. If you see or hear lightning nearby, work your way down to a lower elevation as quickly and safely as possible.

EQUIPMENT. Carry a packable waterproof, breathable rain jacket at all times. Wrap your mind around the fact that you might be out on the course for two nights and pack accordingly. Pack a complete change of clothes in every drop bag (from underwear to outerwear). Trekking poles can help steady your pace on the downhills.

INDISPENSABLE GEAR. An emergency space blanket will take up hardly any space but may prove a godsend if you need to wait out a storm before heading over a pass.

CRUX OF THE RACE. Handies Peak, at more than 14,000 feet, is higher than many people have ever climbed before, much less in the middle of the night after slogging 40-plus miles. The altitude can slow you down more than you expect, but pushing too hard at this altitude can take a lot out of you, so gauge your effort by exertion rather than speed. Once you get over Handies, you can take a breath of relief.

CRITICAL MENTAL CHALLENGE. It's a long race. A good time is under 30 hours, which is the cutoff for other less challenging 100-milers. Even for experienced ultrarunners, the Hardrock will have you on your feet longer than you are used to and running at higher elevations than you may be comfortable with.

The course isn't particularly well marked compared with other races, and that is by design. Racers should know the course before showing up at the start line. During the race, participants (and their pacers) must pay attention to their whereabouts at all times and have solid map-reading skills.

THE PRO KNOWS. "On years when the race runs counterclockwise, you have to watch your pace through the Pole Creek section. You can easily let yourself fly down the course to the Sherman aid station and blow your whole race. Same goes for the descent off the Wasatch saddle into Telluride in the clockwise years. People get so excited to see the town below that they blow out their quads by going too fast."
—*Missy Gosney, fourth place, 2015*

TRAINING TIPS. Training for the Hardrock is about banking as much vertical in the legs as possible. Shoot for long runs with 4,000 to 5,000 feet of climbing/descending on successive days. And take any chance you have to run at altitude, not necessarily to acclimate but to understand how your body responds to it.

CRITICAL TRAINING PHASE. April and May, with lots of hiking and descending. Most athletes cannot match the 680 feet of elevation change per mile in training, but it is critical to do whatever you can. Even for the winners, nearly all the uphills will be hikes, so spend the majority of April and May hiking as much as possible.

CREW TIPS. Crews are allowed only at the designated aid stations, some of which are remote, with no cellular phone service. Crew members need to prepare for a lot of driving on twisting mountain roads and Forest Service roads.

Pacers need to make sure to pack for a long time on the trail, as much as 10 hours, and carry enough water and food accordingly. Because there are no bailouts between aid stations, pacers must understand that they have to be prepared to go the distance.

JAVELINA JUNDRED

The setup for the Javelina Jundred makes it unusual among ultras. The popular race with more than 600 participants takes place entirely inside McDowell Mountain Regional Park, which is situated just outside the sprawl of Scottsdale, Arizona. The race, either a 100K or a 100-miler, is relatively flat and has participants running up to six loops of the 15.3-mile Pemberton Trail. What's unique about the race is that with each lap, runners reverse direction to run the next loop, giving everyone multiple chances to see each other (and for those aiming to win the race, a chance to see where their competition is).

Relatively little elevation change, easy logistics, and timing at the very end of the running season make the Javelina Jundred attractive to ultrarunners looking to qualify for the Western States 100-Mile Endurance Run.

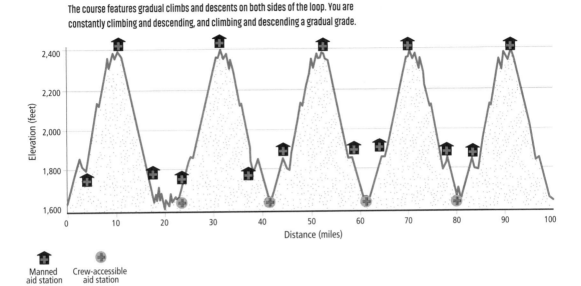

The course features gradual climbs and descents on both sides of the loop. You are constantly climbing and descending, and climbing and descending a gradual grade.

Manned aid station   Crew-accessible aid station

DID YOU KNOW? Because the race occurs on or near Halloween, costumes are encouraged for runners and their crews, with awards given for the best male and female costumes. And because crews are allowed only at the start/finish line, they set up camp for the duration of the race and turn it into an all-day/all-night party. I have run as a Chippendale dancer.

SPECS

Course record:

100-mile: 13:47:43 (Hal Koerner, 2011); 14:52:06 (Devon Yanko, 2015)

100K: 9:29:14 (Karim El Hayani, 2015); 9:42:45 (Susan Barrows, 2015)

Median time in 2015: 100-mile—25:33:16; 100K—16:40:09

Cutoff time: 30 hours for 100-mile; 29 hours for 100K

Climbing:
Total elevation gain/loss: 6,000 feet for the 100-mile

WEATHER. As far as ultras go, the weather is relatively mild, with overnight temperatures in the high 50s to low 60s. Daytime highs can reach the mid-90s. Rain is rare, but it can happen.

UNIQUE WEATHER-RELATED CHALLENGE. The timing of the race at the end of October means that runners from farther north have already spent months running in much cooler fall weather. When they arrive in Arizona, they're not acclimated to running in 90-degree sun, with no shade anywhere on the course. As a result, expect to run slower than you may have planned due to the heat. Sunset doesn't always bring relief, either. Many runners (and crews) aren't prepared for the sudden 40-degree drop in temperature once the sun goes down.

EQUIPMENT. With minimal weather-related issues and regular aid station intervals (you're never more than 6 miles from the next aid station), there's no need to carry any special equipment beyond a water bottle or two. The race rents out large tents with cots for competitors to set up at the start/finish line, a popular choice, since private vehicles aren't allowed to park or camp at the site. Everyone needs to shuttle in from an off-site parking area.

INDISPENSABLE GEAR. Many runners wear gaiters to keep the grit and small pebbles from the sandy washes and trail out of their shoes.

CRUX OF THE RACE. The imperceptible descent from the backside of the course to the start/finish line lulls many runners into thinking they're going to have an A+ day, and they start running faster than they should. When they start the slog back up that incline, they pay the price.

CRITICAL MENTAL CHALLENGE. Despite its easy logistics and relatively flat course, the Javelina Jundred is a deceptively hard race, with a finishing rate of only roughly 50 percent. The reason, beyond the heat, is that with every 15-mile lap, racers return to where all the crews' camps are set up. During the night, the start/finish turns into a party atmosphere, with music, beer trucks, disco balls—it's a hard environment to leave. Even the backside aid station is set up as a party. Help yourself by not sitting down and getting sucked into the scene.

THE PRO KNOWS. "Many people start out this race too fast because of the cool morning temperatures and easy geography. After the first lap, at least a third of the field is usually running a sub-24 hour pace, which is unsustainable unless they're an elite pro. The key to finishing is to force yourself to go slow during the first couple of laps." —*Jamil Coury, race director*

TRAINING TIPS. If you live in a climate that features cool, crisp autumns, train during the heat of the day, not the mornings or evenings. Get comfortable running in sand and gravel—dry riverbeds work well. You don't need to do all of your runs in sand and gravel, but do enough to get used to them. Thanks to the terrain, it's possible to run the entire Javelina Jundred course, which makes pacing discipline a must.

CRITICAL TRAINING PHASE. Both the 100K and the 100-mile Javelina are steady grinders. So EnduranceRun and SteadyStateRun intensity will be your bread and butter in September and October.

CREW TIPS. There may be no easier race to crew than the Javelina Jundred. The hardest part is shuttling in all your gear and camping equipment the afternoon or evening before the event starts. But after setting up camp, the crew doesn't need to move. Accordingly, make sure they—and you—have enough food, fluids, and creature comforts to last for the entire race, since they can't easily hop in a car to go get supplies or a meal.

As soon as the sun goes down on day one, pacers are allowed to join their runners to the finish of the race.

JFK 50

The oldest ultra run in America, the JFK 50 started in 1962. The point-to-point race, held every November between Boonsboro and Williamsport, Maryland, is now the largest ultra in the country, with a cap of 1,000 runners. The course starts in western Maryland on the Appalachian Trail before connecting with the sublime C&O Canal Towpath along the Potomac River on the way to the finish. It's considered a fast and relatively easy course without much climbing (and nearly all the climbing is completed in the first 5 miles). But it's a different kind of race, as champions of western 100-mile races soon discover when they fail to crack the top 10.

DID YOU KNOW? The 50-mile distance came from a challenge to the U.S. Marines by then president John F. Kennedy to hike 50 miles in under 20 hours, as Teddy Roosevelt's marines had done. That led a group of 11 civilians to try it on what is now the JFK 50 course. By 1970, 73 participants had finished. For comparison, the first New York City Marathon held in 1970 recorded only 55 finishers.

SPECS

Course record: 5:34:59 (Max King, 2012); 6:12:00 (Ellie Greenwood, 2012)

Median time: 10:00 (2014)

Cutoff time: 13 hours

Climbing: Total elevation gain/loss: 2,077 feet

WEATHER. Expect crisp fall weather for the Appalachian Mountains: highs in the mid-50s and lows at start time in the high 30s. It can rain, though. It can even snow.

UNIQUE WEATHER-RELATED CHALLENGE. It's rarely uncomfortably hot for this race; it's usually a glorious running day with perfect temperatures. Or it could rain, sleet, or snow. Prepare for the latter by stocking your drop bags with plenty of dry clothes to change into.

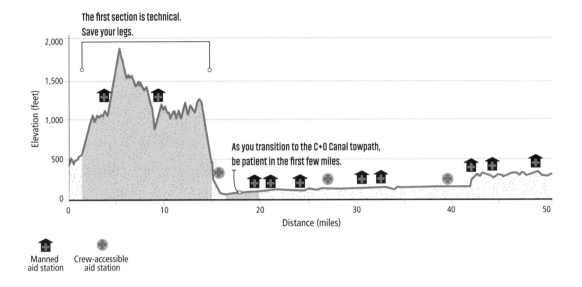

Manned aid station
Crew-accessible aid station

INDISPENSABLE GEAR. A space blanket is a small insurance policy worth carrying in case your day goes south and the cold starts getting to you.

CRUX OF THE RACE. The majority of the climbing takes place within 5 miles of the start, with a lot of it on technical, rocky trail. It will be a conga line up and down the mountains. If you're not careful, this can become a giant energy suck, as you're constantly trying to sprint around people on the trail. If you find yourself stuck in the pack, save your energy, settle in, and carefully pick spots where you can pass more people more easily.

CRITICAL MENTAL CHALLENGE. Once runners hit the flat, soft gravel of the C&O Canal Towpath, many unwisely figure the hard part's over and pour on too much speed in those first few miles. Holding yourself in check and sticking with your race plan is critical here; you've still got 35 miles to go.

TRAINING TIP. Except for parts of the roughly 10-mile stretch along the Appalachian Trail, the JFK 50 is a completely runnable event, and you can easily settle into a rhythm for the duration of the course. You have to train for the trails and for the flats. Versatility is key for success in this event.

CRITICAL TRAINING PHASE. This is a late-season race for many ultrarunners, so starting healthy is a priority. Training during July, August, and September should include TempoRuns and SteadyStateRuns, which will pay off in this race.

CREW TIPS. The horseshoe-shaped route of the race makes it relatively easy for crew members to support their runners. That said, with 1,000 participants, your crew will likely find themselves more stressed out over the battle for parking at aid stations than over helping you, especially for the first few aid stations when the field will still be relatively bunched up. Better to plan on a few strategic meeting points and a smart drop bag strategy for the other points to get you through the race.

Pacers are not encouraged, but they are allowed.

LAKE SONOMA 50

This early-season 50-miler is held every April in the beautiful and lush (at that time of year) Sonoma Valley in Northern California. The out-and-back rolling trail course is considered fast and features many sections through forest shade, across 12 creeks, and around its namesake lake. Trail runners love it; 86 percent of the course is on relatively smooth, nontechnical singletrack trails. The race has a high finishing rate (approximately 90 percent) and is often used as a tune-up race for the Western States 100, which is held in June. Entry is via a blind lottery (i.e., there's no preferential treatment for past entrants or pros).

DID YOU KNOW? The Island View aid station on the course is so remote that supplies and volunteers have to be delivered by boat.

SPECS

Course record: 6:09:39 (Alex Varner, 2015); 7:08:23 (Stephanie Howe, 2015)

Median time: 10:24 (2015)

Cutoff time: 14 hours

Climbing: Total elevation gain/loss: 10,500 feet

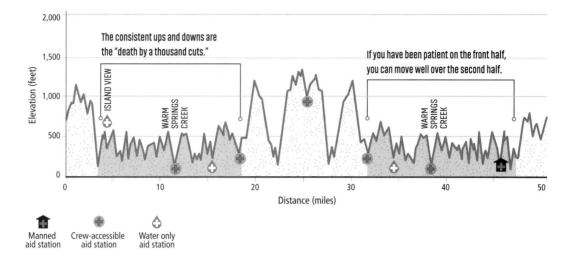

The consistent ups and downs are the "death by a thousand cuts."

If you have been patient on the front half, you can move well over the second half.

ISLAND VIEW

WARM SPRINGS CREEK

WARM SPRINGS CREEK

Manned aid station

Crew-accessible aid station

Water only aid station

WEATHER. April in the Sonoma Valley has near-perfect ultrarunning weather, with lows in the mid-40s and highs in the mid-70s. Even during the heat of the day, much of the trail is under the shade of tree cover. There's one caveat (it's a big one): If it's raining, there's a good chance that it will rain hard throughout the day and that the temperature will stay uncomfortably cool.

UNIQUE WEATHER-RELATED CHALLENGE. None, really. It's California. It's spring. Odds are it's going to be a nice day.

EQUIPMENT. There are no special equipment needs and no need to carry much beyond water and food. Also, water at the more remote aid stations will be limited to drinking, not dousing yourself to cool off; you'll want to do that at the creek crossings or at the lake.

INDISPENSABLE GEAR. Some aid stations are nearly 7.5 miles apart, a long distance during the hottest part of the race. As such, carry more water and food than you think you might need.

CRUX OF THE RACE. From mile 33 to the finish, the race can feel long and lonely, with roughly 5 to 7.5 miles between the last three aid stations. Not helping matters, you won't see many people due to the terrain and how spread out everyone is. For mid-packers and those at the back, the race can suddenly feel like running through the middle of nowhere by yourself.

CRITICAL MENTAL CHALLENGE. For a 50-mile race with no mountains to climb, the Lake Sonoma 50 packs a serious dose of vertical into its rolling course. The relentless ups and downs with few flat sections or gradual inclines to rest can blow racers' quads apart well before the finish. The key, as with any ultra, is pacing, especially on the short downhill sections. "Death by a thousand cuts" is how course record holder Alex Varner describes the multitude of ups and downs.

THE PRO KNOWS. "To do well in this race, you've got to be able to run fast, yet deal with a lot of climbing. That combination is unique in the ultra world, which is why you want to train for running this race—not just speed hiking—uphill and down." —*Dakota Jones, first place, 2012*

TRAINING TIPS. Work on your foot turnover to maintain your speed on the short flats and to mitigate some of the punishment (but not your speed) on the downhill stretches. The race requires a lot of pace changes; work on that in training by including ups, downs, and flats in any specific interval work.

CRITICAL TRAINING PHASE. If you are using this race as a tune-up for your primary ultras later in the summer, some VO$_2$max work leading up to the race is a good idea. Although you will not tap into that energy system much, it will set the stage for those more important upcoming races. If this is your goal event, or your first ultra, you should be doing SSR work in the four to eight weeks leading up to the race.

CREW TIPS. Thanks to the usually mild weather, crewing this race is easy. However, it involves a lot more driving on winding roads than many expect to get to the remote Warm Springs Creek aid station. Crews will need to be self-contained and have a full tank of gas for the day because fuel stations and grocery stores are too far away to dash off for a resupply.

Pacers are not allowed on the course.

LEADVILLE TRAIL 100

Held in late August in the Colorado Rockies, the Leadville Trail 100 is one of the oldest and most iconic 100-mile races in North America. Known for its high altitude (the lowest point of the race is 9,200 feet) and relatively large race field, the race attracts a number of first-time 100-mile runners to the starting line due to the fact that there is no qualifying requirement to enter.

DID YOU KNOW? Leadville local Ken Chlouber started the race in 1983 as a way to generate tourism revenue for the town, which at the time had the highest unemployment rate in the nation.

SPECS

Course record: 15:42:59 (Matt Carpenter, 2005); 18:06:24 (Ann Trason, 1994)

Median time: 28:20 (2015)

Cutoff time: 30 hours

Climbing: Total elevation gain/loss: 18,168 feet

Significant climbs:
Colorado Trail and Hagerman Road: 5.65 miles and 1,338 feet
Hope Pass: 4.48 miles and 3,204 feet
Sheep's Gulch: 2.4 miles and 2,303 feet
Leaving Twin Lakes to the Colorado Trail: 2.7 miles and 1,222 feet
Powerline: 3.88 miles and 1,483 feet

Significant descents:
Powerline: 3.88 miles and 1,483 feet
Colorado Trail into Twin Lakes: 2.7 miles and 1,222 feet
Sheep's Gulch: 2.4 miles and 2,303 feet
Hope Pass: 4.48 miles and 3,204 feet
Hagerman Road and the Colorado Trail: 5.65 miles and 1,338 feet

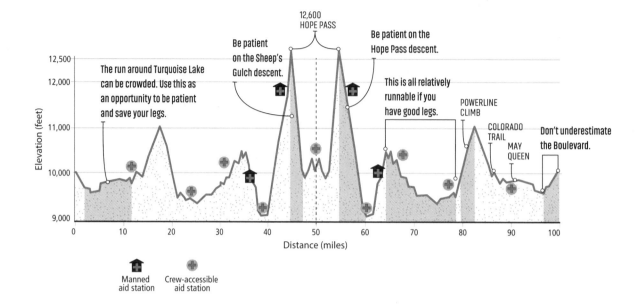

WEATHER. Typically cool, crisp mornings in the low 40s give way to mild afternoon temps in the mid-70s. Fast-moving thunderstorms roll through this area of the Rocky Mountains in the late afternoon, so if you are up high, especially above the timberline, make sure you have gear for nasty weather.

UNIQUE WEATHER-RELATED CHALLENGE. Late August can offer a dry weather window in the Colorado Rocky Mountain monsoon season, but every few years the race falls on the edge of the rainy season. If this is the case, expect heavy rain throughout the day and snow and sleet at higher elevations and during the night. In addition, between 10:00 p.m. and 4:00 a.m., it can be quite cold. Combine that with late-race fatigue and the difficulty generating body heat and you have a recipe for hypothermia. Pack extra clothes for the night.

EQUIPMENT. Leadville is unique in the world of ultras in that pacers, who can join after mile 50, can mule (or carry the equipment) for their runners. The race directors instituted this rule as homage to the area's mining heritage and the miner essential companion, the noble burro. Take advantage of this rule and have your pacer carry extra clothes, water, food, headlamp batteries, and trekking poles should you need them.

INDISPENSABLE GEAR. A pacer/mule to lighten your load.

CRUX OF THE RACE. Although the Hope Pass (12,600 feet) double crossing in the middle of the race always receives the most attention, the crux of the course is the climb up Powerline over Sugarloaf Pass (11,071 feet) and then the descent into May Queen aid station at mile 86.5. This section comes late in the race, and the Powerline climb, although not long, is steep and slow-going. The section of the Colorado Trail leading into the May Queen aid station is one of the more technical parts of the course. Add in the darkness of night and tired legs, and it can be a rough go.

It can also be the weirdest: One of my most notable ultra hallucinations occurred on the Hagerman Road descent, where all the rocks came to life and were dancing and twirling across the gravel road!

CRITICAL MENTAL CHALLENGE. With as many as 600 to 800 participants and an out-and-back course, the race can become quite crowded. Many find this a source of inspiration, but it can also backfire as runners struggle to relax and run their own race among the crowd. Worse, some runners struggling to beat the cutoffs tend to cluster into groups of shared misery around miles 60 to 85, producing a negative feedback loop that slows everyone down to the slowest runner in the group. The result is that some runners who could have easily beaten the cutoffs do not. The key is to realize when you're in such a group and accelerate out of it immediately.

THE PRO KNOWS. "There's a three-mile, gradual uphill finish into town called 'The Boulevard.' Coming at mile 97, it's more difficult than you'd expect." —*Dylan Bowman, second place, 2011*

TRAINING TIPS. Although the course isn't particularly challenging from a technical perspective, many runners fear the altitude with good reason; it exaggerates any weakness in a runner's pacing and nutrition game plan. Thus, it's critical to practice and follow the hydration and nutrition plan you've mapped out for the race in the weeks and months leading up to the event. Come race day, slow and steady will pay off. Last note: If you have the opportunity to use an altitude tent in the several weeks before the event, do it. If you don't, the best course of action is to arrive in Leadville 24 to 48 hours before the start; hanging out for several days in Leadville before the race will only make you more fatigued.

CREW TIPS. With the start/finish in Leadville and the course staying in one general area, logistics for the race are relatively easy. But with so many runners bringing so many crew members to the race, and with few access points to aid stations, tempers among crews can flare up over parking spots and positioning at the aid station. There's no need for it; whether you're right next to the aid station check-in or 30 yards down the trail isn't going to matter to you, the runner. Tell them to chill out.

VERMONT 100

One of the few 100-mile races on the East Coast and one of the oldest in North America, the Vermont 100 takes place every July on a large, looping course in eastern central Vermont. The well-marked, well-supported course follows country roads through bucolic, rolling farmland and New England forests. Unlike ultras out west, there are no sustained climbs or technical sections, but that doesn't mean it's easy. The oppressive humidity of a New England summer and the course can take their toll. Still, its easily accessed location, numerous aid stations and support, and lack of altitude make the Vermont 100 an attractive choice for many runners' first 100-miler.

Entrants to the 100-miler (there's a 100K race run on the same day) need to have completed a 50-mile ultra in under 12 hours or a 100K race in under 14 hours, and also completed a volunteer day at any ultra event that is 50K or longer.

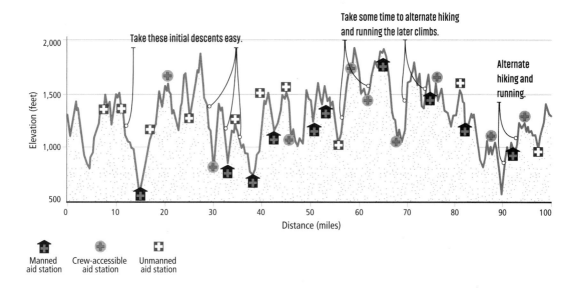

DID YOU KNOW? The Vermont 100 is run congruently with a 100-mile endurance horse race. Runners share the course with the horses, with many of the equine finishing times equaling those of the top runners.

SPECS

Course record: 14:47:35 (Brian Rusiecki, 2014); 16:42:32 (Kami Semick, 2010)

Median time: 24:47 (2015)

Cutoff time: 30 hours

Climbing: Total elevation gain/loss: approximately 14,000 feet

WEATHER. Summer temperatures in Vermont range from 80 to 85 degrees in the day to 55 to 65 degrees at night. As far as ultramarathons go, the conditions are quite pleasant. If you're lucky, you'll get a couple of late afternoon showers to cool things off quickly.

UNIQUE WEATHER-RELATED CHALLENGE. The high humidity will present a struggle for runners who are not acclimated to it. The body's ability to cool itself is hindered by the humidity, and runners will have to get used to running in sweat-drenched gear and deal with the potential for chafing that goes with it.

EQUIPMENT. Runners don't need to haul much with them. The relatively mild weather, easy-access route, and copious aid stations—the max distance between stations is 5 miles; the average distance between them is 3.5 miles—mean that runners can get by with the bare necessities: hat and a water bottle or two.

INDISPENSABLE GEAR. Cushioned road shoes, not trail shoes. Because the Vermont 100 travels along hard-packed gravel farm roads, jeep tracks, and short sections of pavement, it's a runnable course. Those dirt roads often surprise runners with how much pounding they dish out on their bodies. It's better to think of this event as a 100-mile road race rather than a trail run.

CRITICAL MENTAL CHALLENGE. On paper, the Vermont 100 doesn't look too hard— no giant climbs or technical sections—but the saw-edge course profile reveals a relentless series of short climbs and descents that never seem to end. It's difficult to find any sense of rhythm, the kind you might enjoy on the long climbs and descents of ultras out west. At first, running on country roads seems too easy, with sure footing, plenty of space to maneuver, and a well-marked course that's nearly impossible to get lost on. This causes many runners to start out too fast.

THE PRO KNOWS. "The undulating course blows out so many people's quads by mile 70, more so than I see in mountain races out west. You've got to work hard to hold yourself back from charging down all those short downhills. They add up. You can also lose a lot of time stopping in every aid station. They are excessively frequent. Don't freak out about blowing through a bunch of them. I think I skipped about half of them." —*Larissa Dannis, first-place woman, 2013*

TRAINING TIPS. Heat training is vital, and if you can do it in a humid climate, so much the better. After that, your priority should be preparing your quads for the relentless punchy downhill sections on a hard-packed surface. There's no need to worry about altitude. It's a nonfactor because the race tops out at under 2,000 feet in elevation.

CRITICAL TRAINING PHASE. Given that the race is generally rolling, expect to maintain a constant intensity, regardless of where you are in the pack. EnduranceRuns and SteadyStateRuns in the May–June time frame are advised, with your volume reaching its maximum early June.

CREW TIPS. Because the course is a loop, you can camp out at the remote start/finish line the night before the race. This seems like it should be relatively easy, but keep in mind that the nearest town is 35 miles away. Arrive with everything you need for your race and your crew.

Follow the race bible to a T because it is very easy to get lost on the course. The race directors have it dialed to the 0.01th of a mile for a good reason; unmarked dirt roads head off in all directions, and your phone's GPS won't always work in this part of Vermont.

WASATCH FRONT 100

Held the weekend after Labor Day in September, this point-to-point race in Utah starts outside of Salt Lake City and traverses the Wasatch Mountains, heading southeast to finish in Soldier Hollow, Utah. Its unique feature is that the route, which runs between altitudes of 5,000 and 10,467 feet, stays high on the crest of the Wasatch, following various ridgelines, trails, and jeep roads until dropping down to the finish.

Applicants must complete eight hours of supervised trail maintenance work through a local Forest Service office and submit a verified work report to the race before being allowed to start.

DID YOU KNOW? The race ends at 5:00 p.m. on Saturday so that the vast majority of its volunteer force has plenty of time to get home in order to attend church on Sunday.

SPECS

Course record: 18:30:55 (Geoff Roes, 2009); 22:21:47 (Bethany Lewis, 2014)

Median time: 31:32 (2015)

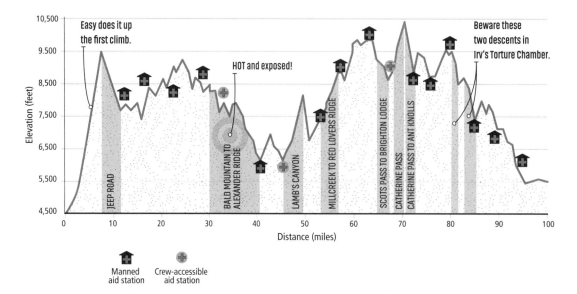

Easy does it up the first climb.

HOT and exposed!

Beware these two descents in Irv's Torture Chamber.

JEEP ROAD

BALD MOUNTAIN TO ALEXANDER RIDGE

LAMB'S CANYON

MILLCREEK TO RED LOVERS RIDGE

SCOTS PASS TO BRIGHTON LODGE

CATHERINE PASS

CATHERINE PASS TO ANT KNOLLS

Manned aid station   Crew-accessible aid station

Cutoff time: 36 hours

Climbing:
Total elevation gain: 26,882 feet
Total elevation loss: 26,131 feet

Significant climbs:
Lamb's Canyon: 4 miles and 2,035 feet
Millcreek to Red Lovers Ridge: 6.5 miles and 2,000 feet
Catherine Pass: 3.6 miles and 1,761 feet

Significant descents:
Jeep road leading to the Francis Peak aid station: 4 miles and 1,715 feet
Bald Mountain to the Alexander Ridge aid station: 5.49 miles and 2,253 feet
Scott's Pass to Brighton Lodge: 3.14 miles and 1,135 feet
Catherine Pass to Ant Knolls aid station: 1.9 miles and 1,423 feet
"The glide" and "the plunge": short, steep plunges starting at mile 79, known as "Irv's Torture Chamber"

WEATHER. The Wasatch is known for extreme temperature swings, ranging from the mid-20s in the early morning to scorching mid-80s in the middle of the afternoon. Between mile 20 and mile 40, the dry heat kicks in.

UNIQUE WEATHER-RELATED CHALLENGE. Having the right gear to handle the 60-degree temperature range. You'll want ice sleeves and ice-filled bandanas to wear during the heat of the day, and double gloves, knit hat, and a down jacket for the nights in the mountains, where the technical trails don't allow you to move fast enough to generate sufficient heat to keep you warm. Some years have recorded snow on the mountain passes. Some years have seen temperatures top 100 degrees.

EQUIPMENT. Make sure you have enough gear to handle any weather conditions, from snow to triple-digit temperatures. Carry more water than you think you'll need, especially if you're at the front of the pack because you'll be running through the hottest sections of the course at the hottest time of the day.

INDISPENSABLE GEAR. A packable down jacket that stuffs down to the size of a water bottle.

CRUXES OF THE RACE. The descents off of Catherine Pass and "Irv's Torture Chamber" are rooted in ultrarunning lore for good reason. They occur late in the race, are tough, and will shred even the most seasoned runner's quads with steep technical descending.

CRITICAL MENTAL CHALLENGE. Getting out of the Brighton Lodge aid station at mile 67.3. It's just before the big climb up to the highest point of the race, Point Supreme, at 10,467 feet. Many runners arrive in the middle of the night, cold and wasted. The check-in is located right inside the A-frame, but all the drop bags are 50-feet farther inside, where it's warm and cozy. Beyond that is a room referred to as "the morgue," so called because racers who enter it to rest often never leave. If you have a drop bag inside, grab it and then head immediately back outside, or else have your crew wait for you outside to help you. Whatever you do, don't spend any more time inside than you have to.

Because this race follows a point-to-point course, there are long stretches where it can get lonely.

THE PRO KNOWS. "The first big climb of the race is one of the hardest. You have to force yourself to be patient because it's still morning and cool, and you can burn up a lot more energy than you think charging up the climb. There are also some running springs with drinkable water along the course. Get a local's knowledge before the race and see if they are flowing." —*Jason Koop, 11th place, 2012*

TRAINING TIPS. Depending on your fitness, you can run approximately 70 percent of the course, much of which follows smooth roads and singletrack. That said, don't be lulled into thinking that it's easy. The relentless climbing and descending will take their toll, and you'll want to train your body accordingly. If running in heat is a known weakness, train for it by running in the hottest part of the day for some of your runs and perhaps using a sauna for additional heat acclimation. And although the altitude is not as extreme as in races in Colorado, it tops out in the last third of the race and hits most runners in the early hours of the morning.

CRITICAL TRAINING PHASE. July and August. Big EnduranceRun miles, lots of climbing and SteadyStateRun intensity.

CREW TIPS. Pacers can join runners at mile 39. Pacers running through the night, and especially those starting out of the Brighton Lodge aid station, should be dressed for hiking—not running—in subfreezing temperatures.

WESTERN STATES 100

The granddaddy of ultramarathons, the Western States 100-Mile Endurance Run was first run officially in 1977. The point-to-point trail race starts in Squaw Valley, California, crosses the Sierra Nevada, and descends to the finish in Auburn, California. Its heritage and global prestige attract the world's best ultrarunners to the race, making this arguably the most competitive ultra race in North America, if not the world. A win here can make a career.

Competitors are chosen by lottery from a pool of those who've completed either a 100-mile or another qualifying ultra race within a year's time (November to November). The sub-100-mile qualifiers come with time cutoffs determined by Western States race officials.

DID YOU KNOW? The Western States race originally began as a 100-mile endurance horse race, the Tevis Cup, after several local horsemen completed the route in 1955. In 1974, Gordy Ainsleigh, a veteran Tevis Cup rider, decided to run the race to see if he could, finishing in 23:42. In 1977, the run separated from the trail ride and became the first official Western States Endurance Run.

SPECS

Course record: 14:46:44 (Timothy Olson, 2012); 16:47:19 (Ellie Greenwood, 2012)

Median time: 26:36 (2015)

Cutoff time: 30 hours

Climbing:
   Total elevation gain: 18,090 feet
   Total elevation loss: 22,970 feet

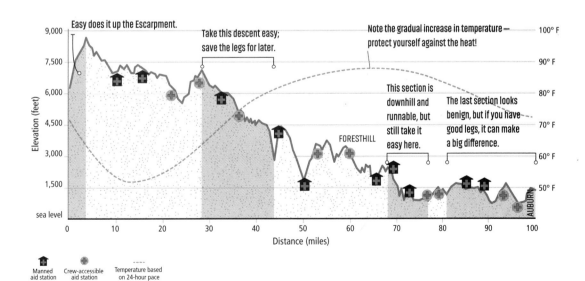

WEATHER. The race is held on the last full weekend in June. The timing, close to the summer solstice, means a short night of chilly temperatures in the high 20s and long days in the hot sun, with temperatures well into the 90s. Temps over 100 degrees are not uncommon. Even at altitudes of 6,000 to 8,000 feet, the heat will make its presence felt. Rain is unlikely, but it can occur.

UNIQUE WEATHER-RELATED CHALLENGE. Fast runners will encounter the most exposed section of the course—with no shade and the possibility of temperatures pushing 110-plus degrees—during the hottest part of the day, between 2:00 and 5:00 p.m. But it's not just fast runners who need to worry; heat is cited as an issue across the pack.

EQUIPMENT. Due to the heat, handkerchiefs, headbands, a hat, or ice sleeves that can be filled with ice will go a long way toward making your day tolerable. But thanks to the high number of aid stations (21), you don't necessarily need to haul extra gear beyond fluids.

INDISPENSABLE GEAR. A headband that you can soak in ice water, fill with ice, and wrap around your head or neck to cool you down.

CRITICAL MENTAL CHALLENGE. The roughly 17-mile descent down the Cal Street section out of Foresthill School, which starts at mile 62, can hit runners during the hottest parts of the day. The relatively gradual decline drops more than 3,000 feet, and it's deceptively easy to go too fast here and blow out your quads. You need to be conscious of when it feels easy during this stretch and hold your speed in check. That way, you'll have enough in your legs to get through the punchy climbs in the last 20 miles.

THE PRO KNOWS. "Every ultrarunner has this race on their bucket list. As a result, you end up with a very competitive international field. If you're not careful, you can get caught up in the competition, reacting to other racers' moves and eventually blowing yourself apart instead of sticking to your own race strategy." —*Dylan Bowman, three-time finisher, third place in 2014*

TRAINING TIPS. Acclimate to running in heat by doing some of your training runs during the hottest parts of the day, making sure to experiment with your fluid and nutrition intake to find out what works. Why? The stomach may react differently to foods and fluids you're used to taking during the cooler temps of your morning or early evening runs. If you can, take advantage of access to a sauna in the last four to six weeks before the race and spend 30 to 40 minutes inside a few times a week. This will help you get used to the heat. In fact, one of my colleagues has taken a thermal imaging camera out to the race to analyze runners' temperatures. Her results? The cooler runners fared better than the hotter ones.

CRITICAL TRAINING PHASE. April and early May with TempoRun work. Western States is one of the few races where I insist that runners find a dry sauna to help them acclimate to the heat. Therefore, it is critical that their cardiovascular fitness is built to a maximum *before* the sauna protocol starts (three to four weeks before the race).

CREW TIPS. Although there are a number of aid stations open to crews, some require shuttles. And because it's a point-to-point race through remote stretches of the Sierra Nevada, crew members spend a lot of time driving, often on twisting, narrow mountain roads.

Pacers can be used starting at the Foresthill aid station at mile 62.

EPILOGUE

One of the hardest things for a coach is seeing one of your athletes fail. Even harder than that is not knowing why. Throughout my career, I have had many athletes succeed. They have run great races and earned incredible results, PRs, belt buckles, and personal levels of achievement. I have also had athletes fail. Sometimes they get lost or roll an ankle and are forced to succumb to things outside their control. Sometimes I mess up their training. Maybe we didn't communicate well enough. Or I pushed them too hard. When I mess up, and I do, I take full ownership. There are times, though, when athletes fail and you have no idea why. Their training went right, they were confident, adapted to the racecourse, and executed their nutrition plan, but for whatever reason, things go south. These are the most heartbreaking moments. You feel as if you have no control. These situations are a reminder that we do not know everything. I, certainly, do not know everything as a coach. Try as we might, athletes will never be solvable math problems, where x plus y always equals z.

Some of the ideas presented in this book will surely run their course and eventually become obsolete. However, I believe that most of the major concepts mentioned here are timeless. Focus on your fitness, train for the specifics of the race, ADAPT when the going gets tough; these aspects will be true regardless of what the future holds. The strategies for *how* you can focus on your fitness, train for the specifics of the race, and ADAPT might change, but the fact that they are important will not!

Particularly when underperformance occurs with a high-profile athlete, the peanut gallery is quick to sound off. Unsolicited e-mails, Facebook messages, and voice mails fill up my in-box, offering up criticism on everything from the athlete's race tactics to how often he or she raced, to the training leading up to the event. Some of the criticism is warranted; some is terribly misguided. I appreciate all of it, however, because it makes me a better coach. I even find some value in the terribly misguided "get your butt over the bar" feedback.

Throughout this book, I have outlined my views on a number of topics ranging from physiology to philosophy. I am sure that some readers will take issue or have an opposing view on ideas that I have presented. Much like the aforementioned feedback, I will appreciate those views. Some readers also might want to inquire further about the methodologies and concepts presented in the book. Feel free to contact me via the following e-mail address, Twitter profile, or website. I am always up for any debate, discussion, or simply just dodging peanuts.

Jason M. Koop

jasonkoop@trainright.com

@jasonkoop

www.trainright.com/ultrarunning

APPENDIX: THE LONG-RANGE PLAN

The template on the following pages may be used as a starting point to develop your long-range plan. Remember to:

- Start at the end (your goal event), and do the most specific things last. You can then work backward and do the least specific things first.
- Get in all three critical intensities (RunningIntervals, Tempo, and SteadyStateRun) at some point during the season.
- Develop your weaknesses furthest from the event and your strengths closest to it.
- Start with 8-week training blocks, working one intensity at a time.
- Shorten or lengthen the block to suit your needs (see Chapter 8).

| TABLE **A.1** | Long-Range Training Plan Template |

	Weeks																					
	1	2	3	4	5	6	7	8	9	10	11	12	13	14	15	16	17	18	19	20	21	22
MONTH	JANUARY					FEBRUARY				MARCH				APRIL				MAY				
RACE NAME																						
RACE PRIORITY																						
PHASE GOAL																						
Recovery																						
EnduranceRun/SSR																						
TempoRun																						
RunningIntervals																						
Taper																						
Other																						
Notes																						

OUTCOME GOALS

1. _____
2. _____
3. _____
4. _____
5. _____

PROCESS GOALS

1. _____
2. _____
3. _____
4. _____
5. _____

Weeks																													
23	24	25	26	27	28	29	30	31	32	33	34	35	36	37	38	39	40	41	42	43	44	45	46	47	48	49	50	51	52
JUNE				JULY				AUGUST					SEPTEMBER				OCTOBER				NOVEMBER					DECEMBER			

REFERENCES AND FURTHER READING

Allan, J. R. 1964. "A Study of Foot Blisters" (research memorandum). United Kingdom: Army Operational Research Establishment.

Allan, J. R., and A. L. Macmillan. 1963. "The Immediate Effects of Heat on Unacclimatized Paratroops: Exercise 'Tiger Brew II'" (research memorandum). Report No. 16/62. United Kingdom: Army Operational Research Establishment.

Bailey, Stephen J., Jonathan Fulford, Anni Vanhatalo, Paul G. Winyard, Jamie R. Blackwell, Fred J. DiMenna, Daryl P. Wilkerson, Nigel Benjamin, and Andrew M. Jones. 2010. "Dietary Nitrate Supplementation Enhances Muscle Contractile Efficiency During Knee-Extensor Exercise in Humans." *Journal of Applied Physiology* 109 (1): 135–148.

Bam, Jenefer, Timothy D. Noakes, June Juritz, and Steven C. Dennis. 1997. "Could Women Outrun Men in Ultramarathon Races?" *Medicine and Science in Sports and Exercise* 29 (2): 244–247.

Barnes, K., A. Kilding, W. Hopkins, M. McGuigan, and P. Laursen. 2013. "Effects of Different Uphill Interval-Training Programs on Running Economy and Performance." *Journal of Science and Medicine in Sport* 15: S14.

Bartlett, Jamie L., and Rodger Kram. 2008. "Changing the Demand on Specific Muscle Groups Affects the Walk-Run Transition Speed." *Journal of Experimental Biology* 211 (8): 1281–1288.

Berg, Kris. 2003. "Endurance Training and Performance in Runners." *Sports Medicine* 33 (1): 59–73.

Beuter, A., and F. Lalonde. 1989. "Analysis of a Phase-Transition in Human Locomotion Using Singularity Theory." *Neuroscience Research Communications* 3 (3): 127–132.

Bigland-Ritchie, B. 1981. "EMG and Fatigue of Human Voluntary and Stimulated Contractions." *Human Muscle Fatigue: Physiological Mechanisms.* London: Pitman Medical, 130–156.

Bijker, K., G. De Groot, and A. Hollander. 2002. "Differences in Leg Muscle Activity During Running and Cycling in Humans." *European Journal of Applied Physiology* 87 (6): 556–561.

Browning, Raymond C., Emily A. Baker, Jessica A. Herron, and Rodger Kram. 2006. "Effects of Obesity and Sex on the Energetic Cost and Preferred Speed of Walking." *Journal of Applied Physiology* 100 (2): 390–398.

Browning, Raymond C., and Rodger Kram. 2005. "Energetic Cost and Preferred Speed of Walking in Obese vs. Normal Weight Women." *Obesity Research* 13 (5): 891–899.

Browning, Raymond C., and Rodger Kram. 2007. "Effects of Obesity on the Biomechanics of Walking at Different Speeds." *Medicine and Science in Sports and Exercise* 39 (9): 1632.

Buczek, Frank L., and Peter R. Cavanagh. 1990. "Stance Phase Knee and Ankle Kinematics and Kinetics During Level and Downhill Running." *Medicine and Science in Sports and Exercise* 22 (5): 669–677.

Byrne, Christopher, Craig Twist, and Roger Eston. 2004. "Neuromuscular Function After Exercise-Induced Muscle Damage." *Sports Medicine* 34 (1): 49–69.

Cappellini, Germana, Yuri P. Ivanenko, Richard E. Poppele, and Francesco Lacquaniti. 2006. "Motor Patterns in Human Walking and Running." *Journal of Neurophysiology* 95 (6): 3426–3437.

Carrio, I., M. Estorch, R. Serra-Grima, M. Ginjaume, R. Notivol, R. Calabuig, and F. Vilardell. 1989. "Gastric Emptying in Marathon Runners." *Gut* 30 (2): 152–155.

Casa, Douglas J. 1999. "Exercise in the Heat. I. Fundamentals of Thermal Physiology, Performance Implications, and Dehydration." *Journal of Athletic Training* 34 (3): 246.

Casa, Douglas J., Lawrence E. Armstrong, Susan K. Hillman, Scott J. Montain, Ralph V. Reiff, Brent S. E. Rich, William O. Roberts, and Jennifer A. Stone. 2000. "National Athletic Trainers' Association Position Statement: Fluid Replacement for Athletes." *Journal of Athletic Training* 35 (2): 212.

Cavagna, G. A., and M. Kaneko. 1977. "Mechanical Work and Efficiency in Level Walking and Running." *Journal of Physiology* 268 (2): 467–481.

Cavanagh, Peter R., and Mario A. Lafortune. 1980. "Ground Reaction Forces in Distance Running." *Journal of Biomechanics* 13 (5): 397–406.

Cavanagh, Peter R., and Keith R. Williams. 1982. "The Effect of Stride Length Variation on Oxygen Uptake During Distance Running." *Medicine and Science in Sports and Exercise* 14 (1): 30–35.

Cermak, Naomi M., Martin J. Gibala, and Luc J. C. van Loon. 2012. "Nitrate Supplementation's Improvement of 10-km Time-Trial Performance in Trained Cyclists." *International Journal of Sport Nutrition and Exercise Metabolism* 22 (1): 64.

Chang, Young-Hui, H. W. Huang, Chris M. Hamerski, and Rodger Kram. 2000. "The Independent Effects of Gravity and Inertia on Running Mechanics." *Journal of Experimental Biology* 203 (2): 229–238.

Chapman, Dale, M. Newton, P. Sacco, and K. Nosaka. 2006. "Greater Muscle Damage Induced by Fast Versus Slow Velocity Eccentric Exercise." *International Journal of Sports Medicine* 27 (8): 591–598.

Cheung, Karoline, Patria A. Hume, and Linda Maxwell. 2003. "Delayed Onset Muscle Soreness." *Sports Medicine* 33 (2): 145–164.

Cheuvront, Samuel N., and Michael N. Sawka. 2005. "SSE#97: Hydration Assessment of Athletes." *Sports Science Exchange* 18 (2): 1–12.

Clarkson, Priscilla M. 2007. "Exertional Rhabdomyolysis and Acute Renal Failure in Marathon Runners." *Sports Medicine* 37 (4–5): 361–363.

Clarkson, Priscilla M., and Monica J. Hubal. 2002. "Exercise-Induced Muscle Damage in Humans." *American Journal of Physical Medicine and Rehabilitation* 81 (11): S52–S69.

Clarkson, Priscilla M., Kazunori Nosaka, and Barry Braun. 1992. "Muscle Function After Exercise-Induced Muscle Damage and Rapid Adaptation." *Medicine and Science in Sports and Exercise* 24 (5): 512–520.

Cox, Gregory R., Sally A. Clark, Amanda J. Cox, Shona L. Halson, Mark Hargreaves, John A. Hawley, Nikki Jeacocke, Rodney J. Snow, Wee Kian Yeo, and Louise M. Burke. 2010. "Daily Training with High Carbohydrate Availability Increases Exogenous Carbohydrate Oxidation During Endurance Cycling." *Journal of Applied Physiology* 109 (1): 126–134.

Davies, C. T., and M. W. Thompson. 1986. "Physiological Responses to Prolonged Exercise in Ultramarathon Athletes." *Journal of Applied Physiology* 61 (2): 611–617.

DeVita, Paul, Joseph Helseth, and Tibor Hortobagyi. 2007. "Muscles Do More Positive Than Negative Work in Human Locomotion." *Journal of Experimental Biology* 210 (19): 3361–3373.

Diedrich, Frederick J., and William H. Warren Jr. 1995. "Why Change Gaits? Dynamics of the Walk-Run Transition." *Journal of Experimental Psychology: Human Perception and Performance* 21 (1): 183.

Di Prampero, Pietro E. 1992. "Energetics of Running." In *Endurance in Sport*, 2nd ed., edited by R. J. Shephard and P.-O. Åstrand, 813–823. Oxford: Blackwell Science.

Ebbeling, Cara B., and Priscilla M. Clarkson. 1989. "Exercise-Induced Muscle Damage and Adaptation." *Sports Medicine* 7 (4): 207–234.

Ejaz, P., K. Bhojani, and V. R. Joshi. 2004. "NSAIDs and Kidney." *Journal of the Association of Physicians of India* 52: 632–640

Enoka, Roger M. 2008. *Neuromechanics of Human Movement*, 4th ed. Champaign, IL: Human Kinetics.

Eston, Roger G., Jane Mickleborough, and Vasilios Baltzopoulos. 1995. "Eccentric Activation and Muscle Damage: Biomechanical and Physiological Considerations During Downhill Running." *British Journal of Sports Medicine* 29 (2): 89–94.

Fallon, K. E., G. Sivyer, K. Sivyer, and A. Dare. 1999. "The Biochemistry of Runners in a 1600 km Ultramarathon." *British Journal of Sports Medicine* 33 (4): 264–269.

Falls, Harold B., and L. Dennis Humphrey. 1976, "Energy Cost of Running and Walking in Young Women." *Medicine and Science in Sports* 8 (1): 9–13.

Ferley, Derek D., Roy W. Osborn, and Matthew D. Vukovich. 2013. "The Effects of Uphill vs. Level-Grade High-Intensity Interval Training on VO_2max, Vmax, V(L), and Tmax in Well-Trained Distance Runners." *Journal of Strength and Conditioning Research* 27 (6): 1549–1559.

Fogoros, Richard N. 1980. "'Runner's Trots': Gastrointestinal Disturbances in Runners." *Journal of the American Medical Association* 243 (17): 1743–1744.

Gandevia, S. C., R. M. Enoka, A. J. McComas, D. G. Stuart, and C. K. Thomas. 1995. "Neurobiology of Muscle Fatigue." In *Fatigue Neural and Muscular Mechanisms*, edited by S. C. Gandevia, R. M. Enoka, A. J. McComas, D. G. Stuart, and C. K. Thomas, 515–525. New York: Springer Science and Business Media.

Gazendam, Marnix G. J., and At L. Hof. 2007. "Averaged EMG Profiles in Jogging and Running at Different Speeds." *Gait and Posture* 25 (4): 604–614.

Giandolini, Marlène, Sébastien Pavailler, Pierre Samozino, Jean-Benoît Morin, and Nicolas Horvais. 2015. "Foot Strike Pattern and Impact Continuous Measurements During a Trail Running Race: Proof of Concept in a World-Class Athlete." *Footwear Science* 7 (2): 127–137.

Gibson, A. St. Clair, E. J. Schabort, and T. D. Noakes. 2001. "Reduced Neuromuscular Activity and Force Generation During Prolonged Cycling." *American Journal of Physiology—Regulatory, Integrative and Comparative Physiology* 281 (1): R187–196.

Gill, S. K., J. Hankey, A. Wright, S. Marczak, K. Hemming, D. M. Allerton, P. Ansley-Robson, and R. J. Costa. 2015. "The Impact of a 24-h Ultra-marathon on Circulatory Endotoxin and Cytokine Profile." *International Journal of Sports Medicine* 36 (8): 688–695.

Glass, Stephen, Gregory Byron Dwyer, and American College of Sports Medicine. 2007. *ACSM's Metabolic Calculations Handbook*. Philadelphia, PA: Lippincott Williams and Wilkins.

Gottschall, Jinger S., and Rodger Kram. 2005a. "Energy Cost and Muscular Activity Required for Leg Swing During Walking." *Journal of Applied Physiology* 99 (1): 23–30.

Gottschall, Jinger S., and Rodger Kram. 2005b. "Ground Reaction Forces During Downhill and Uphill Running." *Journal of Biomechanics* 38 (3): 445–452.

Grabowski, Alena M., and Roger Kram. 2008. "Effects of Velocity and Weight Support on Ground Reaction Forces and Metabolic Power During Running." *Journal of Applied Biomechanics* 24: 288–297.

Graham, T. E., and L. L. Spriet. 1995. "Metabolic, Catecholamine, and Exercise Performance Responses to Various Doses of Caffeine." *Journal of Applied Physiology* 78 (3): 867–874.

Guo, Lan-Yuen, Fong-Chin Su, Chich-Haung Yang, Shu-Hui Wang, Jyh-Jong Chang, Wen-Lan Wu, and Hwai-ting Lin. 2006. "Effects of Speed and Incline on Lower Extremity Kinematics During Treadmill Jogging in Healthy Subjects." *Biomedical Engineering: Applications, Basis and Communications* 18 (2): 73–79.

Hamill, Joseph, and Kathleen M Knutzen. 2006. *Biomechanical Basis of Human Movement*. Philadelphia, PA: Lippincott Williams and Wilkins.

Hannon, Patrick R., Stanley A. Rasmussen, and Carl P. Derosa. 1985. "Electromyographic Patterns During Level and Inclined Treadmill Running and Their Relationship to Step Cycle Measures." *Research Quarterly for Exercise and Sport* 56 (4): 334–338.

Harris, Alon, Alice K. Lindeman, and Bruce J. Martin. 1991. "Rapid Orocecal Transit in Chronically Active Persons with High Energy Intake." *Journal of Applied Physiology* 70 (4): 1550–1553.

Hayashi, Mitsuo, Akiko Masuda, and Tadao Hori. 2003. "The Alerting Effects of Caffeine, Bright Light and Face Washing After a Short Daytime Nap." *Clinical Neurophysiology* 114 (12): 2268–2278.

Heer, M., F. Repond, A. Hany, H. Sulser, O. Kehl, and K. Jäger. 1987. "Acute Ischaemic Colitis in a Female Long Distance Runner." *Gut* 28 (7): 896–899.

Herring, Kirk M., and Douglas H. Richie Jr. 1990. "Friction Blisters and Sock Fiber Composition. A Double-Blind Study." *Journal of the American Podiatric Medical Association* 80 (2): 63–71.

Hicheur, Halim, Alexander V. Terekhov, and Alain Berthoz. 2006. "Intersegmental Coordination During Human Locomotion: Does Planar Covariation of Elevation Angles Reflect Central Constraints?" *Journal of Neurophysiology* 96 (3): 1406–1419. doi:10.1152/jn.00289.2006.

Hickson, R. C., C. Foster, M. L. Pollock, T. M. Galassi, and S. Rich. 1985. "Reduced Training Intensities and Loss of Aerobic Power, Endurance, and Cardiac Growth." *Journal of Applied Physiology* 58 (2): 492–499.

Hodges, G. R., T. W. DuClos, and J. S. Schnitzer. 1975. "Inflammatory Foot Lesions in Naval Recruits: Significance and Lack of Response to Antibiotic Therapy." *Military Medicine* 140 (2): 94.

Hoffman, M. D. 2008. "Anthropometric Characteristics of Ultramarathoners." *International Journal of Sports Medicine* 29 (10): 808–811.

Hoffman, Martin D. 2014. "Pacing by Winners of a 161-km Mountain Ultramarathon." *International Journal of Sports Physiology and Performance* 9 (6): 1054–1056.

Hoffman, Martin D., and Kevin Fogard. 2011. "Factors Related to Successful Completion of a 161-km Ultramarathon." *International Journal of Sports Physiology and Performance* 6 (1): 25–37.

Hoffman, Martin D., Tamara Hew-Butler, and Kristin J. Stuempfle. 2013. "Exercise-Associated Hyponatremia and Hydration Status in 161-km Ultramarathoners." *Medicine and Science in Sports and Exercise* 45 (4): 784–791.

Hoffman, Martin D., and Eswar Krishnan. 2013. "Exercise Behavior of Ultramarathon Runners: Baseline Findings from the ULTRA Study." *Journal of Strength and Conditioning Research* 27 (11): 2939–2945.

Hoffman, Martin D., and Eswar Krishnan. 2014. "Health and Exercise-Related Medical Issues Among 1,212 Ultramarathon Runners: Baseline Findings from the Ultrarunners Longitudinal TRAcking (ULTRA) Study." PLoS ONE 9 (1): e83867. doi:10.1371/journal.pone.0083867.

Hoffman, M. D., D. K. Lebus, A. C. Ganong, G. A. Casazza, and Marta Van Loan. 2010. "Body Composition of 161-km Ultramarathoners." *International Journal of Sports Medicine* 31 (2): 106–109.

Hoffman, Martin D., Ian R. Rogers, Jeremy Joslin, Chad A. Asplund, William O. Roberts, and Benjamin D. Levine. 2015. "Managing Collapsed or Seriously Ill Participants of Ultra-endurance Events in Remote Environments." *Sports Medicine* 45 (2): 201–212.

Hoffman, Martin D., and Kristin J. Stuempfle. 2014. "Hydration Strategies, Weight Change and Performance in a 161 km Ultramarathon." *Research in Sports Medicine* 22 (3): 213–225.

Hoffman, Martin D., Kristin J. Stuempfle, Kerry Sullivan, and Robert H. Weiss. 2015. "Exercise-Associated Hyponatremia with Exertional Rhabdomyolysis: Importance of Proper Treatment." *Clinical Nephrology* 83 (4): 235–242.

Hooper, Sue L., Laurel T. Mackinnon, and Alf Howard. 1999. "Physiological and Psychometric Variables for Monitoring Recovery During Tapering for Major Competition." *Medicine and Science in Sports and Exercise* 31 (8): 1205–1210.

Hopkins, Will G. 2005. "Competitive Performance of Elite Track-and-Field Athletes: Variability and Smallest Worthwhile Enhancements." *Sportscience* 9: 17–20.

Horne, Jim A., and Louise A. Reyner. 1996. "Counteracting Driver Sleepiness: Effects of Napping, Caffeine, and Placebo." *Psychophysiology* 33 (3): 306–309.

Hreljac, Alan. 1993. "Preferred and Energetically Optimal Gait Transition Speeds in Human Locomotion." *Medicine and Science in Sports and Exercise* 25 (10): 1158–1162.

Ingalls, Christopher P., Gordon L. Warren, Jay H. Williams, Christopher W. Ward, and R. B. Armstrong. 1998. "EC Coupling Failure in Mouse EDL Muscle After in Vivo Eccentric Contractions." *Journal of Applied Physiology* 85 (1): 58–67.

Jeukendrup, A. E., and J. McLaughlin. 2011. "Carbohydrate Ingestion During Exercise: Effects on Performance, Training Adaptations and Trainability of the Gut." In *Sports Nutrition: More Than Just Calories—Triggers for Adaptation*, edited by R. J. Maughan and L. M. Burke. *Nestlé Nutritional Institute Workshop Series* (69): 1–17.

Jeukendrup, Asker E., Luke Moseley, Gareth I. Mainwaring, Spencer Samuels, Samuel Perry, and Christopher H. Mann. 2006. "Exogenous Carbohydrate Oxidation During Ultraendurance Exercise." *Journal of Applied Physiology* 100 (4): 1134–1141.

Jeukendrup, A. E., K. Vet-Joop, A. Sturk, J. H. Stegen, J. Senden, W. H. Saris, and A. J. Wagenmakers. 2000. "Relationship Between Gastro-intestinal Complaints and Endotoxaemia, Cytokine Release and the Acute-Phase Reaction During and After a Long-Distance Triathlon in Highly Trained Men." *Clinical Science* 98 (1): 47–55.

Keller, T. S., A. M. Weisberger, J. L. Ray, S. S. Hasan, R. G. Shiavi, and D. M. Spengler. 1996. "Relationship Between Vertical Ground Reaction Force and Speed During Walking, Slow Jogging, and Running." *Clinical Biomechanics* 11 (5): 253–259.

Kenefick, Robert W., Samuel N. Cheuvront, Lisa Leon, and Karen K. O'Brien. 2012. "Dehydration and Rehydration." In *Wilderness Medicine*, 6th ed., edited by Paul S. Auerbach. Philadelphia, PA: Mosby.

Kiistala, U. 1972a. "Dermal-Epidermal Separation. I. The Influence of Age, Sex and Body Region on Suction Blister Formation in Human Skin." *Annals of Clinical Research* 4 (1): 10.

Kiistala, U. 1972b. "Dermal-Epidermal Separation. II. External Factors in Suction Blister Formation with Special Reference to the Effect of Temperature." *Annals of Clinical Research* 4 (4): 236–246.

Kim, Hyo Jeong, Yoon Hee Lee, and Chang Keun Kim. 2007. "Biomarkers of Muscle and Cartilage Damage and Inflammation During a 200 km Run." *European Journal of Applied Physiology* 99 (4): 443–447.

Kim, S. H., S. Kim, H. I. Choi, Y. J. Choi, Y. S. Lee, K. C. Sohn, Y. Lee, C. D. Kim, T. J. Yoon, J. H. Lee, and Y. H. Lee. 2010. "Callus Formation Is Associated with Hyperproliferation and Incomplete Differentiation of Keratinocytes, and Increased Expression of Adhesion Molecules." *British Journal of Dermatology* 163 (3): 495–501. doi:10.1111/j.1365–2133.2010.09842.x.

Knapik, Joseph J., Murray P. Hamlet, Kenneth J. Thompson, and Bruce H. Jones. 1996. "Influence of Boot-Sock Systems on Frequency and Severity of Foot Blisters." *Military Medicine* 161 (10): 594–598.

Knapik, Joseph J., Katy Reynolds, and John Barson. 1998. "Influence of an Antiperspirant on Foot Blister Incidence During Cross-Country Hiking." *Journal of the American Academy of Dermatology* 39 (2): 202–206.

Knapik, Joseph J., Katy L. Reynolds, Kathryn L. Duplantis, and Bruce H. Jones. 1995. "Friction Blisters." *Sports Medicine* 20 (3): 136–147.

Knechtle, B., T. Rosemann, and R. Lepers. 2010. "Predictor Variables for a 100-km Race Time in Male Ultra-marathoners." *Perceptual and Motor Skills* 111 (3): 681–693.

Knechtle, Beat, Brida Duff, Ulrich Welzel, and Götz Kohler. 2009. "Body Mass and Circumference of Upper Arm Are Associated with Race Performance in Ultraendurance Runners in a Multistage Race—The Isarrun 2006." *Research Quarterly for Exercise and Sport* 80 (2): 262–268.

Knechtle, Beat, Patrizia Knechtle, Thomas Rosemann, and Oliver Senn. 2011. "What Is Associated with Race Performance in Male 100-km Ultra-marathoners—Anthropometry, Training or Marathon Best Time?" *Journal of Sports Sciences* 29 (6): 571–577.

Knechtle, Beat, Patrizia Knechtle, Ingo Schulze, and Goetz Kohler. 2008. "Upper Arm Circumference Is Associated with Race Performance in Ultra-endurance Runners." *British Journal of Sports Medicine* 42 (4): 295–299.

Knechtle, Beat, Andrea Wirth, Patrizia Knechtle, Kanai Zimmermann, and Goetz Kohler. 2009. "Personal Best Marathon Performance Is Associated with Performance in a 24-h Run and Not Anthropometry or Training Volume." *British Journal of Sports Medicine* 43 (11): 836–839.

Kowalski, Erik, and Jing Xian Li. 2015. "Ground Reaction Forces in Forefoot Strike Runners Wearing Minimalist Shoes During Hill Running." *Footwear Science* 7 (suppl. 1): S40–42.

Kram, Rodger, Timothy M. Griffin, J. Maxwell Donelan, and Young Hui Chang. 1998. "Force Treadmill for Measuring Vertical and Horizontal Ground Reaction Forces." *Journal of Applied Physiology* 85 (2): 764–769.

Kramer, Patricia Ann, and Adam D. Sylvester. 2011. "The Energetic Cost of Walking: A Comparison of Predictive Methods." *PLOS ONE* 6 (6): E21290.

Kyröläinen, Heikki, Janne Avela, and Paavo V Komi. 2005. "Changes in Muscle Activity with Increasing Running Speed." *Journal of Sports Sciences* 23 (10): 1101–1109.

Larson, Peter, Erin Higgins, Justin Kaminski, Tamara Decker, Janine Preble, Daniela Lyons, Kevin Mcintyre, and Adam Normile. 2011. "Foot Strike Patterns of Recreational and Sub-elite Runners in a Long-Distance Road Race." *Journal of Sports Sciences* 29 (15): 1665–1673.

Laursen, Paul B., and David G. Jenkins. 2002. "The Scientific Basis for High-Intensity Interval Training." *Sports Medicine* 32 (1): 53–73.

Lepers, Romuald, Christophe Hausswirth, Nicola Maffiuletti, Jeanick Brisswalter, and Jacques van Hoecke. 2000. "Evidence of Neuromuscular Fatigue After Prolonged Cycling Exercise." *Medicine and Science in Sports and Exercise* 32 (11): 1880–1886.

Lepers, Romuald, Nicola A. Maffiuletti, Ludovic Rochette, Julien Brugniaux, and Guillaume Y. Millet. 2002. "Neuromuscular Fatigue During a Long-Duration Cycling Exercise." *Journal of Applied Physiology* 92 (4): 1487–1493.

Levine, Robert V., and Ara Norenzayan. 1999. "The Pace of Life in 31 Countries." *Journal of Cross-Cultural Psychology* 30 (2): 178–205. doi:10.1177/0022022199030002003.

Lien, Han-Chung, Wei Ming Sun, Yen-Hsueh Chen, Hyerang Kim, William Hasler, and Chung Owyang. 2003. "Effects of Ginger on Motion Sickness and Gastric Slow-Wave Dysrhythmias Induced by Circular Vection." *American Journal of Physiology—Gastrointestinal and Liver Physiology* 284 (3): G481–G489.

Lohsiriwat, Supatra, Mayurat Rukkiat, Reawika Chaikomin, and Somchai Leelakusolvong. 2010. "Effect of Ginger on Lower Esophageal Sphincter Pressure." *Journal of the Medical Association of Thailand* 93 (3): 366.

Lucas, Wayne, and Paul C. Schroy. 1998. "Reversible Ischemic Colitis in a High Endurance Athlete." *American Journal of Gastroenterology* 93 (11): 2231–2234.

Mackenzie, I. C. 1983. "Effects of Frictional Stimulation on the Structure of the Stratum Corneum." In *Stratum Corneum*, edited by Ronals Marks and Gerd Plewig, 153–160. Berlin: Springer.

Margaria, R., P. Cerretelli, P. Aghemo, and G. Sassi. 1963. "Energy Cost of Running." *Journal of Applied Physiology* 18 (2): 367–370.

Margaria, Rodolfo, 1976. *Biomechanics and Energetics of Muscular Exercise*. Oxford: Clarendon Press.

Martin, Vincent, Hugo Kerhervé, Laurent A. Messonnier, Jean-Claude Banfi, André Geyssant, Regis Bonnefoy, Léonard Féasson, and Guillaume Y. Millet. 2010. "Central and Peripheral Contributions to Neuromuscular Fatigue Induced by a 24-h Treadmill Run." *Journal of Applied Physiology* 108 (5): 1224–1233.

Martin, Vincent, Guillaume Y. Millet, Alain Martin, Gaelle Deley, and Gregory Lattier. 2004. "Assessment of Low-Frequency Fatigue with Two Methods of Electrical Stimulation." *Journal of Applied Physiology* 97 (5): 1923–1929.

Millet, Grégoire P., and Guillaume Y. Millet. 2012. "Ultramarathon Is an Outstanding Model for the Study of Adaptive Responses to Extreme Load and Stress." *BMC Medicine* 10 (1): 77.

Millet, Guillaume Y., and Romuald Lepers. 2004. "Alterations of Neuromuscular Function After Prolonged Running, Cycling and Skiing Exercises." *Sports Medicine* 34 (2): 105–116.

Millet, G. Y., R. Lepers, N. A. Maffiuletti, N. Babault, V. Martin, and G. Lattier. 2002. "Alterations of Neuromuscular Function After an Ultramarathon." *Journal of Applied Physiology* 92 (2): 486–492.

Millet, Guillaume Y., Katja Tomazin, Samuel Verges, Christopher Vincent, Régis Bonnefoy, Renée-Claude Boisson, Laurent Gergelé, Léonard Féasson, and Vincent Martin. 2011. "Neuromuscular Consequences of an Extreme Mountain Ultra-marathon." *PLOS ONE* 6 (2): E17059.

Minetti, A. E, L. P. Ardigo, and F. Saibene. 1994. "The Transition Between Walking and Running in Humans: Metabolic and Mechanical Aspects at Different Gradients." *Acta Physiologica Scandinavica* 150 (3): 315–323.

Minetti, Alberto E., Christian Moia, Giulio S. Roi, Davide Susta, and Guido Ferretti. 2002. "Energy Cost of Walking and Running at Extreme Uphill and Downhill Slopes." *Journal of Applied Physiology* 93 (3): 1039–1046.

Mitchell, Jere H., William Haskell, Peter Snell, and Steven P. Van Camp. 2005. "Task Force 8: Classification of Sports." *Journal of the American College of Cardiology* 45 (8): 1364–1367.

Modica, Jesse R., and Rodger Kram. 2005. "Metabolic Energy and Muscular Activity Required for Leg Swing in Running." *Journal of Applied Physiology* 98 (6): 2126–2131.

Mohler, Betty J., William B. Thompson, Sarah H. Creem-Regehr, Herbert L. Pick Jr., and William H. Warren Jr. 2007. "Visual Flow Influences Gait Transition Speed and Preferred Walking Speed." *Experimental Brain Research* 181 (2): 221–228.

Monash University. 2015. "Extreme Exercise Linked to Blood Poisoning" (press release), June 9.

Montgomery, William H., Marilyn Pink, and Jacquelin Perry. 1994. "Electromyographic Analysis of Hip and Knee Musculature During Running." *American Journal of Sports Medicine* 22 (2): 272–278.

Morgan, W. P., D. R. Brown, J. S. Raglin, P. J. O'Connor, and K. A. Ellickson. 1987. "Psychological Monitoring of Overtraining and Staleness." *British Journal of Sports Medicine* 21 (3): 107–114.

Mujika, Iñigo, and Sabino Padilla. 2000a. "Detraining: Loss of Training-Induced Physiological and Performance Adaptations. Part I." *Sports Medicine* 30 (2): 79–87.

Mujika, Iñigo, and Sabino Padilla. 2000b. "Detraining: Loss of Training-Induced Physiological and Performance Adaptations. Part II." *Sports Medicine* 30 (3): 145–154.

Mujika, Iñigo, and Sabino Padilla. 2003. "Scientific Bases for Precompetition Tapering Strategies." *Medicine and Science in Sports and Exercise* 35 (7): 1182–1187.

Munro, Carolyn F., Doris I. Miller, and Andrew J. Fuglevand. 1987. "Ground Reaction Forces in Running: A Reexamination." *Journal of Biomechanics* 20 (2): 147–155.

Myburgh, Kathryn H. 2003. "What Makes an Endurance Athlete World-Class? Not Simply a Physiological Conundrum." *Comparative Biochemistry and Physiology Part A: Molecular and Integrative Physiology* 136 (1): 183–185.

Nacht, Sergio, Jo-Ann Close, David Yeung, and Eugene H. Gans. 1981. "Skin Friction Coefficient: Changes Induced by Skin Hydration and Emollient Application and Correlation with Perceived Skin Feel." *Journal of the Society of Cosmetic Chemists* 32 (2): 55–65.

Naylor, P. F. D. 1955. "The Skin Surface and Friction." *British Journal of Dermatology* 67 (7): 239–248.

Nevill, Alan M., Damon Brown, Richard Godfrey, Patrick J. Johnson, Lee Romer, Arthur D. Stewart, and Edward M. Winter. 2003. "Modeling Maximum Oxygen Uptake of Elite Endurance Athletes." *Medicine and Science in Sports and Exercise* 35 (3): 488–494.

Newham, D. J., G. Mcphail, K. R. Mills, and R. H. T. Edwards. 1983. "Ultrastructural Changes After Concentric and Eccentric Contractions of Human Muscle." *Journal of the Neurological Sciences* 61 (1): 109–122.

Nicol, C., P. V. Komi, and P. Marconnet. 1991. "Fatigue Effects of Marathon Running on Neuromuscular Performance." *Scandinavian Journal of Medicine and Science in Sports* 1 (1): 10–17.

Nigg, B. M., H. A. Bahlsen, S. M. Luethi, and S. Stokes. 1987. "The Influence of Running Velocity and Midsole Hardness on External Impact Forces in Heel-Toe Running." *Journal of Biomechanics* 20 (10): 951–959.

Nilsson, Johnny, and Alf Thorstensson. 1989. "Ground Reaction Forces at Different Speeds of Human Walking and Running." *Acta Physiologica Scandinavica* 136 (2): 217–227.

Nosaka, K., and P. M. Clarkson. 1996. "Variability in Serum Creatine Kinase Response After Eccentric Exercise of the Elbow Flexors." *International Journal of Sports Medicine* 17 (2): 120–127.

Nosaka, Kazunori, K. E. I. Sakamoto, Mike Newton, and Paul Sacco. 2001. "How Long Does the Protective Effect on Eccentric Exercise-Induced Muscle Damage Last?" *Medicine and Science in Sports and Exercise* 33 (9): 1490–1495.

Novacheck, Tom F. 1998. "The Biomechanics of Running." *Gait and Posture* 7 (1): 77–95.

Nummela, A., Heikki Rusko, and Antti Mero. 1994. "EMG Activities and Ground Reaction Forces During Fatigued and Nonfatigued Sprinting." *Medicine and Science in Sports and Exercise* 26 (5): 605–609.

Øktedalen, O., O. C. Lunde, P. K. Opstad, L. Aabakken, and K. Kvernebo. 1992. "Changes in the Gastrointestinal Mucosa After Long-Distance Running." *Scandinavian Journal of Gastroenterology* 27 (4): 270–274.

Overgaard, Kristian, Tue Lindstrøm, Thorsten Ingemann-Hansen, and Torben Clausen. 2002. "Membrane Leakage and Increased Content of Na+-K+ Pumps and Ca2+ in Human Muscle After a 100-km Run." *Journal of Applied Physiology* 92 (5): 1891–1898. doi:10.1152/japplphysiol.00669.2001.

Padulo, Johnny, Douglas Powell, Raffaele Milia, and Luca Paolo Ardigò. 2013. "A Paradigm of Uphill Running." *PLOS ONE* 8 (7): E69006.

Page, A. J., S. A. Reid, D. B. Speedy, G. P. Mulligan, and J. Thompson. 2007. "Exercise-Associated Hyponatremia, Renal Function, and Nonsteroidal Antiinflammatory Drug Use in an Ultraendurance Mountain Run." *Clinical Journal of Sport Medicine* 17 (1): 43–48.

Papaioannides, D., C. Giotis, N. Karagiannis, and C. Voudouris. 1984. "Acute Upper Gastrointestinal Hemorrhage in Long-Distance Runners." *Annals of Internal Medicine* 101 (5): 719.

Pasman, W. J., M. A. Van Baak, A. E. Jeukendrup, and A. De Haan. 1995. "The Effect of Different Dosages of Caffeine on Endurance Performance Time." *International Journal of Sports Medicine* 16 (4): 225–230.

Peter, Laura, Christoph Alexander Rust, Beat Knechtle, Thomas Rosemann, and Romuald Lepers. 2014. "Sex Differences in 24-Hour Ultra-marathon Performance—A Retrospective Data Analysis from 1977 to 2012." *Clinics* 69 (1): 38–46.

Pfeiffer, Beate, Trent Stellingwerff, Eric Zaltas, and Asker E. Jeukendrup. 2010a. "CHO Oxidation from a CHO Gel Compared with a Drink During Exercise." *Medicine and Science in Sports and Exercise* 42 (11): 2038–2045.

Pfeiffer, Beate, Trent Stellingwerff, Eric Zaltas, and Asker E. Jeukendrup. 2010b. "Oxidation of Solid Versus Liquid CHO Sources During Exercise." *Medicine and Science in Sports and Exercise* 42 (11): 2030–2037.

Pongrojpaw, Densak, Charinthip Somprasit, and Athita Chanthasenanont. 2007. "A Randomized Comparison of Ginger and Dimenhydrinate in the Treatment of Nausea and Vomiting in Pregnancy." *Journal of the Medical Association of Thailand* 90 (9): 1703–1709.

Proske, U., and D. L. Morgan. 2001. "Muscle Damage from Eccentric Exercise: Mechanism, Mechanical Signs, Adaptation and Clinical Applications." *Journal of Physiology* 537 (2): 333–345.

Proske, Uwe, and Trevor J. Allen. 2005. "Damage to Skeletal Muscle from Eccentric Exercise." *Exercise and Sport Sciences Reviews* 33 (2): 98–104.

Pyne, David B., Cassie B. Trewin, and William G. Hopkins. 2004. "Progression and Variability of Competitive Performance of Olympic Swimmers." *Journal of Sports Sciences* 22 (7): 613–620.

Qamar, M. I., and A. E. Read. 1987. "Effects of Exercise on Mesenteric Blood Flow in Man." *Gut* 28 (5): 583–587.

Quinn, J. 1967. "The Effects of Two New Foot Powders on the Incidence of Foot Infection and Blisters in Recruits During Basic Training" (research memorandum). Report No. P/6. Farnborough, United Kingdom: Army Personnel Research Establishment.

Raglin, John S., David M. Koceja, Joel M. Stager, and Craig A. Harms. 1996. "Mood, Neuromuscular Function, and Performance During Training in Female Swimmers." *Medicine and Science in Sports and Exercise* 28 (3): 372–377.

Rebay, M., A. Arfaoui, and R. Taiar. 2008. "Thermo-mechanical Characterization of the Interaction Foot-Athletic Shoe During the Exercise." Paper presented at the Fifth European Thermal-Sciences Conference.

Reyner, Luise A., and James A. Horne. 1997. "Suppression of Sleepiness in Drivers: Combination of Caffeine with a Short Nap." *Psychophysiology* 34 (6): 721–725.

Reynolds, Katy, Andre Darrigrand, Donald Roberts, Joseph Knapik, Jon Pollard, Kathryn Duplantis, and Bruce Jones. 1995. "Effects of an Antiperspirant with Emollients on Foot-Sweat Accumulation and Blister Formation While Walking in the Heat." *Journal of the American Academy of Dermatology* 33 (4): 626–630.

Rønnestad, B. R., J. Hansen, and S. Ellefsen. 2014. "Block Periodization of High-Intensity Aerobic Intervals Provides Superior Training Effects in Trained Cyclists." *Scandinavian Journal of Medicine and Science in Sports* 24 (1): 34–42.

Rønnestad, Bent R., Joar Hansen, Vetle Thyli, Timo A. Bakken, and Øyvind Sandbakk. 2015. "5-Week Block Periodization Increases Aerobic Power in Elite Cross-Country Skiers." *Scandinavian Journal of Medicine and Science in Sports* 26 (2): 140–146.

Ryan, Julie L., Charles E. Heckler, Joseph A. Roscoe, Shaker R. Dakhil, Jeffrey Kirshner, Patrick J. Flynn, Jane T. Hickok, and Gary R. Morrow. 2012. "Ginger (*Zingiber officinale*) Reduces Acute Chemotherapy-Induced Nausea: A URCC CCOP Study of 576 Patients." *Supportive Care in Cancer* 20 (7): 1479–1489.

Sakaguchi, Masanori, Haruna Ogawa, Norifumi Shimizu, Hiroaki Kanehisa, Toshimasa Yanai, and Yasuo Kawakami. 2014. "Gender Differences in Hip and Ankle Joint Kinematics on Knee Abduction During Running." *European Journal of Sport Science* 14 (suppl. 1): S302–S309.

Sanders, Joan E., Barry S. Goldstein, and Daniel F. Leotta. 1995. "Skin Response to Mechanical Stress: Adaptation Rather Than Breakdown—A Review of the Literature." *Journal of Rehabilitation Research and Development* 32 (3): 214–2164.

Saporito, Bill. 2012. "Who Is the Fittest Olympic Athlete of Them All?" *Time*, July 19.

Sawka, Michael N., Louise M. Burke, E. Randy Eichner, Ronald J. Maughan, Scott J. Montain, and Nina S. Stachenfield. 2007. "Exercise and Fluid Replacement." *Medicine and Science in Sports and Exercise* 39 (2): 377–390. doi:10.1249/mss.0b013e31802ca597.

Shepley, B., J. D. MacDougall, N. Cipriano, J. R. Sutton, M. A. Tarnopolsky, and G. Coates. 1992. "Physiological Effects of Tapering in Highly Trained Athletes." *Journal of Applied Physiology* 72 (2): 706–711.

Shorten, Martyn R. 2000. "Running Shoe Design: Protection and Performance." In *Marathon Medicine,* edited by D. Tunstall Pedoe, 159–169. London: Royal Society of Medicine.

Sloniger, Mark A., Kirk J. Cureton, Barry M. Prior, and Ellen M. Evans. 1997. "Lower Extremity Muscle Activation During Horizontal and Uphill Running." *Journal of Applied Physiology* 83 (6): 2073–2079.

Smith, Judith L., Patricia Carlson-Kuhta, and Tamara V. Trank. 1998. "Forms of Forward Quadrupedal Locomotion. III. A Comparison of Posture, Hindlimb Kinematics, and Motor Patterns for Downslope and Level Walking." *Journal of Neurophysiology* 79 (4): 1702–1716.

Swanson, Stephen C., and Graham E. Caldwell. 2000. "An Integrated Biomechanical Analysis of High Speed Incline and Level Treadmill Running." *Medicine and Science in Sports and Exercise* 32 (6): 1146–1155.

Telhan, Gaurav, Jason R. Franz, Jay Dicharry, Robert P. Wilder, Patrick O. Riley, and D. Casey Kerrigan. 2010. "Lower Limb Joint Kinetics During Moderately Sloped Running." *Journal of Athletic Training* 45 (1): 16.

Temesi, John, Pierrick J. Arnal, Thomas Rupp, Léonard Féasson, Régine Cartier, Laurent Gergelé, Samuel Verges, Vincent Martin, and Guillaume Y. Millet. 2015. "Are Females More

Resistant to Extreme Neuromuscular Fatigue?" *Medicine and Science in Sports and Exercise* 47 (7): 1372–1382. doi:10.1249/mss.0000000000000540.

Thompson, Paul D., Erik J. Funk, Richard A. Carleton, and William Q. Sturner. 1982. "Incidence of Death During Jogging in Rhode Island from 1975 Through 1980." *Journal of the American Medical Association* 247 (18): 2535–2538.

Tiidus, Peter M., and C. David Ianuzzo. 1982. "Effects of Intensity and Duration of Muscular Exercise on Delayed Soreness and Serum Enzyme Activities." *Medicine and Science in Sports and Exercise* 15 (6): 461–465.

Volek, Jeff S., Timothy Noakes, and Stephen D. Phinney. 2015. "Rethinking Fat as a Fuel for Endurance Exercise." *European Journal of Sport Science* 15 (1): 13–20.

Vonhof, John. 2011. *Fixing Your Feet: Prevention and Treatments for Athletes.* Birmingham, AL: Wilderness Press.

Wharam, Paul C., Dale B. Speedy, Timothy D. Noakes, J. M. Thompson, Stephen A. Reid, and Lucy-May Holtzhausen. 2006. "NSAID Use Increases the Risk of Developing Hyponatremia During an Ironman Triathlon." *Medicine and Science in Sports and Exercise* 38 (4): 618–622.

Wickler, Steven J., Donald F. Hoyt, Andrew A. Biewener, Edward A. Cogger, and L. Kristin. 2005. "In Vivo Muscle Function vs Speed II. Muscle Function Trotting up an Incline." *Journal of Experimental Biology* 208 (6): 1191–1200.

Wylie, Lee J., James Kelly, Stephen J. Bailey, Jamie R. Blackwell, Philip F. Skiba, Paul .G Winyard, Asker E. Jeukendrup, Anni Vanhatalo, and Andrew M. Jones. 2013. "Beetroot Juice and Exercise: Pharmacodynamic and Dose-Response Relationships." *Journal of Applied Physiology* 115 (3): 325–336.

Yack, H. John, Carole Tucker, Scott C. White, and Heather Collins. 1995. "Comparison of Overground and Treadmill Vertical Ground Reaction Forces." *Gait and Posture* 3 (2): 86.

Yokozawa, T., N. Fujii, Y. Enomoto, and M. Ae. 2003. "Kinetic Characteristics of Distance Running on the Uphill." *Japanese Journal of Biomechanics in Sports and Exercise* 7: 30–42.

Yokozawa, Toshiharu, Norihisa Fujii, and Michiyoshi Ae. 2005. "Kinetic Characteristics of Distance Running on Downhill Slope." *International Journal of Sport and Health Science* 3: 35–45.

Zaryski, Calvin, and David J. Smith. 2005. "Training Principles and Issues for Ultra-endurance Athletes." *Current Sports Medicine Reports* 4 (3): 165–170.

Zingg, Matthias Alexander, Klaus Karner-Rezek, Thomas Rosemann, Beat Knechtle, Romuald Lepers, and Christoph Alexander Rüst. 2014. "Will Women Outrun Men in Ultra-marathon Road Races from 50 km to 1,000 km?" *SpringerPlus* 3: 97. Grabowski, Alena M., and Roger Kram. 2008. "Effects of Velocity and Weight Support on Ground Reaction Forces and Metabolic Power During Running." Journal of Applied Biomechanics 24: 288–297.

ACKNOWLEDGMENTS

JASON KOOP. I am fortunate that I have had fantastic coaches, teammates, educators, and mentors throughout the course of my life. Each of the individuals mentioned here has influenced both me and this book. I would be remiss if I failed to mention them and how they have impacted my career.

The coaches I have had in my life, Lyndall Weaver, Tom Clark, Chuck Estill, Billy Cox, Terry Jessup, and Dave Hartman: There's a piece of each of you in this book.

Jim Lehman and Chris Carmichael: You took a kid who couldn't coach his way out of a wet paper bag and helped him become a pretty OK coach. I am forever grateful for the initial risk you took in hiring me and the countless hours you each spent helping me develop as a coach.

My coauthor, Jim Rutberg, thank you for pushing me to pursue this project and for bringing it to life (and making sense of all my run-on ramblings along the way).

To Frank Pipp and the folks at TrainingPeaks, thank you for your help with many of the illustrations.

To Rodger Kram, PhD, thank you for your guidance in the early development of Chapters 4 and 5. More important, thanks for helping with the bloopers.

To Martin Hoffman, MD, thank you for your guidance in the early development in Chapters 4 and 5. More important, thank you for being a leader in the ultraendurance community.

To Dakota, Missy, Kaci, Dylan, and Erik: Thank you for letting me share your stories. It is an honor to guide you through your ultrarunning adventures.

To the coaches at CTS: Many, if not all, the ideas represented in this book are ones we as a team have developed over the course of many years, debates, and continuing education sessions. I am proud to call you my colleagues.

To Coach Noah Collins and Nick White: Thank you for your help, guidance, and expertise along the way.

To Casey Blaine, Connie Oehring, Vicki Hopewell, and the rest of the crew at VeloPress for your tireless work and believing in me as a naive rookie author.

Finally, to my parents and brother: Thank you for all your love and support.

JIM RUTBERG. I knew Jason Koop was a smart guy long before I proposed the idea of writing an ultrarunning training book with him. Jason and I have been colleagues and friends for nearly 15 years, and as he alluded to in his Acknowledgments, I've been around to watch him develop from a kid fresh out of college to one of the most respected and knowledgeable coaches in ultrarunning. But sometimes you don't realize how smart someone is until you push them, and cajoling Jason into writing a book on ultrarunning opened my eyes to how truly expansive his knowledge is on the subject. His knowledge of the science and training of ultrarunning is second only to his passion for the sport, and I am extraordinarily proud to play a role in bringing his work to a larger audience.

I have had the pleasure and honor to coauthor several books on training and sports nutrition, and I am thankful to Chris Carmichael, Jim Lehman, Dean Golich, Renee Eastman, Clayton Feldman, and the entire coaching staff at CTS for providing their knowledge and the opportunity to devote time, energy, and resources to writing books. A special thanks to Noah Collins for his invaluable assistance wrangling data and citations.

Thank you to Ted Costantino, Dave Trendler, Casey Blaine, and everyone else at VeloPress for their trust, confidence, and guidance in the development of this book and the Time-Crunched Athlete series of books.

And thank you to Leslie, Oliver, and Elliot for your boundless love and support.

INDEX

Italicized page numbers indicate a table or figure.

ABOUT THE AUTHORS

PHOTO BY JIM RUTBERG

Jason Koop walks the walk—or runs the run, as the case may be—when it comes to ultras. His journey from a cross-country runner at Texas A&M to ultra coach started with a postgraduation internship at CTS in the summer of 2001. A runner in a company of predominantly cycling coaches, Koop was quickly drafted and trained to be the company's lead running coach. In 2006 he traveled around the United States coaching and supporting Dean Karnazes as the "Ultramarathon Man" ran 50 marathons in 50 states in 50 days. Karnazes again tapped Koop's expertise in 2011 for "Regis and Kelly's Run Across America with Dean Karnazes," a nearly 3,000-mile cross-country run.

As the director of coaching for CTS, Koop coaches runners, cyclists, and triathletes in his role as a CTS premier coach. He also oversees the recruitment, education, and ongoing evaluation of more than 30 full-time endurance coaches and has developed CTS's quality assurance system for coaching as well as the CTS Coaching College. His personal ultrarunning resume includes two top-10 finishes at the Leadville Trail 100 Run and finishes at some of ultrarunning's most formidable events, including the Western States Endurance Run, the Badwater 135, the Wasatch 100, and the Hardrock 100.

Jim Rutberg is the media director and a coach for CTS and is coauthor, with Chris Carmichael, of *The Time-Crunched Cyclist*, *The Time-Crunched Triathlete*, *The Ultimate Ride*, *Chris Carmichael's Food for Fitness*, *Chris Carmichael's Fitness*

Cookbook, *The Carmichael Training Systems Cyclist's Training Diary*, *5 Essentials for a Winning Life*, and innumerable web and magazine articles. His work has appeared in *Bicycling, Outside, Men's Health, Men's Journal, VeloNews, Inside Triathlon*, and more. A graduate of Wake Forest University and former elite cyclist, Rutberg lives in Colorado Springs with his wife, Leslie, and their two sons, Oliver and Elliot.